American Murder

American Murder

Volume 1

Homicide in the Early 20th Century

Gini Graham Scott

PRAEGER

Westport, Connecticut
London

Library of Congress Cataloging-in-Publication Data

Scott, Gini Graham.
American murder / Gini Graham Scott.
p. cm.
Includes bibliographical references and index.
ISBN 978-0-275-98388-8 (set : alk. paper) — ISBN 978-0-275-99977-3 (v. 1 : alk. paper) — ISBN 978-0-275-99978-0 (v. 2 : alk. paper)
1. Murder—United States—History—20th century. 2. Murder—United States—History—20th century—Case studies. 3. Murder—Investigation—United States—History—20th century. 4. Murder in mass media—History—20th century. I. Title.
HV6524.S35 2007
364.15209730904—dc22 2007028409

British Library Cataloguing in Publication Data is available.

Library of Congress Catalog Card Number: 2007028409
ISBN-13: 978-0-275-98388-8 (set)
ISBN-13: 978-0-275-99977-3 (vol. 1)
ISBN-13: 978-0-275-99978-0 (vol. 2)

First published in 2007

Praeger Publishers, 88 Post Road West, Westport, CT 06881
An imprint of Greenwood Publishing Group, Inc.
www.praeger.com

Printed in the United States of America

The paper used in this book complies with the Permanent Paper Standard issued by the National Information Standards Organization (Z39.48–1984).

10 9 8 7 6 5 4 3 2 1

Contents

Preface

TODAY, HOMICIDE INVESTIGATORS have an arsenal of scientific techniques for investigating murder. DNA analysis of the genetic material in the blood or body fluids is just the latest in a series of scientific breakthroughs. There are also highly sophisticated information systems for tracking down suspects, weapons, and witnesses and learning personal histories, including internationally linked crime databases, telephone records, and credit reports. Additionally, police departments all over the nation and the world share information by phone, fax, and the Internet. The international media plays a part in spreading information that helps solve crimes.

This is very different than the way it was in the beginning of the twentieth century, when there were few techniques for investigating homicides. Fingerprinting was then in its infancy, and chemists could only identify the most common poisons. There was no ballistics, no hair and fiber analysis, no tests to distinguish blood types. Investigators were only just beginning to tell if a blood type was animal or human.

Police departments were not actively in touch with each other. There weren't readily available telephones then; messages had to be sent by telegraph or letter. Most travel was by horseback or train; the motorcar was still a blip on the horizon. In fact, the police did not have active homicide divisions or investigators; typically, little priority was given to solving homicides. Generally, people in the community may have seen who had done the crime or had a good idea who it was—because they may have known who was fighting or who was harboring a long-term grudge. After some interviews with people in the community, the police would make an arrest. Sometimes, people would informally form their own posses to help. In turn, in a world of mostly small towns and farms, a suspect couldn't easily hide, though from time to time some fled someplace else. As a result, homicides were typically solved fairly quickly or not at all. There was little investigation and very few trials.

At the same time, homicides were typically the result of everyday conflicts, like barroom fights, jealousies over straying spouses, killings for revenge, or murder for money. There were generally no lurking serial murderers or sex murderers, as there are today—and no psychiatrists and psychologists defending killers because of their dysfunctional childhoods or other sources of insanity. Perhaps in the beginning of the century, community ties were still relatively close; sex was still kept very much in the closet; the theories of Freud and later psychologists were not yet part of the culture; and killers couldn't jump into a car to get away or dispose of a body that easily. The best they could do was hop a train.

Then everything began to change. As society was transformed with new technologies and communities, norms and values changed as well, and so did the types of homicides—and the techniques used to investigate them. For example, when Prohibition in the 1920s and 1930s contributed to the rise of gang warfare and killings—and the newly popular car provided a way to get away quickly, making robbery a more popular crime—the police fought back with new investigative techniques. For example, the FBI began creating a fingerprint database in the mid-1920s and then linked police departments nationally in the first national crackdown on crime. The 1920s also marked the beginnings of the first serious scientific investigation of the trace evidence left at a crime when a chemist at the University of California at Berkeley, Edward Heinrich—called the "Wizard of Berkeley"—broke the D'Autremont brothers case by examining some overalls found near the scene of a train robbery and murder.

The science of homicide investigation was developing, and it picked up steam over the next decades as the types of murders themselves became more difficult to solve. This occurred because killers now had more ways to dispose of the body and more mobility to get to the crime scene and get away. As cities expanded, victims and killers were less apt to be known to each other; an increasing number of killers were picking out very casual acquaintances or strangers, often driven by sex, a deep general rage, or both—especially beginning in the 1950s.

To fight back, homicide investigators developed even more techniques—such as more sophisticated methods of firearms and ballistic analysis, better methods for analyzing blood and trace evidence, and better lie detector, interviewing, and interrogation techniques.

It was like an escalating cat-and-mouse game, in which the homicide investigator had to keep getting better to outwit increasingly wily killers—as well as a growing battery of defense attorneys, as these difficult cases turned into longer, harder-fought court battles in the 1950s.

This volume examines these developments from the early twentieth century to the end of the 1950s. Volume 2 continues to look at developments from the 1960s through the end of the twentieth century.

Throughout the century, even as the nature of homicides and the techniques used to investigate them has changed, there has been one constant. There have always been some cases that are very baffling and hard to solve or prove—even today. For various reasons, these cases have mystified the police and the public. In some cases, this mystery has captured the public imagination, turning these cases into front-page or TV news thrillers.

American Murder is about such cases, tracing the main developments in the types of homicides and investigative techniques from decade to decade. After a discussion of the trends, each chapter highlights a few of the most interesting, and baffling cases of each decade. These are the cases where the investigators had a hard time figuring out who did it—or even if they suspect who had done it, they had a hard time proving it. In some cases they were never able to discover the killer or prove it; in these cases, the crime has remained officially unsolved. A Selected Bibliography lists source material and further reading.

This volume begins at the turn of the century with one of the first cases involving the national mails from Delaware to San Francisco—the Cordelia Botkin case, in which a jealous woman poisoned the wife of her lover. The volume ends with the mysterious murder of fourteen-year-old Stephanie Bryan in Berkeley, California. This case eventually led police to the cabin of a University of California accounting student, Burton Abbott (who was convicted as a sexual psychopath), in part because of the trace evidence he left in his car, such as woolen fibers and hairs showing that Stephanie had been there. It was evidence that might not have been possible to find and use decades before.

As this volume describes, advances in investigative techniques and technologies contributed to solving many cases, although in other cases, even these new methods were not enough. The killers have proved to be good students of criminology, too, making the murders especially challenging to solve in these mysterious, baffling, and intriguing cases. In fact, they are the kind of cases that might be crafted by a scriptwriter in Hollywood writing an exciting mystery or legal thriller, leaving the audience on edge with the unexpected turns of plot. And they all are true.

American Murder

Chapter 1

The Turn of the Century and Early 1900s

THE TURN OF the century and early 1900s was a time when the United States was rapidly transforming from an innocent rural nation of farms and small towns to growing cities. Women were dressing up in long skirts with tight waists and wore frilly blouses and wide-brimmed hats, while men looked their best in starched suits. In the cities, men went to gentlemen's clubs with cigars and spittoons, while women, described as the "fairer" or "weaker" sex, went to literary gatherings and used smelling salts. Meanwhile, the traditional country values of hard work, religion, and chastity were being replaced by the new city values of the Gilded Age. Such changes were pushed by the money barons and Wall Street speculators like Jay Gould and James Fisk, who envisioned a new America built on feverish capitalism, acquisition of money, and lavish living. The rise of gala opera houses and music halls typified this age.

Meanwhile, the crime of murder changed with the times, and investigators struggled to keep up as new scientific techniques began to slowly change traditional ways of finding criminals. Before the growing urbanization of America in the mid-1800s, murder was rare—even rarer than it was in Europe. In a nation of farms and small towns, people were part of close-knit local communities. Many owned their own land or at least had roots in the area, and most murders developed out of local quarrels with fellow workers, neighbors, and spouses. Aside from a small number of sheriffs and constables, there were no paid law enforcement officers. Mostly murderers were caught because they were seen committing their crimes or were caught by a posse of angry citizens organized by neighbors who knew of ongoing conflicts and suspected the murderer, who had fled the scene. Other murderers got away entirely by heading out to the frontier in the West. In the 1830s, 1840s, and 1850s the first professional police departments began to appear in the major cities, though the officers had no training—usually they got their position because they knew someone in the political party in power, and their main job was breaking up fights and keeping order.[1]

Before the mid-1800s, there were no detectives who tried to investigate and solve murder cases in which the killer wasn't immediately known. The first detectives in the big cities were private entrepreneurs or moonlighting cops or constables who were hired to recover stolen goods for a reward. If there was any mystery about who killed someone, the coroner had the job of trying to identify who might be the killer, and typically he conducted a brief inquest of a few hours near where the body was found to establish the physical cause of death. Then the inquest jurors—typically local citizens paid $1 a day by the party in power—would name a suspect if one was easily identified. The locals knew of a fight or a jealous spouse, or a crowd of bystanders had already chased down the suspect. Once captured, the suspect was quickly referred to the local district attorney, who did little investigating and simply presented the case to jurors in a trial that usually lasted a morning, followed by deliberations that were typically over in a few minutes to an hour. A big case might take a week.[2] About half the suspects were convicted—and many guilty people got away because even if they were seen doing the crime, there was little evidence that could be used to convict them. Blood evidence or fingerprinting wasn't available in those days.

Then, in the late 1800s, as cities grew and the United States was filled with floods of immigrants, there was a growing pressure for creating order in society and discovering who done it through more sophisticated crime detection techniques. Now, too, prosecutors began to offer guilty pleas, once very rare, in exchange for lower sentences to help settle a case. Mostly, these cases still involved personal crimes of anger and jealousy between people who knew each other. Some murders grew out of robberies and riots. With occasional exceptions, there were no rape and sex killers and no multiple or serial killers like today.

The new detection techniques actually got their start in Europe before they spread to England and then to North America. They developed there first because the big European centers of the time—Paris, Berlin, and London—were far more "civilized" with their centuries of development of high culture. They had a centralized government, an educated nobility or class of wealthy landowners, and well-reputed universities from the Sorbonne in Paris to Oxford and Cambridge Universities in England. Plus they had a tradition of culture, which included high-class publishers, opera houses, and art patrons supporting favorite artists. Meanwhile, European medical doctors and chemists led the way in developing new techniques for anatomy and physiology that revolutionized the then-haphazard world of crime detection.

Ironically, these medical techniques developed and spread to the United States at a time when there was not only a growing number of homicides as society became more urban, but also an increasing concern with actually solving homicides. Before then, unsolved homicides were a low priority. A historian of homicides, Philadelphia professor and author of *Murder in America*, Roger Lane explains.

> In the great majority of cases, the facts that homicide was obvious and that there was an immediate suspect made detection easy and cheap. When the dead person was a known member of the community, coroners and police, with the press looking over their shoulders, were increasingly willing at least to begin the often expensive and time-consuming business of finding out what had happened and who was responsible. But it was a different matter when anonymous "floaters" were pulled from the river, or under suspicious circumstances the bodies of poor people were found in the street, and no one of any influence or standing had reported them missing. The business of "detective work" as we now know it had been made a public responsibility only a few days earlier; even public prosecution was a relatively recent American invention. And in the late nineteenth century homicide detection was still a relatively low priority.

Unlike the professional crime fighters of today, around the turn of the 1900s, the police detectives really had no tools, power, or special expertise that set them apart from other citizens. Though they might make some homicide arrests, they had the same ability to do so that coroners, judges, and often private citizens enjoyed. Commonly, urban crowds would corner a suspected killer. About the only thing the police did then was to make dragnet arrests in frustrating or high-publicized cases, such as that shown in the famous movie *M* with Peter Lorre (except there it was the underworld instead of the public). Mostly, the police acted to prevent homicide by breaking up small fights and bigger riots. They didn't detect much of anything.

That's one of the reasons Lizzie Borden probably got away with murder in the most famous case of the times—the ax murder of her father and stepmother in 1892 in Fall River, Massachusetts. As virtually all true crime and history buffs know, the case began when Lizzie Borden called upstairs to the family maid, Bridget Sullivan, "Come down quick. Father's dead. Someone came in and killed him." Bridget brought back the family doctor and a friend, followed soon after by the police. Andrew Borden was found face down on the downstairs parlor couch, his head smashed by dozens of blows. Soon his second wife, Abby, was found upstairs, similarly battered. The country was riveted by the news, and though the police heard rumors of a "wild-eyed" or "bushy-haired" stranger in the neighborhood, neighbors saw no one enter or leave and heard no sound at the time of the killing. So Lizzie was soon suspected, especially because her demeanor seemed so cool and restrained, and she told some contradictory and odd stories. One was that she had burned a blue dress with dark stains that morning because it had blue paint on it. But in the end, since she seemed so primly respectable, and there was no blood and no weapon found, the jurors found her not guilty in just over an hour, though most people then and now believe she did it. Or as the popular ballad puts it:

Lizzie Borden took an axe
And gave her father forty whacks;
When she saw what she had done,
She gave her mother forty-one.

Unfortunately, there was a lack of evidence to convict her if she did, because the detectives were unable to check into such things as whether Lizzie or Bridget might have smuggled a package out of the household with the weapon and bloody clothes.

Around the turn of the century, things began to change with the introduction of new methods that eventually cracked some of the most baffling crimes of the late 1890s and early 1900s. It was the beginning of modern criminology.

These beginnings go back to 1879 in Paris, when a young man named Alphonse Bertillon was working for the French police, copying and filing descriptions of criminals. At the time, Queen Victoria was in the midst of her long reign in England; France was still a colonial empire ruled by Napoleon III; and a German emperor, William I, king of Prussia, was still on the throne. It was a period when notions of royalty and elegance still prevailed, and the world of art and letters was still ruled by notions of order and sensibility, typified by Renoir's painting of *Madame Charpentier and Her Children* and Rodin's *John the Baptist* sculpture. Yet there were signs of change pushing against the old order, such as Henrik Ibsen's play *A Doll's House* and Henry James's *Daisy Miller*, suggesting the growing eagerness of women for independence.

But most of all, change came through the propagation of new scientific discoveries, like the first electric train (introduced at the Berlin Trade Exhibition) and London's first telephone exchange established in 1879. That's also the year when Bertillon first asked the Paris police if he could take various measurements of convicts passing through headquarters on the theory that no two human beings would have identical physical measurements, and he finally received permission to begin doing so in 1892. He began measuring the length of the forearm, the circumference of the skull, and the size of the chest. Soon he had a few successes—first identifying a petty crook who gave a false name and then identifying several nameless corpses found floating in the River Seine. Within a few years, police forces all over the world began adopting his system of anthropometrics. He even used his system to trap an anarchist bomber named Ravachol who was wanted for murder under another name—Koenigstein—in 1892.[3]

But also in 1892—the same year Lizzie Borden went free—William Herschel invented the system of fingerprinting, which soon became and remains a major tool for identification and detection. Herschel invented this system when he was working as a civil servant in India and had the job of paying pensions to Indian ex-soldiers. They all looked very much alike to him, so to prevent the claimants from collecting twice, which some did, he asked them to sign for their pensions by putting an inky fingerprint next to their name, and he published his book *Fingerprinting* that year. Over the next few years, ideas about fingerprinting spread, since the Bertillon system of anthropometrics seemed overly complicated.

In 1897, another British civil servant in India, Edward Richard Henry, took the next big step of creating a fingerprint classification system that has become the standard throughout the world. The system is based on identifying five basic types of loops, arches, and whorls. After Henry used this new system to solve a number of murder cases in 1897, it became the sole means of identifying criminals in England, and after he published a description of his system in 1901, it spread around the world through the 1900s. Finally, in 1904, it arrived in America, when a New York policeman, Inspector Joseph A. Faurot, who studied fingerprinting at Scotland Yard, used it to catch a hotel thief and later to solve a murder.[4] When Faurot was able to tell the judge in a burglary case which fingerprints on a window and table were identical, his testimony convicting the thief made headlines throughout the United States.

Meanwhile, other big steps in the late 1890s and early 1900s were the development of tests of blood and bones to determine whether they were animal or human. The blood test was discovered by a German doctor, Paul Uhlenhuth, who showed that if a rabbit was injected with human blood, its serum would develop a defense against it that would show up in a milk color.[5] In France, meanwhile, starting in the 1880s, Professor Alexandre Lacassagne, a doctor of pathology and forensic medicine at the University of Lyons, began determining the cause of death from the types of wounds and the condition of the heart and lungs. He was able to identify bodies from bits of hair, bones, and teeth; when he looked at bloodstains under a microscope, he was able to tell the difference between human and animal cells.[6]

The year 1902 also brought the beginning of ballistics in the United States, showing whether a bullet came from a particular gun. The science actually got its start in France in 1888, when Professor Lacassagne found that a specific bullet could be traced to a specific revolver by counting and measuring the unique rifling marks of each gun.[7] Before then, gunsmiths had occasionally been called to testify whether a bullet came from a large- or small-caliber gun or whether a suspected murder weapon had been fired recently. Then, in 1902, Judge Oliver Wendell Holmes of the Supreme Court of Massachusetts set up a demonstration at a murder trial in which the defendant's gun was fired into a wastebasket filled with cotton, after which the bullets were compared to those found in the victim's body. The bullets were a match, and after the killer's conviction, news spread around the country. The science of ballistics was launched.[8]

Meanwhile, scientists were gaining skills in identifying different poisons, which were typically the weapon of choice in high-class murders—especially those committed by women, who typically sought to kill due to feelings of jealousy, greed, and lust. Arsenic was one of the most popular of these poisons, though as other poisons were used more frequently, medical examiners gradually became more skilled at identifying these as well.

In short, this explosion of new techniques turned homicide detection into a real skill that helped solve otherwise baffling murders. Of course, there were still many more ordinary murders, including a growing number of bank robbers, especially in the West and Southwest, who continued the Jesse James gang tradition, and there was a spreading problem of gangs, extortion, and corrupt cops in the cities.

By contrast, the baffling murders were generally more quiet, personal, domestic, or unusual crimes. They were characterized by men and women who murdered lonely suitors for their money (like Johann Otto Hoch, who murdered lonely and rich widows in Chicago for about ten years until discovered in 1905); wealthy men who killed women they didn't want to marry (like Chester Gillette, who drowned a lower class girl he got pregnant in Utica, New York, in 1906, and was later written about in Theodore Dreiser's novel *An American Tragedy*); and men who killed out of jealousy and rage (like Henry Thaw, who killed the famous architect Stanford White point blank at a theater in New York in 1906 because White was having an affair with Thaw's wife, Evelyn Nesbit).

But most baffling of all were four cases of killings for love, sex, jealousy, and money that involved poisoning or buried bones. The new techniques of detection enabled the investigators to better solve these cases. While the detectives tried to solve them, these unusual murders often captured the imagination of the public, because they were so difficult to solve or prove or they involved bizarre methods that were hard to understand.

One was the case against Cordelia Botkin in San Francisco for the murder of Elizabeth Dunning, the wife of her lover, with poisoned candies in 1898. Another was the murder charge against sausage-maker Adolph Luetgert in Chicago, who allegedly killed his wife for money and hid her body in a sausage vat in 1898. A third was the claim that a high-society New Yorker, Roland Molineux, had poisoned or tried to poison several people he didn't like; he was finally convicted and sentenced to the Tombs in 1902, though he got a retrial on a technicality and was acquitted. The most famous of all was the case of Belle Gunness, a dowdy farmwoman from La Porte, Indiana, who was believed to have killed and buried a former husband, her children, and many lovers at her farm. But after it burned down in 1908, she was never seen again, though whether she escaped or died in the fire has been a subject of continuing debate.

Following are the stories of Cordelia Botkin and Belle Gunness to illustrate some of these trends and how the investigations were handled.

THE CASE OF CORDELIA BOTKIN

Dover, Delaware, and San Francisco, California, 1898–99

The murder of Elizabeth Dunning baffled police because it involved solving and proving a whodunit in the first cross-country case of poisoning in the United

States. Could the police actually make the connection given the undeveloped science of poisoning and other detection methods at the time?

The case began when Elizabeth Dunning received a colorful box of chocolate bonbons from the postman on September 9, 1898, in Dover, Delaware. She was sitting on the porch of a Victorian-style row house with her family, trying to get cool. As she opened the parcel postmarked from San Francisco, she saw the chocolates nestled under a lacy handkerchief with the price tag attached to it. Just a nice gift from a San Francisco friend, she thought. Three days later, she and her older sister, who had also eaten the chocolates, were dead after being racked with spasms and stomach pains. But at first not even their doctor realized that they had been poisoned, by whom, or why.

When Elizabeth opened the securely wrapped parcel, she didn't suspect anything, because sending long-distance parcels wasn't unusual since the expansion of railroads had linked cities coast to coast in turn-of-the-century America. Besides, when she saw the friendly note at the bottom of the box—"With love to yourself and baby, Mrs. C."—she thought the bonbons were from a close friend she had known in San Francisco, Mrs. Corbally. The chocolates still looked firm and tasty. So she passed the box around the porch to her parents, the Peningtons, with whom she was living, and to her sister Mrs. Joshua Deanne, Mrs. Deanne's child, and her own young daughter, then just seven years old. Though her parents passed on the bonbons, the children had a few bites, and her sister eagerly joined her in eating several pieces. A nice treat for a hot and lazy afternoon, she thought.

As she and the others ate the bonbons, she was reminded of a San Francisco she had left two years before. She had come home because she was tired that her once respectable journalist husband John Dunning had been carrying on a wild affair with his older mistress, Cordelia Botkin. He had even lost his job as the Associated Press bureau chief in San Francisco that had led him to move there in the first place. But now, she hoped he would come to his senses and return to her, because he had moved away from his mistress when the AP called him to cover the Spanish-American War. He had jumped at the chance to work again. As the war was winding down, Elizabeth hoped John would at last settle down and come back to her. His letters to her from the war gave her the chance to hope.

Then, she imagined, everything would return to the normal and proper life she had become used to. After all, she had been raised a very proper Victorian lady, the daughter of a U.S. congressman from Dover, and she believed in following the niceties of the times. For a well-bred woman that meant staying at home, raising children, visiting with friends and relatives, going to the theater or literary salon with other women, reading gentle magazines like *Godey's Lady's Book*, and going to church. It was a time when women dressed demurely in long dark skirts with cinched waists, wore gloves when they went to visit, and had high collars. It was an age of drawing room theater and literature about aristocrats, such as Edmond Rostand's *Cyrano de Bergerac* and Henry James's

The Turn of the Screw. Also, it was a time when the rules and morality of Victorian England, celebrated by Queen Victoria's Diamond Jubilee of 1897, were pervasive in U.S. life, too.

After Elizabeth married John in 1895, life had continued like that ideal, until he had been offered the job of bureau chief. Suddenly, everything changed. He began courting a woman (Cordelia) he met while riding his bike in a park on his way to work. Cordelia led him into a wild and crazy secret life of drinking, gambling, and partying before Elizabeth found out; after that, he had the audacity to move in with his lover and carry on at all hours of the night. It affronted Elizabeth's sense of propriety, and after he lost his job and began living off the money his mistress got from her own deserted husband, Elizabeth had enough. She sold her furniture and jewels to pay for her trip back to Dover. Taking her daughter with her, she moved back in with her parents.

After that, as she waited and hoped her husband might return to the respectable life they once knew, she got a few strange letters from San Francisco describing how he was still cavorting with an interesting and pretty Englishwoman, enjoying the bohemian life. The first letter, signed from "a friend" had warned her not to resume living with her husband. When Elizabeth contacted her estranged husband, he said the handwriting looked like that of Cordelia, the woman with whom he was living. However, after Cordelia huffily denied writing the letter, Elizabeth turned over the others that came without reading them to her father, and he put them away in a drawer.

Now it looked like John finally would be coming back, and as she ate the chocolates, recalling their happier days in San Francisco before he took up with the awful Cordelia, that's what she hoped. But the next day, she and her sister and their two children felt strangely ill. At first, they just had stomach aches, and the children were soon better. "It's just a *cholera morbus*," said the physician who came over to see them. "Probably due to eating corn fritters." But the following day, Elizabeth and her sister were much worse. They were having painful spasms, and after a specialist her father called examined them, he told him the grim news. "I believe they have been poisoned." But by then it was too late to save them. A day later, on September 12, they both died.

Who had tried to poison Elizabeth and why? That's when Mr. Penington and his wife remembered how Elizabeth had passed around the box of candy. He also recalled how she, her sister, and the children had made a few joking comments about some gritty lumps inside the candies, though Elizabeth and her sister kept eating them anyway. "It must be the chocolates!" he exclaimed.

Immediately, Mr. Penington rushed around the house, looking for the box of candy. Fortunately he had kept it. He even had the wrapping and the note. Then he remembered the strange letters that Elizabeth had received the previous summer from San Francisco, and he pulled them out of his drawer to compare the handwriting. Yes, he concluded. They looked exactly the same. But from whom?

He sent a quick telegram with the grim news to Dunning, who was still following soldiers in Puerto Rico. As quickly as he could, Dunning rushed back to Dover to be with the family. It took him several days, because he had to go by boat and train and then take a horse carriage from the station. After he sat down in the drawing room, Mr. Penington brought out the candy box and letters. Dunning read them, shocked at their contents and the obvious parallels in the handwriting. "Yes, they must have been written by the same person, and it must be Cordelia," he said grimly. He knew her handwriting, and though Cordelia had previously denied writing that first letter a year before, he felt sure she must be the writer.

At once, the local Dover police referred the case to San Francisco, because the candies had been sent from there, and they described the suspicions expressed by Dunning and Penington. Now it would be up to the San Francisco police to find Cordelia and show that she had in fact sent the poisoned chocolates. The specialist concluded that Elizabeth and her sister had been poisoned and their symptoms suggested arsenic, then the poisoning drug of choice, but could the police to find enough evidence to prove it? Not only had all the chocolates been eaten, but the victim had been poisoned from 3,000 miles away.

Isaiah W. Less, San Francisco's chief of police at the time, was determined to do everything he could to find Cordelia and bring her to justice. He was particularly incensed after hearing John Dunning describing his life with her. Everything about her offended his sense of law, order, and morality, as he heard the tale of this depraved, immoral woman who had abandoned her own husband and then had drawn a previously respectable hard-working man into a life of adultery, drunkenness, and sin in San Francisco's bohemian red light district. Chief Less knew the area well—a seedy section known as the Barbary Coast, from Broadway to the edges of Chinatown, full of small bars, prostitutes, whorehouses, and opium dens. The area was frequented by sailors, out-of-work drifters, and travelers seeking a wild night on the town. Ironically, this was a time when San Francisco was trying to present a respectable face as a proper and cultured Victorian city, where people enjoyed the finer pleasures of high culture, arts, and elegant dining; the tawdry part of San Francisco represented exactly the opposite of this high-toned image.

As Dunning described it, shortly after he had moved there with Elizabeth to take over the AP bureau, he was riding his bicycle to the office one morning when he met Cordelia. Bicycles had become a very popular and fashionable means of transportation, so it was quite ordinary to go to work that way. As he rode on a path through a small park, his bike broke down near a bench where Cordelia was sitting, and as he fixed it, they started talking. Though Cordelia was ten years older, heavy set (even dumpy), in her tight-fighting bodice and long skirt there was something wild and intriguing about her that captivated him, and soon he joined her in exploring the bohemian side of San Francisco. In fact, he soon threw caution to the wind, excited by the wild parties, drinking, gambling, dancing, and passionate sex with her. Often they formed a foursome with Cordelia's heavy-set son, Beverly, and his mistress, Louise Seeley, and they partied until late at night. He especially enjoyed the racy stories Cordelia told as the four of them lay around on two beds in the darkness. After a while, he didn't care about the normal proprieties of being a married man and moved in with Cordelia, Beverly, and Louise. Though he soon lost his job, he was quite content to let Cordelia support him with the money she got from her husband, a businessman in the farming town of Stockton, whom she had left a few years before.

Why would Cordelia send the chocolates to Elizabeth, Chief Less wondered. "Perhaps she was afraid I would return to Elizabeth after the war," Dunning reflected sadly. "I had talked about Elizabeth fondly before I left to go off to the war and moved out of Cordelia's apartment. So I think she thought I was ready to settle down and go back to work once the war was over. She felt I was ready to end my fling with her."

Thus, that must be the motive, Less reasoned. If Cordelia could eliminate her rival, then Dunning would come back to her. Less could imagine what probably happened. Probably Cordelia had written the letters describing how Dunning had met the "interesting and pretty" English woman and loved the bohemian life to scare Elizabeth off from trying to get back together with Dunning. Then after Dunning had left for the war, Cordelia was probably very lonely, especially after she applied for a position as a front-line nurse to follow him there but was turned down. Less imagined she must have been very sad and despondent, feeling Dunning might be gone for good after the war, back to the arms of her rival. But if his wife wasn't there, she could resume that wild and passionate life with him.

But was his theory right? Could he find the evidence to back it up? Immediately, Less set to work, trying to find Cordelia to arrest her as a suspect. At the same time, he tried to find out more about the candy, whether she purchased it, and whether she had put any arsenic in it. It was a tall order for a case where the victims were 3,000 miles away and the only evidence so far was an empty box of chocolates, a wrapping box from San Francisco, and some similar handwriting on the box and some letters. Unfortunately, handwriting was not then admissible as evidence in the courts of California. Without that, would he be able to find enough evidence to prove Cordelia sent the package? Since the candy had been eaten, would there be any evidence to show it was the source of the arsenic poisoning? Or would a woman he was sure was the killer get away?

With the information Dunning gave him, Less finally tracked down Cordelia at the Hotel Victoria, a small Victorian-style hotel that had the lacy trim. After he walked down a narrow corridor to Cordelia's room and she met him at the door, he was surprised that a gentleman like Dunning would be attracted to her in the first place. She was heavy-set and dumpy-looking, with an ample bosom that made her look like an overstuffed turkey squeezed into a tight dress. Her cheeks were full, and her dark brown hair was piled up in a swirl on the top of her head, so she looked like somebody's grandmother. Could this be the wild, sensual creature that attracted Dunning to exotic nights of debauchery?

Putting aside his impressions, Less announced he was there to arrest her on suspicion in the death of Mrs. Dunning and her sister. Cordelia immediately protested, "But I'm innocent. I did nothing." He searched her room. At once his eye was caught by a suspicious candy wrapping from the George Haas candy store, and he took it with him.

Then, after depositing Cordelia at the San Francisco jail, Less went to the store and spoke to the clerk, showing her the wrapping. Immediately, the clerk recognized the box and remembered Cordelia. "Oh, yes," she said. "That's from our store. She bought a box of candy here."

Then, he chased down the next clue—the lace handkerchief with the price tag that covered the candies. He went to several stores, showing the handkerchief, and finally he found a sales clerk at the elegant City of Paris department store who recognized the tag.

Next, back at Cordelia's hotel, he questioned several servants. Some recalled how Cordelia had returned to the hotel with a box of candy from Haas's candy store and went to her room. "It was surprising," one said, "because she stayed there for several days." Then, when the servants saw her leaving the room, she was carrying a large box with wrapping paper around it. "It looked like she was taking it to the post office," one said.

But did he have enough information to prove anything? All Less could show now was that Cordelia had apparently sent a package of candies, as well as some provocative letters, to the wife of her lover. But what about the poison?

Looking for that proof, Less began checking the drug stores near the Victoria Hotel. He wasn't sure he could learn anything, because at the time, customers didn't have to sign the register when they bought poison. (The Poison Act that would make this mandatory didn't go into effect until 1907.) So it was a long shot, but with Cordelia firmly denying she committed any crime, he had to find some way to connect her to the poison.

Less checked store after store with no luck. Finally, at one small drug store, he asked the clerk if anyone had recently purchased arsenic. The clerk thought back, remembering. Then he suddenly recalled. "Oh, yes, a few weeks earlier I did sell a woman two ounces of arsenic, and I asked her why she was buying it. I thought her answer: 'I want to clean a straw hat,' a little curious, since I never heard of anyone using arsenic to clean hats." But he sold her the arsenic anyway.

"So do you have a record of who bought it?" Less asked, hoping desperately that the man did, even though such a record wasn't required.

The man looked in his book, because he did keep an informal sales record. And yes, there was the woman's name. He had written down: "Mrs. Bothin" of the Victoria Hotel.

The name was close enough to suggest Cordelia had bought it. Now the district attorney would have the difficult task of proving there was a strong enough chain of circumstances for a conviction. Though the case would go forward in San Francisco, the Delaware officials were interested, too, because the victims were in Delaware. So Attorney General White of Delaware took the train across the country to prosecute the case, scheduled for December 28, 1898. He knew it would be a tough case to prove, because he had only a chain of circumstantial evidence to link Cordelia to the crime—primarily Dunning's statements about his relationship with Cordelia, the package wrapping found in her room, the box and note found by Mr. Penington, and the statements of the City of Paris and drugstore clerks.

For three hours that morning, he argued passionately to the jurors, emphasizing the horrors of the crime, the tremendous suffering of Mrs. Dunning and Mrs. Deanne, and Mrs. Dunning's defenselessness when she opened the box of bonbons, suspecting nothing of the poisoned candy inside. Was the jury convinced? That afternoon, for three more hours, Cordelia's attorney, George Knight, a noted criminal defense lawyer with the reputation as a skilled orator, argued that she was just an innocent, persecuted woman. In fact, he accused the "machinations of the police" for building a completely fabricated case against her, based totally on suspicion. Meanwhile, Cordelia sat at the defense table, looking the picture of Victorian propriety as she listened attentively to her lawyer argue on her behalf. After that, San Francisco District Attorney Hosmer and a second defense attorney, McGowan, gave the final arguments. Afterward, the jury retired with the case.

It was nerve-wracking, waiting for the jury to decide. Would they be connect this chain of circumstantial evidence to Cordelia? Would they be able to see the evil underneath her seemingly proper and matronly veneer? Less waited nervously outside the courthouse for the news.

Finally, after their brief deliberations, the jury was back with the verdict. "We find Cordelia Botkin guilty of murder in the first degree," they agreed, and then they announced her penalty: "imprisonment for life." Immediately Cordelia's lawyer petitioned for a new trial, arguing that California had no jurisdiction in a death that had occurred in Delaware. But Judge Carroll Cook refused. After all, the weapon of murder had been sent from California. So he proceeded to sentence Cordelia to life imprisonment in San Quentin State Prison on February 4, though first he asked her if she had anything further to say in her own defense. "I'm totally innocent of this horrible crime," Cordelia stated firmly, unrepentant to the end. She served her sentence until she died in 1910, never confessing, still claiming her innocence.

THE CASE OF BELLE GUNNESS

La Porte, Indiana, 1908

What was so baffling about this case was not only that Belle Gunness was accused of the most horrendous crimes—luring dozens of suitors to their death and butchering them—but the fact that her Indiana farm burned in a mysterious fire. The big question was whether she died or escaped in the fire. The debate about what happened to her went on for years; it is still going on today.

The mystery of what happened on Belle's farm near La Porte, Indiana, that came to be called "Murder Hill," erupted on April 28, 1908, when a spectacular fire seen for miles burned down Belle's house and barn. At the time, La Porte was a quiet Midwestern farming community in northwest Indiana. Belle had been born as the daughter of a poor sharecropper and occasional stonemason in a little fishing and farming hamlet in Norway in 1859. She had hired out as a cattle girl or dairymaid in surrounding farms as a teenager and had joined the immigrants heading from Norway in the early 1880s. Like them, she viewed America as a land of opportunity where rags-to-riches stories came true.[9]

In those days, women gained their piece of the American dream through marriage. At first, this is what Belle did. At age twenty-five, she married Norwegian farmer Mads Sorensen in 1884 in Chicago at the height of the Victorian period. Even her wedding picture showed her as a respectable middle-class woman, wearing a simple long-sleeved black dress with long billowy skirts and a white lace collar—standard dress at a time when women were quiet homebodies and men were considered their chivalrous protectors.

Belle was ambitious, and she got a taste of independence when she opened a small confectioner shop in Chicago in 1896, though she soon encountered a series of odd misfortunes. Soon after it opened, her shop burned down when a kerosene lamp exploded. After she and her husband bought their first house, it too burned down, killing two of her four infant children, but she had insurance on them. In 1900, her husband died. Though the symptoms suggested strychnine poisoning, Belle convince her family doctor she had only given him a powder to help his cold and the death certificate said natural causes.

That's when Belle moved to La Porte. She used the $8,500 insurance money from her husband's death to buy a forty-eight-acre farm a mile outside of La Porte in the fall of 1901. It was an impressive spread with a beautiful, luxuriously furnished farmhouse. It had once belonged to a former madam who had decorated the rooms like a Victorian palace for entertaining her upper-crust clientele. Belle lived a much more quiet and spartan life, though neighbors soon noticed a trail of gentlemen callers who answered her matrimonial ads.

A year later, she married another Norwegian farmer, Peter Gunness, though he mysteriously died soon after in December 1902. When the coroner found him, he was lying face down in the parlor with a broken nose and a hole in the back of the head. Nearby in the kitchen, a bowl of brine and a sausage grinder were on the floor. Belle calmly explained what happened. Her husband had been helping her make sausage during hog butchering season, and shortly before he died, she found him in the kitchen holding his head and moaning. She guessed he had knocked the brine off the stove, burning himself, and the sausage grinder had fallen on his head. Without much investigation, the coroner described the death as an accident, though the first rumors about Belle began circulating then.

Had she killed him with the grinder?, the neighbors wondered quietly, though no one dared openly say anything.[10]

Belle otherwise appeared to be a proper respectable widow who mostly kept to herself and lived quietly. After a while, though, the neighbors began to wonder about this, too, because she seemed too distant from other folks in a community where neighborliness was the usual way for the farmers who lived near one another. Then, too, the neighbors thought it curious when Belle's foster daughter, Jennie Olsen, suddenly disappeared in 1906, though Belle said she had gone to a finishing school in Los Angeles. They also gossiped about how she worked the farm with a series of hired hands after her husband died and got lots of letters and out-of-town visitors who seemed to disappear after a few weeks. Back then, though, their curiosity was just talk, and perhaps they considered Belle unusual because her city background in a newly urbanizing America made her so different in her ways than her farming neighbors.

She seemed so different because the farms of the Midwest at this time were like an outpost of a rapidly disappearing America that embraced the old values of family, hard work, religion, and Puritan virtues. Growing cities like New York and Chicago represented the fast-paced new America, excited by new machines, technology, material possessions, and making money. The first trial flight of a zeppelin had been launched in 1900; Marconi had transmitted his first telegraphic radio message and the first motor-driven bicycles had been produced in 1901; in 1903, the Wright brothers flew their first airplane. Over the next few years, new inventions and ideas rapidly transformed America—among them the founding of the Ford Motor Company and the first coast-to-coast crossing of the North American continent by car in sixty-five days (1903), the first telegraphic transmission of photographs (1904), and the first neon light signs (1905).

Meanwhile, a new generation of writers was describing the quickening pace of life in the cities, such as George M. Cohan, who wrote and produced *Forty-five Minutes from Broadway* in New York in 1906, and Mary Roberts Rinehart, who wrote *The Circular Staircase*, a mystery of the cities in 1908. Politically, it was the age of Teddy Roosevelt, for whom Richard Steiff designed the first teddy bear in 1903. Roosevelt's air of ebullient optimism and possibilities typified the spirit of America in the 1900s, while the opulence of the city elite inspired those in other parts of the country, like Belle Gunness, to seek the good life, too.

It was in such a world that Belle's farm went up in smoke on the night of April 28, 1908, and soon the police, her neighbors, and then the world began to discover the horrors under her soil. The gory discoveries began the next day, when Sheriff Smutzer and several men came out to investigate the smoldering ruins of what had been a large brick mansion. As they picked through the wreckage, they could still see the remnants of a marble fireplace with mirrors on many walls and bars on the windows, left over from the house's sporting house days. Nearby was a large barn and hog pen, and around the property a row of pine trees created a wall of privacy between Belle and her neighbors—unusual in a world of normal small town openness.

As they dug around, Smutzer and his men quickly discovered four badly burned bodies in the basement—three small ones and one headless adult. The police immediately surmised the small ones belonged to Belle's three children, Myrtle, Lucy, and Philip, aged 11, 9, and 5, and the headless body must be that of Belle. But was it? The headless body was badly shriveled and appeared to weigh much less than Belle, who tipped the scale at a hefty 200-plus pounds at the time of the fire. At first, though, Smutzer didn't immediately pay attention to this discrepancy.

He wondered where the head was. At first, the coroner speculated that it had been cut off by a falling beam. If so, then, where was it? The police kept digging, but the head still did not turn up. Soon they began to speculate that perhaps a killer had cut off the head and set fire to the whole building.

Meanwhile, thinking Belle had died in the fire with her children, Sheriff Smutzer arrested Belle's former handyman, Ray Lamphere, as his prime suspect. He suspected Lamphere after the neighbors reported that Belle had fired him two months earlier. Perhaps, Smutzer reasoned, Lamphere was angry he had been fired or even jealous when Belle introduced one of her suitors as the man she planned to marry next, because he had hoped she would marry him. Thus, at first it seemed a fairly open and shut case.

But then Smutzer and his men began to turn up more bodies. The grisly discoveries began searching after the brother of one of Belle's suitor's, Asle Helgelien,[11] arrived, worried about his missing brother, Andrew. They had worked together on neighboring ranches in South Dakota for fifteen years after immigrating from Norway, and Asle was worried about Andrew, because he knew his brother had left about four months earlier for Indiana to visit a rich widow he had been corresponding with to consider marriage. But after two weeks, Asle hadn't heard anything from him, and by March he was even more concerned when other hired men in the area told him that the woman had been advertising in a Norwegian paper for a Norwegian husband. So if Andrew had gone to marry her, why would she still advertise?

Asle became even more worried when he found Belle's letters from Andrew's two-year correspondence with her and he discovered that Andrew had withdrawn some of his savings to pay for a mortgage on Belle's home. As he told Sheriff Smutzer, he had even written to Belle himself in early April, and she told him that Andrew had come to visit but gone back to Norway. But that didn't sound right. Why would Andrew go without telling his brother? He was even more concerned.

On May 1 Asle received a newspaper clipping about the fire in the mail from a helpful La Porte bank clerk, and he was on the next train to La Porte. He arrived on May 3, and after he poured out his strange story, Sheriff Smutzer and about twenty of his men continued to dig in the remains of the fire. They went back on May 5, and soon they had to tell Asle the sad news. They had found the cut-up remains of Andrew's body.

Nearby, they found the body of a young woman. Who was it? Soon they concluded it was probably Jennie Olsen, since neighbors told them she had never returned after Belle claimed she had gone to school in Los Angeles. Digging on, they found three more bodies—a woman and two adult males.[12] It was the beginning of a search that eventually turned up a dozen bodies.

Just what was going on at the farm? Smutzer theorized that Belle might have helped Lamphere kill Andrew and Jennie, but he still thought Lamphere killed all of them, telling the *New York Times* of May 6 that Lamphere probably did so because of "cupidity and jealousy." He described how Asle told him that Mrs. Gunness had been trying to get a loan from a local bank, and Andrew agreed to lend her the money, sending her $4,500. But then, Smutzer believed, Lamphere had butchered him, since he was a carpenter, and Andrew's body was found dismembered, with his arms, legs, trunk, and hand put in different sacks and buried. As Smutzer told the *Times*, "the way in which the body was dismembered indicates that someone familiar with the use of a saw did the work." He also believed that Jennie was murdered when two other men were killed out of fear that she might reveal what she knew.

But was the killer Belle, Lamphere, or both? As Smutzer began to hear more of Belle's history and learned the suspicious circumstances under which her previous husbands died, he began to wonder. Then a possible would-be victim, Carl Peterson of Waupaca, Wisconsin, came forward with some letters he exchanged with Belle after he answered one of her ads. "I wanted to marry her," he said. "But when she asked for more money than I had and I asked her if she could consent to be a poor man's wife, she backed down."

Could there be even more potential suitors that disappeared? Smutzer asked the local postmaster to learn the names of her other correspondents over the previous four years, thinking this might help him identify the two skeletons found near Jennie's body. As his men continued digging, even more bodies turned up—four more the next day in the yard and by the barn. This time the remains were in rotting gunny sacks, with quicklime scattered about to promote faster decomposition. Now the police began theorizing that maybe Belle didn't perish in the blaze after all. For with all the bodies they had dug up, they still hadn't found the head of the body supposed to be hers. It didn't make sense, Smutzer reasoned. How could her head be totally destroyed, when the remainder of the body believed to be hers was only slightly scorched? Besides, those who saw the body stated that it was smaller than Belle, and they remembered that she had a mouthful of gold teeth. So where were the teeth? Had Belle put a false body in the grave so she could escape?[13]

In case she was still alive, Smutzer quickly notified every police department in the country to be on the lookout for her. His big fear was that she might be on her way back to Norway, and he wanted to catch her first.

Meanwhile, the story of Belle's matrimonial adventures were rapidly coming out. The La Porte postmaster told the prosecutor that after her second husband died in 1903, Belle began getting four to ten letters a day from all over the country in response to her ads for marriage prospects. A typical ad from a Chicago publication read: "A rich and good-looking woman, the owner of a big farm, desires to correspond with a gentleman of wealth and refinement. Object matrimony. Scandinavian preferred." The postal workers joked about the flood of mail, because Belle was anything but good-looking. Rather, they called her "fat, unkempt, and far from attractive in features." But the letters poured in, and soon neighbors began to notice strange men coming to the farm. However, after they gossiped about how Widow Gunness was going to marry again, the suitors were soon gone. One neighbor recalled that one had come wearing a magnificent fur coat, and afterward, she saw Belle wearing it. "Oh, the owner went to Chicago and said he would send for his coat, but he never did," Belle said. As it turned out, it was Andrew's coat.

At this point, on May 6, the police began looking into whether Belle had a private graveyard in Chicago before she moved to La Porte. "Can you exhume the bodies of her former husbands?" Smutzer asked the coroner. Meanwhile, Belle's sister, Mrs. Nellie Larson, provided a public baffled by the horrors unearthed at Belle's farm a reason Belle might have done what she did. "My sister was crazy for money," she declared. "That was her great weakness. As a young woman she never seemed to care for a man for his own self, only for the money or luxury he was able to give." In fact, Belle had told her that she would never have stayed with her first husband "if it was not for the nice home he has."[14]

The next day, May 7, brought even more shocking news. Dr. Charles Jones, who had attended Belle's first husband, Mads Sorensen, when he died in 1900, described her as a "religious fanatic" who was "self-hypnotized into crime," as a result of receiving insurance money after her first husband died. As he theorized, this money affected a mind that was already "unhinged by religious eccentricities," showing her how easily she might obtain money. He opined that is where "her temptation to commit the alleged atrocities may have had its birth."[15]

Meanwhile, with nine bodies dug out of the ground, theories multiplied about where Belle was. One theory was that she had been killed by a Chicago gang. Another was that she was still trying to evade police and make her way to Norway.

Meanwhile, one *New York Times* editorialist expressed the sense of horror that was spreading around the country about the killings. As he wrote:

> The supposed murderess and her victims seem to be in a class apart from the generality of mankind. If the widow of Laporte was really what she now seems to be, she had little or none of the attributes which distinguish man from the beasts: she must have been a stranger to sympathy and sentiment, devoid alike of pity and fear, unmoved by the sight of blood, and free from any sensibility.[16]

It was the beginning of turning Belle from murderess into myth.

Eventually, fourteen bodies were dug up on Belle's property, and though Belle was never found again, Smutzer pieced together the sordid story. Besides probably killing at least two of her former husbands and three of her children, she had lured about a dozen hapless suitors to her farm with promises of marriage and happiness. Then, just as she had butchered her hogs, she had drugged them while they slept, crushed their skulls, and cut them up, burying them around the farm. He estimated that she had stolen over $30,000 from her victims (equivalent to several hundred thousand dollars today). Though Smutzer brought in a former gold prospector to search the Gunness property with sluicing equipment on May 20 to find the missing skull or a jawbone with teeth to identify the headless body, his findings didn't quiet the rumors that Belle had planted someone else's body and escaped. Though Schultz did find a set of teeth belonging to Belle Gunness and coroner Charles S. Mack concluded at the inquest that the body was Belle's, doubters challenged the sheriff: "What's to prevent Mrs. Gunness from having removed her teeth and thrown them into the fire before she left?"[17]

So what of Lamphere? Did he help her? Did he kill her? Ray professed his innocence, claiming he did not set the fire, though he saw it on the road. He also insisted he did not see or help Belle kill Andrew or anyone else. Rather, as the defense tried to show using Belle's eighty love letters to Andrew, she was a woman of deception who had duped poor Andrew and likewise had duped Lamphere and set him up as the prime suspect in her own supposed murder.[18]

In the end, with no absolute proof that Belle had died in the blaze, the jury found Lamphere only guilty of arson, and the judge sentenced him to two to twenty-one years in prison, where he eventually died. But before he did, he contributed even more to the growing mystery when he told a cellmate this story. As he related, he had known about Belle's murders and helped her by burning her victim's bodies. Then, he claimed, Belle had lured a Chicago woman to her farm, gave her a whisky with strychnine, decapitated her, and put her in bed with her children. Afterward, she burned the house down and fled. But before she did, he claimed, she pulled out some of her teeth so the police and coroner would think she had died in the blaze. Then he took her to the train station in Stillwell, Indiana, as the fire raged,[19] and supposedly she was going to contact him and they were going to escape together. But of course, she never did.

Meanwhile, the legends and myths about her grew. On July 9, some of Belle's neighbors—Daniel Hutson and his daughters, Eldora and Evaline—reported seeing her on the road walking in the orchard with a man. Fifteen years later, in 1923, another neighbor, John Nepsha Jr., who was using her land for pasture, reported seeing her in the orchard, too, and when he went to check, he found fresh footprints of a man and a woman.

An even greater shocker occurred in 1931, when an L.A. Deputy District Attorney George Stahlman wrote to the new La Porte sheriff saying that the defendant in a pending murder case might be Mrs. Gunness under the alias of

Mrs. Esther Carlson. She was accused of poisoning an eighty-one-year-old man she was taking care of for his bank account, and she looked very much like an older Belle Gunness, plus she had pictures of children who looked a lot like Myrtle, Lucy, and Philip. But the woman denied being Belle, and after a sensational story in the press, there was no proof, though speculation continued.

Later, in 1955, Lillian de la Toree wrote a book called *The Truth About Belle Gunness*, in which she claimed that Belle did escape but was killed by her conspirators soon afterward to get the money she stole from the men she killed. Some even thought that Sheriff Smutzer might have been in on it. And in *Women Who Kill*, published in 1980, Ann Jones argued that Belle had about a week to travel before police began searching for her. In fact, on May 8, she reported, the police even pulled one wealthy widow, Mrs. Flora Belle Heerin, traveling from Chicago to New York off the train in Syracuse, New York, thinking she was Belle Gunness, and later the woman sued the police and train officials for false arrest.[20]

Eventually, the story of her escape was memorialized in a variety of ballads, including this one that concluded with these verses:

They looked for her in Texas
In sunny Tennessee
They sought her most from coast to coast
O where, O where is she?

Perhaps she's gone to heaven
There's none of us can say
But if I'm right in my surmise
She's gone the other way.[21]

The search for what really happened has continued and in some mysterious ways, too. Since the 1970s, some La Porteans and others have gone to the site of Belle's farmhouse and called her spirit in a séance; at one such gathering, a friend of a friend reported that one of the girls began to scream, and when they turned on the lights, the girl who screamed was dead, her back covered with the wounds from a knife.[22]

Thus, whether Belle died in the fire or escaped, the baffling mystery of Belle Gunness lives on.

Chapter 2

The 1910s

IF THE 1900s were a time of transition to a more urban, cosmopolitan, scientific America, the 1910s were even more so. It was a time when the beginnings of scientific detection in homicides made even more headway, and murder was taken even more seriously. There were pioneering techniques that spread from Europe to England and slowly to the United States after the turn of the century, and there was an increasingly professional police department in major cities around the country. In fact, more frequently a professional medical examiner took over from the coroner (who had often been an inexperienced political appointee) and the citizens who formed a coroner's inquest in determining how the victim died. At the same time, teams of professional prosecutors now emerged to charge these cases. More and more, the police began to seriously investigate the difficult cases that might have previously been written off as unsolvable if the killer was not immediately known or easily discovered from reports of witnesses or readily available clues.

In fact, as police departments became more professional, and as the killers themselves became more mobile, the police began to work together as a sort of national network to share information and capture suspects for one another. The Federal Bureau of Investigation (FBI), which was formed in Washington, D.C., in 1908 (as the Bureau of Investigation), began expanding its operations during the decade, although initially it had only limited power. Not until J. Edgar Hoover took over in 1924 did it start to develop into a major crime-fighting force.

Still one sign of the times was the passage of the Mann Act in 1910 to prohibit transporting women across state lines for immoral purposes. It was a response to the growing breakdown of traditional America and the rise of prostitution in the growing cities.

The period was also characterized by the United States becoming more linked to Europe and England, as the American newspapers reported the growing signs of turmoil that eventually led to World War I—such as the Kaiser making a speech in Hamburg to assert Germany's "place in the sun" and the beginning of the Turkish-Italian war in 1911, followed by war beginning in the Balkans in 1912 and 1913. When Europe went to war in 1914, the United States, led by Woodrow Wilson, soon emerged from the shadows of Europe into a period of great prosperity and progress, as the European Allies looked to manufacturers in North America, outside the war theater, to supply their war goods. So the war helped make America rich and promoted even more growth in American cities. The United States become the new leader in crime fighting and homicide-detection techniques by the end of the decade. Though the developments had started in Europe in the late 1880s and 1890s through the turn of the century, U.S. investigators began to run with the ball.

Meanwhile, American cities were being energized and transformed by the growing hordes of immigrants—mostly from Southern and Eastern Europe between 1905 and 1914. The expanding silent cinema was starting to create the first generation of stars like Charlie Chaplin, who reflected the rising power of an urban workforce in his film *Making a Living* (1914), while D. W. Griffith's epic *Birth of a Nation* (1915) highlighted an America more aware of its own history and destiny separate from Europe. New technologies helped contribute to progress and the sharing of crime detection information, too—such as the first transcontinental telephone call between Alexander Graham Bell in New York and Thomas A. Watson in San Francisco in 1915, the millionth car produced by Ford in that same year, and the first regular airmail service established between New York and Washington in 1918.

At the same time, the decade was characterized by a kind of growing freneticism in daily life, reflected in the cubist style of abstract art of painters like Pablo Picasso and Paul Klee; the dramatic modernist architecture of Frank Lloyd Wright, who designed the Imperial Hotel in Tokyo; the spread of excitement in orchestral music by composers like Stravinsky, whose *Rite of Spring* unleashed a new wildness in music in 1913. Jazz began sweeping the United States in 1916, and literature was marked by a new concern with the somewhat alienated urban hero set adrift by the changing times, such as when Theodore Dreiser wrote *The Genius* in 1915, which was suppressed by New York censors, and the U.S. Post Office burned installments of James Joyce's *Ulysses*, published in the *Little Review* in 1918.

Significantly, too, it was a time when women were starting to break out even more against the Victorian strictures of the quiet, prim, nurturing woman—and some of the most baffling crimes of the decade involved these newly domineering or independent women or the men who tried to victimize these women who had money. Some signs of the times were in 1916, when Margaret Sanger opened the first birth control clinic; when the new bobbed hair fashion for women swept the United States and England in 1917; and when the women-led Prohibition movement resulted in twenty-four states voting against alcoholic beverages in 1916. Women still didn't have the vote yet nationally, since Wilson's suffrage bill was turned down in 1917 (they didn't get the vote until 1920). Nonetheless, more and more women were stepping out, and their new role perhaps contributed to crimes by them or against them.

Meanwhile, another growing crime trend of the age was the rise of gangs in the mushrooming cities, especially among the immigrants who poured into cities like New York and Chicago. It was the beginnings of the notorious gangs and killers, which took center stage in the 1920s and 1930s. There was the spread of the notorious Black Hand, led by Sicilian and Italian gangsters, that organized extortion and counterfeiting rackets in New York, Chicago, St. Louis, Kansas City, and New Orleans. Meanwhile, Dion O'Banion, Thomas O'Conner, and others Irish gangsters began to develop their own criminal connections in Chicago and other cities. A new generation of Italian gangsters, like Al Capone, Bugs Moran, and Johnny Torrio, set up their own organizations. They started with other kinds of rackets, like O'Banion, who early on worked as an enforcer for Hearst papers to make sure newsstand owners carried Hearst publications and beat them if they didn't. Thus, they were primed to move into bootlegging in the next decades when Prohibition made drinking illegal.

Ironically, the most common crimes were still those among the lower-income groups, who were more likely to get into fights over "cards, words, and dirty looks" to quote a historian of murder in America, Roger Lane,[1] at a time when upper- and middle-class Americans were still guided by notions of propriety, refinement and proper behavior. But the more dramatic and baffling (though less common) crimes that captivated the nation were those that involved the members of the more respectable and moneyed classes. What made their crimes harder to solve is they were more apt to use stealth, trickery, or more private means of concealing their crimes.

Increasingly, the police were more equipped to go after the more high-status, sophisticated killers. More and more the police, with the backing and funding of the city population behind them, were dedicated to solving these mysterious homicides—and the medical examiners and professional prosecutors were better equipped to support them in gathering evidence and pursuing criminal charges. Meanwhile, a growing popular press helped fan interest in these mystifying cases, turning them into national soap operas—a trend that has continued to today.

Some of these cases turned into international manhunts, such as the search for Dr. Hawley Harvey Crippen, a Michigan homeopath who moved to England in 1900 and worked in London for a patent medicine firm. He killed his wife, Belle Elmore, a would-be opera star, in January 1910 at the urging of his lover, Ethel Le Neve, with hyoscine poison from a medical supply shop. After pawning her jewelry, dismembering her, and burying her, he told friends she had gone back to America. After police searched his house (at the urging of friends who couldn't locate her) but found nothing, they were ready to let him go. However, when Crippen tried to return to the United States with his lover dressed like a boy using the name Mr. Robinson and son, the police got suspicious, returned, and searched, this time finding human remains covered with quick lime under the cellar floor. The police took a faster boat to America, meeting Crippen at the dock. The media and the new technology played a role in his capture, when the London *Daily Mail* printed a story about how the police were looking for a wanted "cellar murderer" and the captain of Crippen's ship recognized his photograph. Using the new Marconi wireless telegraphy, he contacted London to report his suspicions, and then Crippen was captured.

The new advances in forensic medicine made it possible to prove the case against Crippen. Since all that was left of Mrs. Crippen was a pile of flesh and internal organs, the pathologist on the case, Sir Bernard Spilsbury, had to be able to show the remains belonged to Belle Crippen. He did this by using toxicology tests to show that the remains contained traces of hyoscine, and then he was able to show that a piece of flesh found at the scene came from the abdomen by proving that the cells came from the rectus muscle of the abdominal wall and also showed a scar from an operation Mrs. Crippen previously had. Ten years before, forensic scientists couldn't have done this. But now, along with other evidence, such as showing that Belle was wrapped in Crippen's own pajama jacket bought in 1909, the new science helped convince the jury. In less than a half hour, they found Crippen guilty and he was hanged in November 1910, less than a year after committing the crime.[2]

In 1910, another major advance was the use of the microscope, which was able to detect clues invisible to the naked eye that could reveal a killer. This time, the first steps occurred in France, by Edmond Locard, who set up his own laboratory in two attic rooms at the Palace of Justice and worked on turning forensic medicine into an exact science. Among other things, he established the "exchange principle," in which he was able to show that the criminal always leaves something or takes something away from the crime scene. Typical leavings might be samples of his skin under the victim's fingernails, footprints, fingerprints, or clothing fibers. Typical things a criminal might take away include soil on the soles of his shoes or hair or blood from the victim.[3] Then, too, there might be tire marks from a car; tool marks on windows or doors; bits of ink, paint, or blood dropped or taken away; saliva and sweat; vegetation; or pollen.

Locard showed the effectiveness of the process by helping the Paris police break a counterfeit gang that was making metal coins. The police had no proof, but Locard brushed dust from their clothing and examined it under a microscope. He saw metal fragments, and when he used chemicals to test them, he discovered that the fragments contained tin, antimony, and lead in the same proportions in the counterfeit coins. It was a compelling test, and it led to the conviction of the three counterfeiters.[4] This showed the power of the microscope and careful forensic investigation to use trace evidence. Over the next few years, this technology spread to England and to America.

Key progress in fingerprinting was also occurring. This began after a New York policeman, Inspector Joseph A. Faurot, went to London in 1904 to study fingerprinting at Scotland Yard and started to introduce the new Henry method of classifying prints to the United States. It was slow going in the 1900s, even though he caught a hotel thief soon after his return and solved a murder in 1908. He then solved a simple burglary case when he found the fingerprints of the burglar on the window of the shop. Faurot presented a demonstration in court in which he waited outside while the judge invited several members of the public to press their index fingers on a courtroom window and one of them placed a fingerprint on a glass tabletop. After Faurot was able to tell which fingers on the window and table were identical, the case made headlines, captivating the American public.[5] Increasingly, fingerprinting became acceptable in the United States.

These developments, along with improvements in the identification of blood traces into A, O, B, and AB groupings in old bloodstains (discovered by Dr. Leone Lattes in 1915); advances in the identification of poisons; and better methods to distinguish the markings on the bullets of different guns (such as in the Charles Stielow case from upstate New York in 1915 that gained an innocent man a governor's pardon),[6] gave investigators and prosecutors new tools to discover what really happened in these difficult cases.

More and more they needed these tools, as killers were able to use the mobility and anonymity of the growing cities to hide their crimes. Then, too, neighbors were less aware of the odd doings of their neighbors, so more investigators had to piece together what happened after the fact. Meanwhile, it would seem that the killers became more devious and plotting, particularly when it came to staging the growing number of murders motivated by money that resulted in many of the baffling crimes of the 1910s. While the big mysteries of the turn of the century and early 1900s had been inspired by love and jealousy (Luetgert, Botkin, and Molineux), now money from estates, insurance scams, and property of the deceased became the big draw. In turn, killers used innocence, family ties, and love of their victims to pull them into their net.

This can be seen in cases from East to West, with women drawn to one method and male killers to another. The cases with female killers include the case of Linda Burfield Hazzard, a Washington doctor who promoted an unusual fasting cure and starved many of her patients to death for their estates, and the saga of the Wardlaw sisters, from a once prominent Southern aristocratic family, who starved one of their daughters to death to collect insurance money. As for the male murderers, they involved men who found their vulnerable women victims by promising or offering the possibility of marriage and then killing them for their money. One was Henry Spencer, who wooed and killed a spinster with a big bank account; the other was Helmuth Schmidt, called "the American Bluebeard," who found his eager victims in the lovelorn columns and killed perhaps three dozen of them for their money and jewels.

Following are the stories of Spencer and Schmidt. They are examples of these trends and show the development of new investigative techniques.

THE CASE OF HENRY SPENCER

Chicago, 1913–14

When police found Mrs. Mildred Allison Rexroat's body lying on the railroad tracks in Wheaton, Illinois, on the night of Friday, September 26, 1913 (or in June 1914 according to some accounts),[7] she looked like she was planning to travel on the train before she was shot in the head. She very much looked the proper lady, dressed in the long skirts and high-necked blouse of the day. Piles of clothes were scattered around her, as if they had been dumped out of a large suitcase or trunk.

So what had happened? This was a time when proper young ladies still didn't travel around very much on their own, despite the growing suffragette movement. All the clothing suggested the woman, at that time unidentified, was about to go somewhere before she was so suddenly delayed.

Over the next few days, the police, led by Captain Halpin of the Chicago Detective Bureau, began to piece together the strange story of what happened to Mrs. Rexroat.

As it turned out, Mrs. Rexroat was a dancing teacher in Wheaton, as police learned from some of her effects on the tracks. As they asked questions, they learned she had been seeing a seemingly nice young man who looked like a well-bred, mild-mannered store clerk, dressed quite properly in a vest, shirtsleeves, and spectacles. He variously described himself as a salesman or one-time gentleman farmer, and Mrs. Rexroat, who had recently divorced her first husband, had met him at one of her dancing lessons. Over the next two months, they had become a couple, and friends reported how eager she was to get married again.

But who was this mysterious beau? Fortunately, the story of the Wheaton dance teacher had captivated the Chicago papers, and soon a woman came forward describing how a man named Henry Spencer had been boarding with her. She described how on the night of September 26, when Rexroat was found murdered, Spencer had come to her house. "His shoes were covered with dust and he showed a diamond ring resembling the one that had been worn by Mrs. Rexroat. He also took a revolver from his pocket and removed an empty shell, which he threw from the window."[8]

It was an amazingly fortunate lead, and when the police came to question Spencer further on October 5, they found the suitcase that Mrs. Rexroat carried the night of her murder, which was stained with blood, as well as the revolver believed to have shot her. Spencer began the first of his long confessions of the many people he had murdered, which baffled police and gave rise to a kind of urban legend about how he killed.

Spencer began with his story about how he had met Mrs. Rexroat at the dance hall, suggesting that she thought he was a farmer and that she could "work me the same way" as she had her first husband, who was also a farmer. After luring her to go to Michigan with him to be married, he killed her and took the few dollars she had and her diamond ring. Then he took the next train back to Chicago.[9]

There were more, he told Captain Halpin, many more, giving him a list of thirteen other persons, most in the past year. He spoke calmly, without the slightest trace of emotion. He claimed he had killed one man and woman fourteen years earlier, and two policemen he recalled by name—Charles Pennell and Timothy Devine—when he was escaping arrest for a burglary twelve years before. Then there were two girls at Pawpaw Lake in Michigan in August, two girls at Lake Develvan in Wisconsin, and a woman in Belle Island, Michigan, the previous summer. There were two men and two women in Chicago, including one near the Cook County Hospital a few days before, whom he had hit in the head with a hammer, which he left by the railroad tracks. Though the police thought the hammer had something to do with the Rexroat murder, it was only used in this other killing. Supposedly, the recent killings began after he was released from the Illinois State Penitentiary in September 1912, and the other killings had occurred before that.

The only problem was that the police began to sense that most of these confessions and murders weren't really true. They were a little skeptical as Spencer poured out his confessions, since he admitted he was addicted to opium, and it was bizarre for a person, when arrested, to admit what he had done so easily. Still, the police were duty-bound to check, and they decided to investigate each of the homicides Spencer claimed within the last twelve months.

They sent out telegrams to police headquarters around the country where Spencer claimed to have killed his victims, and within a day responses from these other departments came in asserting that no such crimes had ever been committed. As Halpin soon discovered, Spencer had spent half of his life behind bars, and during times when many of these alleged crimes occurred, he was already in jail. Apparently, starting when he was eight years old, he had been sent as an orphan to the Chicago Home for the Friendless, ran away, was picked up by the police, was sent to another institution, ran away again, and was in and out of more institutions until he was sixteen. He was sent to a penitentiary for receiving stolen property for eight years, and after violating his parole, was sent to the Joliet State Penitentiary. In fact, the two policemen he claimed to have killed were killed when he was in Joliet.

Spencer tried to stammer out an explanation. "Oh, the man who did that job was a 'pal' of mine, and I just thought that it wouldn't do any harm for me to take his place. I've got to hang anyway, so what's the difference."[10]

At this point Halpin became increasingly skeptical of most of Spencer's tales of murder, especially when he tried to claim he was involved with the notorious Chicago car bandits and had killed two farmers with them. Unfortunately, he would have been in the Joliet penitentiary then, too. The same was true for a series of lone-man restaurant hold-ups Spencer now confessed to. He described the grisly murder of the maid of a wealthy woman in Orange County, whom he promised to marry for her money—that also proved to be without foundation. There was no such murder in the county records.

Thus, Halpin and the other detectives concluded that most of his tales were "purely the result of a disordered imagination," since Spencer's mind had been "weakened by his indulgence in drugs." As Halpin told one *New York Times* reporter, "Except for possibly two murders, Spencer's weird story seems to be a pure fabrication. His imagination, stimulated by drugs, poured out one of the most fantastic tales of murder that has ever come from a man whose mind is given to dreams of crime."[11]

But why? Why tell these bizarre, incriminating stories? That's what baffled the police and the public. Apparently, the source of the tales was the daily crime news, which had become a popular feature of the city newspapers. Spencer connected himself with many high-profile murders and robberies and was able to describe in detail how he had done what was described in the press. But of details not in the news, he could only describe what he did very vaguely or say, "I don't remember."[12]

The one thing Halpin was sure of was that Spencer had killed Mrs. Rexroat, because he had her suitcase and had put her savings in his name at the bank. That was enough for the jury, which convicted Spencer of her murder, and on November 29 he was sentenced to hang at Wheaton on December 19. At his sentencing hearing, Spencer argued for a new trial himself and repudiated his confession of murder. The judge overruled him, and he was scheduled to hang.

Oddly, Spencer presumably embraced religion, and the story of how he killed Mrs. Rexroat metamorphosed into a somewhat more romantic story that seems to combine elements from several of his claimed killings—and turned Spencer into a more romantic lothario as well. As described in two popular accounts of noted crimes—Martin Fido's *The Chronicle of Crime* and Jay Robert Nash's *Bloodletters and Badmen*—Spencer appeared in town in June 1914, describing himself as a salesman. He met and courted the older and wealthy Rexroat. Supposedly, he impressed the town's leading citizens, and after they announced their engagement, Spencer took Rexroat on a picnic on the outskirts of Wheaton. Presumably, they brought along a picnic basket, and Spencer also brought along a hammer and shovel. During the picnic, as Rexroat lay on her back, her eyes closed, Spencer lifted the hammer, bashed in her head, pulled two rings from her fingers, dug a small grave, and buried her.

But then Spencer attracted the suspicions of a local banker when he went to the bank and drew out her savings. Supposedly, he convinced Rexroat to put her savings in his name, and the banker and bank tellers wondered why Rexroat would permit a comparative stranger to have access to her assets. They were suspicious when he returned to town from the picnic without her. As a result, they called the local sheriff, who stopped Spencer for questioning as he waited for the 1 p.m. train to take him from town. Though Spencer claimed to know nothing, he was arrested and held for questioning for a week about where Rexroat was. Then, his story continues, a farmer who had seen the couple on a hillside reported this to the sheriff, helped them locate Rexroat's grave, and they dug out the body. After this, under heavy questioning, Spencer confessed he had battered her head with a hammer and told them where they could find it. At his trial, Spencer claimed this confession had been beaten out of him and wasn't true.[13]

Shortly before his execution (postponed until August 14, 1914), Spencer was visited by two evangelists, and he renounced his previously evil ways and joined "the ranks of God's children" or "God's holy crusade," as he later told the vast crowd that came to witness his hanging and told reporters Wallace Smith and Ben Hecht of the Chicago *Daily News*. He claimed he had repented. His soul had been "washed of all wickedness," and he felt certain he would go to heaven. As a result, as he was led to the gallows and a long white robe was put over him, he had a big smile on his face, and he continued to smile as his hands were strapped to his side and the rope was placed around his neck. In his last moments, he addressed the crowd, saying, "This is the happiest day of my life," describing how he had never had a home before, but now had a father in heaven waiting to receive him. He was happy because he had made his peace with God, by giving him "the truth of my soul."[14]

But had he? After reciting several psalms before the gallows was finally sprung, Spencer withdrew his confession, saying, "I'm innocent of the murder of Allison Rexroat. . . . I never harmed a hair on her head! So help me God!"

Then the trap sprung, and Spencer went to his death, leaving all sorts of baffling questions about who he really was. Why did he confess? What crimes did he really commit and how? About the only thing clear is that he did kill Rexroat, but beyond that he seems to have woven a story of mystery and illusion, caught up in creating a fantasy world based on identifying with the murderers and criminals of the day, gaining a kind of notorious glory in the popular press. It's as if he wanted to make himself more than he was as a homeless boy who became a petty crook and robber. Through murder—and admitting to more murders than he ever really committed—his name would live on. So it has in the more glorified stories about the thin, bespectacled killer who looks more like a Mr. Milquetoast than a lady killer who killed for money.

THE CASE OF HELMUTH SCHMIDT

Chicago, 1918

When Augusta Steinbach took the train from New York to Detroit in February 1918, she thought she was going to meet a man named Herman Neugebauer and they were going to be married. She had read his advertisement for a wife in the *New York Herald* when she was working for a wealthy man, and after they corresponded for some time, she arrived on the train with all her money and possessions, eager to leave the past behind. Even though he didn't meet her at the train (she telegraphed her departure), she was still hopeful and went to a Detroit rooming house, expecting the marriage to take place in mid-March. She even wrote to her longtime friend Agnes Domanecki telling her, and Agnes sent a wedding present to her rooming house. But by then, she was already missing. Where was she? Who was Herman Neugebauer, the man she was supposed to marry?

At the time, even his name raised concerns, because World War I was just ending and there was strong anti-German sentiment in the United States. Many immigrants from Europe had been arriving for the past few years, fleeing the turmoil in Europe. Yet this European turmoil and influx of immigrants was also making America an even more exciting place to be. The economy was in high gear; cities were booming; the first airmail delivery had started between New York, Washington, and Chicago; and the literature, art, and music of the day reflected this excitement, concern with war, and new European influence, such as Rebecca West's *The Return of the Soldier*, Paul Nash's painting *We Are Making a New World*, and Charlie Chaplin's film *Shoulder Arms*. There was much distrust of Germans, reflected in the decision by the New York Philharmonic Society to ban compositions by living German composers and the arrest of Karl Muck, the German conductor of the Boston Symphony Orchestra, as an enemy alien.

Then the odd Steinbach case came to the attention of the Oakland County police. Based on what Agnes Domanecki told them, by April 22, 1918, they believed Steinbach was probably murdered for the money and possessions she had brought with her, and her remains had been burned or buried. But they didn't know where, and they were still seeking positive proof of her death.

Their investigation began soon after Domanecki sent her wedding present, wasn't able to get in touch with her friend, and asked a Detroit woman to check on Steinbach and the Mr. Neugebauer she was supposed to marry. The woman reported back that Mr. Neugebauer *was* married and had a seventeen-year-old daughter. What was going on?

As the police began checking, they found more mysteries. They soon learned that a few days after the wedding present was delivered, the owners of the rooming house went to an address where Mr. Neugebauer was supposedly staying with his sister, but the woman at the door, who gave her name as Mrs. Schmidt, said she knew of no such person. Her manner was so strange, the owners went to the express agent, who told them that Steinbach's trunks had been delivered to the Schmidt home as well.[15]

That's when the Oakland County officers stepped into the case. When they went to visit the Schmidts, Schmidt claimed that Neugebauer had introduced him to Miss Steinbach and had asked him to take care of her trunks until she sent for them. "He even gave me the key," Schmidt claimed. The officers were skeptical, believing Schmidt, a forty-one-year-old engineer at the Ford Manufacturing Company, was really Neugebauer, and they arrested him and his wife, Helen, and seventeen-year-old daughter Gertrude.

Then they carefully searched their house and found buried under the floor of the porch a box filled with bloodstained feminine apparel. A neighbor they spoke to had some suspicious news as well. In mid-March, she told police, she saw the windows of the Schmidt basement covered with newspapers and heard a woman crying there. Afterward, Mrs. Schmidt cleaned out the furnace, took a box to a nearby creek, and carefully scrubbed it with water.

Thus, police told the press, Miss Steinbach had been murdered for her money and property by Schmidt posing as Neugebauer, and he had burned or buried her remains somewhere. They still needed positive proof of her death because they didn't have her body. They added this ominous note for the press—that Schmidt was registered as an "alien enemy" and that U.S. Department of Justice officials had helped the local authorities in their search of the house.

By the next day, however, the police were convinced when, after intensive questioning, Schmidt finally confessed, telling Prosecutor Gillespie, Sheriff Cross of Oakland County, Chief Seymour of Highland Park, and other deputies and detectives that he had in fact lured Steinbach to his home through a matrimonial advertisement in a New York paper and had cut up and burned her body. Although he at first tried to claim that Steinbach had taken poison when he refused to leave his family and marry her, the police caught him in so many conflicting details that he finally put his arms around Gillespie's shoulders, promising that he would make a formal confession to a stenographer. "And then I'll tell you even more. Just let me have some lunch first."

The officers took him back to his cell, and he fell to the floor on his knees, apparently praying when they left.[16] He never did tell anything more. Shortly after he confessed, he killed himself in his cell. He pulled down a heavy iron bed railing, suspended from the wall, so it fell on his head and crushed his skull.

After his death, more evidence of a long career of collecting and killing women came out. Before World War I, he had placed ads in newspapers using an alias in New York, New Jersey, Missouri, and Michigan, advertising for a "suitable lady to marry soon."[17] His ads were designed to appeal to the young immigrant girls who had recently arrived from Europe. After finding a likely prospect, he would travel to that area to meet her. Then he would rob and usually kill the women, although some early victims he just robbed. They came forward after news of Schmidt hit the papers. One was a woman in Chicago, who thought she was still Mrs. Schmidt. She had answered one of his ads and married him in Chicago in 1915; after a few days he left with $2,000 of her money. Another woman in New York asserted that Schmidt married her using the name John Swift; another woman in New Jersey described how she had lived with Schmidt for a month, and then he disappeared with $400.

At least they survived. On May 2, the police found a body of a woman believed to be Irma Pallatinus wrapped in canvas under the floor of Schmidt's cellar. The body looked like an Egyptian mummy when unearthed. About a year earlier, Irma had disappeared, and after neighbors wondered about what happened, the police had questioned Schmidt. Schmidt calmly said she had died in a hospital and he had told both his daughter, Gertrude, and Irma's sister, Mrs. Edward Rederer, that she had run away with $700 of his money. At the time, lacking a body, police had not pursued the matter. Now, her body contributed to their belief, as they told the *New York Times*, that "Schmidt engaged in the business of luring women through matrimonial ads, obtained their savings, and then killed them." They also believed he had moved from a house in Detroit to a new home near Royal Oak to have more space to dispose of his victims' bodies.[18] They estimated that he may have killed as many as three dozen women who fell for his ads, and it's no wonder that the press dubbed Schmidt the "American Bluebeard."

Now that Schmidt was dead, they had no way to know for sure what had happened to most of the women or why they fell for his charms. By killing himself, Schmidt left the police, the press, and the public even more baffled.

Chapter 3

The 1920s

BY THE 1920s, the United States had finally become an urban, cosmopolitan culture—but it became much more lawless, too. There had been a growing pressure in the major cities—most notably New York and Chicago—from the influx of immigrants and rural residents to the cities, creating problems of poverty, labor agitation, and gangs. In the 1920s, all this exploded after the passage of the Eighteenth Amendment to the U.S. Constitution and the Volstead Act in January 1919 beginning a decade of Prohibition, a year before the Nineteenth Amendment gave women the vote in 1920. A growing temperance movement made up of religious leaders and women with increasing political clout had contributed to the passage of Prohibition, thinking it might help to get men out of the saloons and back to the family. In actuality, what it did is turn millions of otherwise law-abiding Americans into "criminals," led to the establishment of thousands of speakeasies where patrons came to drink illegal alcohol, and fueled the expansion of gangs into a national network of organized crime, making heroes of names like Dutch Schultz, Al Capone, and Bugs Moran. Meanwhile, in the Midwest, gangs of bank robbers like Pretty Boy Floyd and Bonnie and Clyde roared through the small towns with cars and machine guns—heirs to Jesse James and the James-Younger gang, who established the glamorous outlaws of the West tradition. This spirit of lawlessness continued on into the dark days of the Depression in the 1930s.

Many people and the press were fascinated, and a new literature of crime thrillers emerged that helped glorify these outlaws, at the same time that they were terrorizing many Americans. While these outlaws represented one kind of breaking away from old traditions, the growing independence of women reflected another—not only did they get the vote, but many women turned the tradition of the quiet, proper Victorian ideal of women on its head, letting loose as a new, more independent urban woman free to kick up her heels. It was an image captured by the flapper girl, who went out dancing, smoking, and drinking with men or on her own in the speakeasies. In turn, the films of the time reflected this outlaw spirit—such as *Robin Hood* (1922) and *The Thief of Bagdad* (1924), both with the swashbuckling Douglas Fairbanks, and *Don Juan* (1926) with John Barrymore.

Meanwhile, other art and literature reflected this wild and frenetic spirit of liberation that came to be known as the Jazz Age—as expressed in various F. Scott Fitzgerald books, like *This Side of Paradise* (1920), *Tales of the Jazz Age* (1922), and *The Great Gatsby* (1925); the steamy love stories by D. H. Lawrence in *Women in Love* (1920) and *Lady Chatterley's Lover* (1928) that quickly spread to America from England; and the religious shocker by Sinclair Lewis, *Elmer Gantry*, published in 1927. Major artists and composers echoed this spirit of wild release and abandon, too—such as Joe "King" Oliver and Jelly Roll Morton, who recorded their New Orleans–style jazz record in 1923; Rudolf Friml, who presented *The Vagabond King* in New York in 1925, while George Gershwin provided a kind of comic reminder of the need for control in his song "Lady Be Good." But songs like "Crazy Rhythm" and "Makin' Whoopee" in 1928 were more in tune with the spirit of the times, as was the Charleston, which became a fashionable dance in 1925, the first year when female fashions began to feature straight dresses without waistlines and skirts above the knees. It was like a decade celebrating a national release and liberation from the spirit of Queen Victoria and America's brief participation in World War I.

New technologies and new changes in daily life helped contribute to these wild and crazy times. It was the beginning of big sports, with the formation of the American Professional Football Association in 1920, the sale of Babe Ruth to the New York Yankees by the Boston Red Sox for $125,000 that same year, and a knockout by Jack Dempsey in 1921 that made Dempsey the first truly popular national boxing hero. The first radio stations began broadcasting, starting in 1921 with the first radio broadcast of a baseball game and the founding of the first commercially licensed radio station—KDKA in Pittsburgh. The auto became a popular means of travel, as Ford Motor Company produced the ten millionth car in 1924, and a network of highways began to connect all parts of America.

In response to this explosion of independence, freedom, and lawlessness, there was a corresponding reaction. As historian Roger Lane notes in *Murder in America*, "Many thoughtful Americans were both fearful and embarrassed about murderous violence and what it seemed to imply about 'the national character,' judicial institutions, race relations, and other sensitive issues."[1] As a result, in a kind of parallel universe, there was also a reform and strengthening of the police, especially in the form of the national presence of the Federal Bureau of Investigation (FBI) under J. Edgar Hoover. Gradually, Hoover strengthened and professionalized the bureau, using it to declare war on the growing gangs in the cities and the small-town bank robbers, though it wasn't until the 1930s that the big crackdowns happened.

Though the overall national murder rate was down in this decade due to an overall increase in education, urbanization, and other factors, what was new was the way it was concentrated in certain major urban centers and involved an increase in the use of guns, which were now more affordable due to urban prosperity. Also new was that crime became the focus of much popular attention with the help of the press. And the crime rate was much higher than other developed nations. As professor H. C. Brearley reported in *Homicide in the United States*, the first scholarly study of homicide ever published in 1932, in the 1920s, the U.S. homicide rate was 8.4, and even higher in certain regions (notably the South, followed by the far West and Midwest) and states like Florida where it was 30.0, compared to only 0.05 in England and Wales and 0.18 in Switzerland.[2]

As Lane describes it, the organized urban gangs became a way up the American ladder for "ambitious young urban entrepreneurs, once Irish, more recently Italian and Jewish." Though there had been organized gangs since the nineteenth century involved in gambling, extortion, labor racketeering, persuading voters to vote their way, and sometimes liquor sales, now more than ever crime required not only bullets but organized planning and cooperation. This was necessary to import illegal alcohol and then distribute it across a city or state and avoid the interference from rival gangsters or local, state, or federal authorities. Much like the cocaine trade today, the amount of money pouring into the coffers of these illegal marketers was huge, so intimidation or killing became a way of life, as necessary, to control or expand one's territories. New technology helped, because now criminals could buy mass-produced automobiles to use when attacking a target and then quickly get away. Automatic weapons were more readily available, and many of the newly minted gangsters had just come back from the war trained to kill. This was a deadly combo that contributed to the glorious lawlessness of the age, as did the difficulty of solving any of these gangland crimes.[3] For example, the Chicago Crime Commission estimated that there were about 400 gangland murders, virtually all officially unsolved, during the 1920s; 130 of them were in Chicago alone between 1926 and 1927.[4] Typically, the killers would speed away leaving dead victims behind them, or the bodies would turn up in the river, a park, or an abandoned lot. Witnesses were either dead or unwilling to talk. The other major type of killing that mushroomed and was often unsolved were the armed robberies, made much easier by the car—whether by modern Jesse James–style gangs or the lone gunmen who robbed grocery stores, gas stations, and people on the streets late at night.[5]

Meanwhile, all the press and literary attention created an even greater fascination with sensationalized violence. In a day before the popularity of radio and TV, people eagerly read about the latest crime news and trials. For example, when Lane reviewed the 1926 issues of the *New York World* and the tabloid

New York Daily News for one month—from November 8 to December 8—he found that 15 percent of the *World*'s total space was devoted to crime news, and the *Daily News* devoted 33 percent of its coverage to the topic. True crime had started to become part of popular culture.

As in previous decades, the most highly publicized cases were the scandals of improper behavior by those in the higher reaches of society, such as in 1922 when the Rev. Edward Wheeler Hall was found dead with his mistress, Eleanor Mills, in a lovers lane, their bodies arranged in a grisly embrace and love letters strewn around them. It was covered by some 200 reporters and 50 photographers.[6] In 1926 the body of film director William Taylor was found in a Hollywood bungalow, raising hints of a secret double life, jealous lovers, and angry drug lords. The American public ate up that story, as well as the Judd Gray and Ruth Snyder case in 1927, after the lovers faked a bungled burglary to cover up their killing of Snyder's husband, Albert, in suburban Long Island. There wasn't much mystery, since they were soon caught and turned on each other. Perhaps like the Long Island Lolita saga of Amy Fisher and Joey Buttafuoco in the 1990s captured the imagination with its seamy suburban ordinariness, so did the Gray-Snyder case, and for about two weeks they held center stage in the national press.[7]

In turn, all of this interest in crime perhaps sparked the beginning of something new—the killers who killed just for the thrill, excitement, or intellectual challenge of it. Before now, killing had largely arisen out of everyday feelings of anger, greed, jealousy, unrequited love, revenge, and personal and social conflicts. An example of this is the notorious Leopold and Loeb case in Chicago that hit the papers in 1924, when eighteen-year-old Richard Loeb and his friend nineteen-year-old Nathan Leopold, both exceptionally bright university graduates who had started to study law at the University of Chicago, decided to commit the perfect crime. Spurred on by Loeb, the two imagined themselves as superior "Supermen" emancipated from contemporary standards of right and wrong.[8] To show their superiority, they carefully planned a kidnapping and murder, typed up a ransom note on a typewriter, randomly picked fourteen-year-old Bobby Franks, a friend of Loeb's younger brother, and enticed him into their rented car. Then, in accordance with their plan—developed with the help of the crime literature of the day—they hit the boy with a chisel, stuffed his mouth with rags after he was unconscious, wrapped his body in a lap robe, drove about 20 miles while he bled to death, and dumped his body in a marshy culvert after pouring hydrochloric acid over his face to make it unrecognizable. However, because Leopold dropped his rare horn-rimmed prescription eyeglasses at the scene, the men were soon caught and the evidence of the body, chisel, and typewriter readily found. They also confessed, and at their trial—widely covered by the press—noted attorney Charles Darrow pleaded to a judge that they were guilty but were mentally abnormal, as well as very young, so they weren't fully responsible. The judge sentenced them to life without parole because they were so young.[9]

The case both fascinated and appalled the nation because such seemingly well-educated, respectable, highly intelligent boys, the sons of wealthy parents given every opportunity, had apparently killed just for the challenge of doing it successfully without getting caught. That's what was suddenly very different—like an early warning sign of the explosion of unusual crimes to come. In a sense, the public fascination had contributed itself to the motive to kill by glorifying crime and criminals. It made accomplishing a murder something to achieve.

Then, too, this decade also marked the beginning of the first sex and serial killers in the United States. One was the mysterious Earle Leonard Nelson, whose nationwide killing spree of over twenty women, almost all of them landladies, between 1926–27 baffled police in the United States and then in Canada. Another was Edward Hickman, the first widely known pedophile, who kidnapped, held for ransom, murdered, and mutilated twelve-year-old Marian Parker in Los Angeles.[10]

Perhaps a reason for this sudden upsurge in all types of criminality might be, according to Brearley, because of the decline in traditional social restraints—an early version of the same kind of arguments heard today. As Brearley observed in his study, the divorce rate in the United States was now so much higher than any other country—1 out of every 8 marriages, compared to 1 in 96 in England and 1 in 161 in Canada. In turn, he, like other experts, believed this high level of family instability was not only related to juvenile delinquency but to homicide and to the creation of a "homicidal personality"—basically a person who was stuck in the infantile stage of ego development, rather than becoming a more socialized, altruistic person.[11] Such a person simply lacks the usual self-controls and is prone to erupt when triggered, such as when under stress.

Then, too, in explanation of the increase in crime, experts pointed to the legal availability of guns, especially concealed revolvers, and an especially lax and inefficient justice system compared to other countries, due to a weakness in police detection and an American court system that tended to be more tolerant of violence and more sympathetic toward the slayer than in other countries. In fact, early on, as Lane points out, "rich defendants with skillful lawyers fared far better than poor folks," and the legal profession used legal niceties that "allowed the guilty to escape or win new trials on the barest of technicalities."[12]

In any event, as this spirit of lawlessness and fascination with crimes increased in the 1920s, so did the efforts of the police to combat crime, and in this they were aided by new developments in the art of investigation and detection. Increasingly, in part because of the development of the FBI, America now began to take the lead in the forensic sciences and other detection techniques.

One key development was in the science of ballistics, led by three Americans, Calvin Goddard, Charles A. Waite, and Philip Gravelle. A key impetus to this development was the fact that the majority of murder cases now involved guns. An important reason was that guns were now mass produced and less expensive than ever due to the growing prosperity of the cities.[13] Though killers often ditched their guns to avoid detection, they left their bullets or bullet shells behind, and now, with the aid of a new invention, the comparison microscope, investigators were able to look at two bullets and their unique markings at the same time to see if they came from the same gun. In 1927, Goddard was able to use this invention to show that a gun found on Nicola Sacco was the same .32 Colt used in the high-profile Sacco-Vanzetti case, in which two anarchists were accused of shooting paymaster Frederick Parmenter and his guard, Alessandro Berardelli, at a factory in South Braintree, Massachusetts, in 1920.[14] Although Vanzetti himself might not have been guilty, his testimony helped convince the Lowell Commission that hired Goddard to perform the ballistics analysis, and despite intense political pressure to free the men, they were both executed on August 23, 1927.

A new generation of criminalists, like Edward Oscar Heinrich, called the "Wizard of Berkeley," was beginning to develop a systematic study of crime evidence. Heinrich began carefully analyzing each step of the crime—the entrance, approach, attack, retreat, and exit—in a systematic way and collected every bit of detail from the scene for analysis. Then, using a test tube, microscope, or camera, he began the careful analysis of bits of evidence, including bullets, blood, fibers, hairs, fingerprints, inks, typewriter pressures, pen markings, even a grain of sand.[15] He drew on the methods of the early forensic scientists from Europe—and then helped bring U.S. criminology into the modern age. Police departments all over the country began calling on him; in the 1930s, the FBI laboratory began to take over this function.

In sum, in the 1920s, crime in America truly stepped to center stage—and the most well-known killers or killings of the decade were characterized by several major trends. There were the high-profile gangsters from New York, Chicago—among them Louis "Lepke" Buchalter, known for creating the first national crime syndicate; Owney Madden, a top New York bootlegger; Salvatore Maranzano, the "boss of bosses" who founded La Cosa Nostra in 1930 when he brought together major gang leaders,[16] Dutch Schultz, one of the most vicious gangsters; Charles "Lucky" Luciano, a debonair crime syndicate chief; Johnny Torrio, one of the earliest gang organizers; "Machine Gun" Jack McGurn, believed to be one of the killers at the 1929 St. Valentine's Day Massacre in Chicago; Earl "Hymie" Weiss, another Chicago gangster; plus several brothers—the Gennas and the O'Donnells—who controlled various Chicago gangs.

Then there were the notorious bank robbers who variously terrorized and captivated the Midwest, like Pretty Boy Floyd, who was protected by the country people as a kind of Robin Hood who gave money and clothes away, and John Dillinger, who was the most famous bank robber who led Hoover on a long chase as public enemy number one before being killed at the Biograph Theater, when a lady in red gave him away. Or was another man killed in his place, and did he really get away for good?

There were also assorted individuals who gained fame when they killed for love, money, or anger. Among them was Charles Henry Schwartz of Walnut Creek, California, who set up a scheme to fake his own death in 1925 but was discovered in Oakland after criminalist Heinrich discovered from a molar that the dead body wasn't Schwartz's. Two others were Judd Gray and Ruth Snyder, discussed earlier. Another was Jesse Watkins, a stablehand who killed his former employer, Henry Chambers, in his apartment in San Francisco in 1927 because he was fired after a fight. Though the scene was ransacked to look like a murder and there were no fingerprints, Heinrich again helped break the case by showing that a bullet in Watkins's cheek had been fired by Chambers's gun and that the worn-down sole of an old pair of Watkins's shoes had been imprinted in the blood on the floor. He could tell because the unusual wear pattern left the imprint "vere" (from the Revere brand). Carl Otto Wanderer killed his pregnant wife in Chicago in 1921 because he didn't want a child and he really hated women and only married her for her money; he, too, was caught after he killed the killer he hired when a curious detective wondered why a dead man with a revolver would have only $3.80 in his pocket and soon discovered that Wanderer once owned the gun.

Most baffling of all were the officially unsolved cases of the deaths of William Taylor and Rev. Edward Hall and choirgirl Eleanor Mills and the killings by Earle Leonard Nelson and the D'Autremont brothers. The first two cases were baffling because many of the clues simply disappeared or were destroyed, either inadvertently by a too-eager press or public who invaded the crime scene or intentionally by others who didn't want the case solved. The Nelson case was mystifying because the murders by this "Gorilla Killer" were so bizarre and hard to understand. Then this first American sex killer led the police on an eighteen-month chase through the United States and Canada. Finally, the D'Autremont brothers baffled the police with a failed train robbery that resulted in four deaths until the police brought in the first major American criminalist to help them discover who did it—and then they had to search another four years to bring in their men.

Following are their stories illustrating the trends and developments in homicide investigative techniques for the 1920s.

THE CASE OF EARLE LEONARD NELSON

San Francisco, Santa Barbara, and Oakland, California; Portland, Oregon; Council Bluffs, Iowa; Kansas City; Philadelphia; Buffalo, New York; Detroit; Chicago; Winnipeg, Manitoba; Killarney, 1926–28

For eighteen months, the police in a dozen different jurisdictions were baffled trying to find the first and most elusive serial killer who seemed to have it in for landladies after he came with a Bible in hand. But who was he and why was he doing it? The police seemed almost helpless as they confronted the first known American serial killer on a spree across the continent.

The crime spree occurred at the height of the Jazz Age. Bootleg whiskey and beer and speakeasies were everywhere. Flapper chorus girls and newly liberated women who walked around in short dresses and cloche hats had become common. Gangsters like Dutch Schultz, Al Capone, and Bugs Moran reigned like barons in their Prohibition-fueled fiefdoms, while Midwest bank robbers like Baby Face Nelson glamorized hit-and-run crime for the masses, who had their own dislike for heartless rich bankers who were foreclosing on farms, throwing many off the land as the financial crunch leading to the Depression built up.

Meanwhile, those who were religious decried what they considered the fall of America into a lawless world of Sodom and Gomorrah, and literature and films reflected uncertain feelings about religion in these irreverent times. The peak of Nelson's spree, 1927, was the year Sinclair Lewis published *Elmer Gantry*, about a dissolute evangelist; Willa Cather published *Death Comes for the Archbishop* and John Erskine published *Adam and Eve*; one of the most popular songs of the day was "My Blue Heaven," and Greta Garbo starred in the popular film *Flesh and the Devil* (released late 1926). Religion was very much alive, yet also uncertain in these changing times—and it played a part in influencing the first American serial killer, too.

Nelson's spree began on February 20, 1926, in San Francisco when the killer, then unidentified, appeared at the boarding house of Mrs. Clara Newman, a widow of about sixty, who had placed an ad for a boarder. "Yes, I have three vacant rooms," she told him, when he appeared, carrying a folded newspaper, at her two-story Victorian perched on hill near downtown San Francisco. It had once been a family house, but she divided the rooms on the second floor and attic so she could take in boarders. She tried to be selective, taking in respectable widowers and bachelors who would be good, responsible boarders who would pay their rent on time, even at a time when jobs were starting to decline with the beginnings of the Depression. Apparently, Earle looked like a fine, upstanding man with a Bible in his hand; he spoke about being a divinity student or Bible salesman as she stood at the door wearing a matronly black dress and a strand of pearls. Then she led him upstairs to show him a room, passing her nephew, Richard Newman, who was coming down the stairs, on the way.

Later that evening, when Richard returned to call on his aunt, he found her naked body sprawled on the floor in an upstairs bathroom and immediately called the police. The scene shocked them because not only did they find she had been strangled by her own pearl necklace, which had been tightly twisted around her neck before it was ripped off by whoever had killed her, but her legs were pulled apart, and she appeared to have been raped repeatedly. Even worse, as police discovered when they investigated further, the rapes occurred *after* she died. "He killed her first and then he raped her," the coroner reported. So this was no ordinary rapist but a necrophiliac. When they interviewed the nephew, all Richard could tell them from his glancing look at the prospective lodger on the stairs was that he was about five feet, six inches tall, had a dark complexion with thin dark hair and blue eyes, and was wearing a light-colored baggy suit. He also thought he might have seen a small pocket Bible with gold lettering on the cover in his suit pocket.

It wasn't much to go on, but the one thing the police was sure of was that he would probably rape again. They concluded he was a sex nut who had killed to rape. Because he had obviously raped Mrs. Newman's body again and again, he had certain enjoyed it and would probably want to kill and rape again. He would very likely want to keep the pearl necklace as a kind of memento of the crime, if he didn't try to fence it, making the crime even more difficult to solve.

Meanwhile, the San Francisco papers headlined the Newman story, describing the police speculations about the mysterious killer and rapist, who might be on the loose in San Francisco and could strike again.

On March 2, 1926, he did, striking at Mrs. Laura Beale's boarding house, also in San Francisco on Russian Hill. The police found her similarly strangled and raped after she died in one of the rooms of her boarding house, and once again witnesses had a similar description of the murderer. They had seen a short, dark-complexioned man with piercing blue eyes leaving her house around the time of the crime. The police were sure it was the same person; it was the same modus operandi, the same type of landlady-advertising-for-boarders killing. The San Francisco press nervously described this second similar killing.

For over three months, there was silence. Perhaps the news had scared the killer off. Perhaps he had moved on. With no clues apart from a vague description, the police felt they couldn't do much more than wait.

On June 10, there was another killing. A landlady, Mrs. Lillian St. Mary, was found, her naked and raped body stuffed under a bed in her rooming house. On June 26, the police learned from a wire that a similar killing of a landlady, Mrs. George Russell, had occurred in Santa Barbara. The killer could be anywhere, though the police in San Francisco felt a special link to the crime since the killing had started here. So what was going on?

For help they turned to an outside consultant—Edward Oscar Heinrich in Berkeley, who by now was developing a reputation as a preeminent crime analyst with his Berkeley crime lab. He was among a new generation of criminologists who regarded crime analysis as an orderly procedure, starting with a series of logical questions: "Precisely *what* happened? Precisely *when* did it happen? Precisely *where* did it happen? *Why* did it happen? *Who* did it?"[17] Then, he looked carefully at the succession of methods used by the criminal—from his entrance, approach, and attack to his retreat and exit. For him, the one clue always present after any crime was the criminal's method, which exposed his knowledge, skill, and habit.[18] Using a test tube, microscope, or camera, Heinrich looked for clues in poison, the remnants of bullets, blood clots, fiber, fingerprints, differing inks, typewriter flaws, and the slips of a pen, and he emphasized the importance of seeking to identify every bit of debris, no matter how small.[19] This was a far cry from the level of investigation a decade before—and Heinrich was a helpful adviser in searching for insights into this unusual killer, particularly because he had some observations about what even a Bible could tell. He once said, "By their books ye shall know men. The Bible, through its underscorings and a few marked passages, has given me an index on many occasions to the character of a man involved in a crime. One book often will lead to a minute description of its owner. Give me a well-used book and I will describe to you the man who read it."[20] This interpretation would be helpful later on, but for now, all the police knew was that this was a serial rapist/necrophiliac who was oddly attracted to middle-aged or elderly landladies; he looked outwardly ordinary and respectable, and was short and strong, apparently able to overpower the women when they let him in and showed him a room, and then within an hour or so he fled. Perhaps he carried a Bible, or at least, he was seen carrying what looked like one on his first murder.

Meanwhile, in Santa Barbara, Capt. Ben Schuttler continued the investigation, which showed a growing pattern of madness. This time investigators had found the landlady's naked body in the pantry with a rug beater, which the killer apparently found hanging on the wall and plunged into her after he raped her. The scene made even the experienced homicide detectives shudder in disgust. Clearly this was a deranged, sadistic sex killer—something that quiet Santa Barbara (much less the nation) had ever seen before. Apparently it was the same killer, because a neighbor had seen the man go in and out, and similarly described him as short, stocky, and carrying a little book. So perhaps again it was a Bible, and perhaps he used it to disarm any suspicions. After all, who would suspect a man with a bible might be planning horrible crimes? Now he was gone again.

Schuttler announced some warnings on the radio and put up some posters around town, warning rooming house owners to be on the lookout for a dangerous criminal with a short, stocky build and polite, quiet nature who might be carrying a Bible. Perhaps that helped scare the killer away, maybe to take the Southern Pacific train back to the San Francisco Bay area and get off in Oakland, where he killed and raped his next victim, Mrs. Mary Nesbit, on August 16, 1926. Now the police in a third city were involved in what had become a statewide concern, as the newspapers described this fifth slaying and rape by a dark, mysterious killer they now began calling the "Dark Strangler." Meanwhile, as terrified women bolted their doors against strangers, the newspapers reported how baffled the police were. "Police have no clues in strangler case—a dead end," went a typical account.[21] In fact, women were so scared that one woman in Bakersfield shot her husband in the legs when he came home drunk one night, thinking he was the strangler.

Fortunately, the Oakland police did have one small clue that they brought to Heinrich to check out. There was a page of a Bible that had been found on the train, and there was a smudge on the bottom of the page showing a fingerprint. At the time, only a few departments in the state kept fingerprints, and Hoover was only in the beginning stages of setting up a complete fingerprint system at the FBI, but there was a clearinghouse for prints in Chicago—then the largest collection in the country. Heinrich said he would send the print there.[22]

While a fearful Bay area worried when the Dark Strangler would strike again, he did—but this time in Portland, Oregon, where in the space of a week he raped four women between October 20 and October 26. Beta Withers was found strangled in the attic by her teenage son when he was going upstairs to look for his kite.[23] Nelson stuffed her body into a trunk, like a rag doll. Another, Mrs. Mabel Fluke, who lived a few blocks away, was found behind the furnace of her boarding house by her handyman.[24] This time, some money, jewels, and clothing were taken. The next day another Portland landlady, Mrs. Virginia Grant, became a victim; her body was also found in an attic, a knotted scarf tied tightly around her bruised and cut body.[25] It's as if the killer was becoming more creative in his style.

This time, Captain Wranley of the Portland police homicide department sent circulars to every boarding house in the city and had his men canvass every boarding house looking for clues. He also asked the Portland newspaper to publish descriptions of the jewelry that had been stolen from some of the victims. That finally brought some new clues. Two ladies at a Portland boarding house recalled buying a few pieces of jewelry from a young man who stayed with them a few days. He had seemed quite pleasant and ordinary at the time, but just in case, they brought it to the police, and it matched the stolen items from one of the victims. "And he's a short, blue-eyed young man with a round face," one of them said, adding that he had a slightly "simian mouth and jaw." "But he's quietly spoken and claims to be deeply religious," the other said.[26] He's like a gorilla, one of the Portland reporters commented, and after that the mysterious killer had a new label that followed him everywhere: the "Gorilla Killer." The new moniker made him sound even more mysterious and scary—like some evil creature from the jungles of darkest Africa. In turn, the name spread with him as he began to move now beyond the West Coast and into Canada. "Gorilla Murderer Strikes Again" read a typical headline.

Oddly, the mysterious killer made a quick foray back to San Francisco in mid-November, killing Mrs. William Edmonds on November 10, before returning a few days later to murder his fourth Portland landlady, Mrs. Blanche Meyers, on November 15. But why go back and forth?

Nothing made sense until the first thumbprint ID came back telling who Nelson was.[27] As it turned out, he had a long history of run-ins with the law. He had been orphaned as an infant when his parents died of syphilis. Then, his aunt, Mrs. Lillian Fabian, took him in and raised him in a religious Christian household, where he was encouraged to read his Bible each day and say grace at each meal. At first, he was a quiet, withdrawn, moody child who spent a lot of time alone. But then, when he was ten, he was in a serious accident in which he was hit by a cable car, either because his bike collided with it or because he was chasing a runaway ball in the street, according to varying accounts. He was near death for days and in a coma because of the injury to his head. After that his whole personality changed. He became even more quiet and moody, lapsing into periods of sullenness, when he would retreat to his room, where he would read his Bible for hours. As he grew into a teenager, his aunt found him peeping through a keyhole at his cousin Rachel getting undressed.

In 1915, Nelson first came to the attention of the law, though the accounts become somewhat murky as to whether he was raised by his aunt in Philadelphia and then came to San Francisco or was raised in San Francisco. In any case, by one account, he was arrested in 1915 for burglary, sentenced to two years in San Quentin, signed up to serve in the navy, but after lying on his cot and refusing to get up while babbling about the Great Beast of Revelations, he was sent off to a mental institution, where he remained during the war. After he was discharged and briefly married a sixty-year-old spinster who soon left him, he attacked a twelve-year-old girl and was returned to the mental institution where he remained until 1925. Soon after his release, he began his deadly rampage.[28] Alternate stories go that he was first arrested in 1917 or 1918 after he tried to rape a neighbor girl in the basement. He was convicted and sent to the state reformatory penal farm for two years, and after several escapes, he was transferred to the state penitentiary, escaped again, and married a young schoolteacher on August 12, 1919, using the alias Roger Wilson. Supposedly, Nelson's jealousy and ravings led her to have a nervous breakdown and she was sent to a hospital, where one night Nelson broke in and tried to rape her before the doctors and nurses pulled him away.[29]

In any case, the fingerprint record that came back at least provided the Gorilla Killer with a name, although it wasn't clear just how helpful that was, because Nelson was a master of using aliases. Besides using Roger Wilson, he had and used many other names. Still, having his name and prison photo was helpful, and after Nelson killed Mrs. William Edmonds in San Francisco on November 10, leaving her body in the basement before his return to Portland, the San Francisco police released his prison photo and true identity to the press, and papers all along the West Coast published it. Although Nelson had certainly changed since the old photo was taken, becoming heavier and more jowly over the years, at least this was a way to alert the public to be more cautious. Yet Nelson was such a chameleon, using all sorts of names and identities, that the police knew he would be hard to find, especially since it was easy to mix with an increasingly mobile population of down-and-out men who were now drifting about, among them the veterans of the war, farmers who had lost their land, and other jobless, homeless men who were becoming part of a hobo society in the late 1920s. The best they could do was spread the warning and hope this would alert the public or other police departments. Then maybe Nelson might finally make a mistake.

Meanwhile, feeling that all the publicity was making things too hot for him on the West Coast, Nelson began his murderous journey around the country that led him to kill other landladies in still more cities—including the next in Council Bluffs, Iowa, in December; another woman and her eight-month-old child in Kansas City, Missouri, a few days later; and others in Philadelphia (April 27, 1927), Buffalo (May 1, 1927), two sisters in Detroit (June 1, 1927), and a woman in Chicago (June 3, 1927).

In turn, armies of police (and the press) were looking for him, literally dragnetting the country and putting pins in the map as he struck again. The pattern of attacking landladies and raping them was clear, as were repeated sightings of a fleeing short, blue-eyed, gorilla-like killer after various attacks. But he always managed to elude the police by running quickly through streets and yards and then apparently blending into a nameless underworld.

So where was Nelson? Not surprisingly, with the law and press on his tail, he quickly slipped out of sight into Canada. But it wasn't long before he turned up, when he continued the same pattern as in the United States. On June 8, he appeared at the lodging house of Mrs. August Hill in Winnipeg, carrying a Bible, and she rented him a third-floor room. That night a sixteen-year-old girl, Lola Cowan, disappeared, and police began searching for her.

The next night, when a man named William Patterson returned home, his sobbing children told him their mother had been gone all day, but Patterson couldn't find her anywhere in the neighborhood. As he knelt by his bed in prayer for his wife's safe return, he noticed a hand sticking out from under the bed, and when he looked more closely, he gasped in horror. It was his dead wife, who lay naked under the bed. After he called the police, they determined she had been strangled and then raped.

At once, Chief Detective George Smith realized that the mad serial rapist from the United States had come to Canada, because he had gotten the warning from the U.S. police to be on the lookout. It was the same modus operandi, though Emily Patterson wasn't a landlady. Plus he had done something he hadn't done before. He had left behind his old clothes, as well as taking a set of Mr. Patterson's clothes, which included corduroy pants and a plaid shirt, along with some money, Mrs. Patterson's wedding ring, and a Bible.

Immediately, Smith sent his men out to search the boarding houses, in case Nelson was still in the area, and that's when they encountered Mrs. August Hill, who told him her only new boarder was a nice man named Mr. Wilson. He's "short, dark haired, and with blue eyes," she explained. A match! The detectives went racing to his room, though Wilson had already gone. But they noticed a heavy smell he had left behind, and when they checked, they discovered that under the bed was a naked girl's body that had been cut up and mutilated. It was the body of Lola Cowan, who had disappeared three days before.

After that, the police launched the largest manhunt in Canadian history for Nelson. Briefly he surfaced 200 miles away in Regina, when he rented a room and tried to attack a woman boarder. But after she screamed and the landlady came running, he fled again; the police were on their way after him a few minutes later.

At this point, Smith guessed Nelson would probably head for the border and alerted the police there to be on the lookout. A few days later, two constables outside Killarney, a small farming town, noticed a man walking along the roadway wearing a plaid shirt and corduroy pants. Though the man gave his name as Wilson and calmly claimed to be a local stockhand on a nearby ranch, the officers said they had to take him in just to check on his story to be sure because there was a killer on the loose. "Sure," Nelson said, and the officers locked him in a jail cell while they want to check, leaving him in handcuffs. They called Smith in Winnipeg, who was certain they had the right man, since he had used the name Wilson there and once before in San Francisco.

Once again, when they got back to Nelson's jail cell, he had picked the locks of the handcuffs and the cell door and was gone. As a 500-man local posse began a search, Chief Smith headed to the area with 50 of his own men. Ironically, Nelson spent the night in a barn only one block from the jail. But in the morning, Chief Smith and his team spotted Nelson as he walked calmly toward the train station, ready to board the morning express.

With that, the search for Nelson finally ended. He was tried in Winnipeg for the murder of Mrs. Patterson, and he listened with a strange, icy coolness as the grisly testimony about him continued. He showed no emotion when his aunt and wife came to visit him during the trial. On November 14, 1927, he was found guilty and condemned to death, going to the gallows on January 12, 1928. As he stood waiting for the black hood to be placed over him, he finally said his last words, saying, "I am innocent before God and man. I forgive those who have wronged me and ask forgiveness of those I have injured. God have mercy!"[30]

The strange and baffling saga of Earle Leonard Nelson was over. Though he had killed twenty-two women, twenty of them landladies, he died protesting his innocence to God in the end. Did he believe in the Bible? Did he kill out of some strange religious and sexual compulsion? Was the Bible just a cover to convince others to trust him? Nelson took his secrets to his death while proclaiming his innocence. No one will ever know.[31]

THE MURDER OF REV. EDWARD HALL AND ELEANOR MILLS

New Brunswick, New Jersey, 1922–26

De Russey's Lane, three miles outside New Brunswick near the Phillips farm, had the reputation of being a quiet lover's lane. It was several hundred feet long and a small loop branching off it called Phillips Lane was surrounded by thickets of brush, occasional cedars, high grass, the currently unoccupied Phillips farmhouse, and a crabapple tree. Lovers would go to "spoon" as they called it in the 1920s, sometimes picnicking on the grass under the trees, or discreetly necking and petting in the boxy Model T Fords of the period.

On September 15, 1922, the lane was anything but quiet as the New Brunswick police and the Somerset County sheriff soon discovered. The following morning the police got a frantic call from Mrs. Edwards, who lived a mile away. As she described it, a young couple had suddenly come pounding on her door, describing how they had seen the dead bodies of a man and woman in the lane.[32]

The police and a reporter were the first to arrive, and the couple who found the bodies—Raymond Schneider and Pearl Bahmer—guided them to the scene, explaining that they had been simply picking mushrooms at the time. (Later it turned out they had been doing something quite different.) When the couple arrived, they saw a shocking scene. Under a crabapple tree, several yards from Phillips Lane, lay two bodies, soon identified as the Reverend Edward Hall and Eleanor Mills, a married choir singer at his church. The two bodies lay on their backs, like lovers who might have been enjoying the sun. The minister, age forty-one, who wore a dark gray suit, stiff-collared white shirt, and white tie, lay with his head about two yards from the tree, his feet pointing toward Phillips Lane, a wide Panama hat over his head. Underneath the hat, Hall's glasses were perched on the bridge of his nose. Next to him, her head resting in the crook of his outstretched right arm, was Eleanor Mills, wearing a simple blue dress with small red polka dots, a blue velvet turban on her head, and black hose. A fold of a brown woolen scarf covered her bloody face and neck. Scattered on and around them were several dozen love letters, written in pencil in a woman's hand. It was as if someone had carefully arranged them in repose of death, and then left one of Hall's calling cards by his feet to let the world know who these people were and that they were having an affair. Both had been shot in the head—Hall with one shot, Mills with three shots. As it came out in the autopsy, which was mostly concealed for four years, whoever had killed the couple had slashed Mrs. Mills's throat from ear to ear, cut off her tongue, and then slashed through her vocal cords—as if to say she wouldn't be singing in the choir anymore.

Over the next few hours, detectives, the coroner, and because the crabapple tree was in Somerset County, just beyond the Somerset-Middlesex County line, the sheriff of Somerset County arrived, and so did the press and neighboring public en masse. The case was a sensation because Reverend Hall was the prominent minister of the 500-member Church of St. John the Evangelist in New Brunswick, and his wife was the richest woman in New Brunswick, the daughter of the wealthy Stevens and Carpender families. The dead woman was the lead soprano in the choir whose husband, Jim Mills, was the part-time church sexton and janitor at a local school. Plus it was a well-known secret among many in town that the two had been having a passionate and adulterous affair; a few even heard or suspected that they were contemplating running away together.

The affair was also very much a shocker, because despite the lawless image of the roaring twenties, small cities in America were still very much tied to more traditional Victorian notions of propriety. Despite Fitzgerald's stories of loose living in *Tales of the Jazz Age* and *The Beautiful and the Damned*, the image of innocence and virginity conveyed by actresses like Mary Minter, who figured in her own Hollywood scandal after director William Desmond Taylor's death the following year, was very much in vogue. The ideal was still womanly purity, virtue, and family monogamy, as portrayed in works like Katherine Mansfield's *The Garden Party*, Booth Tarkington's small-town novel *Alice Adams*, and in Harold Lloyd's nostalgic film *Grandma's Boy*.

Unfortunately, all of this attention quickly compromised much of the crime scene. By early afternoon, as detectives tried to investigate the scene, throngs of people converged, began going through the paths and fields, and crowded around the crabapple tree, straining for a glimpse of the bodies. The detectives didn't think to quickly cordon off the crime scene to keep out the growing mob, and as dozens and then hundreds of gawkers arrived, they were unable to do so. In fact, within a few hours there were vendors selling hot dogs, soda pop, and popcorn.

They did manage to find a few useful clues, though others were lost to history. Detective Totten of Somerset County, who was by now in charge of the scene, found a number of empty .32 cartridge shells from an automatic pistol near the bodies, and he picked up the business card to check it for prints. Meanwhile, Dr. William H. Long, the county physician, did a brief examination, which was later roundly criticized for its lack of precision. Initially, he reported that both victims had been shot by one bullet each and that Mrs. Mills's throat wound might have been made by the tightness of her scarf. Although he spoke about performing autopsies on both bodies and had them removed to nearby Somerville, the autopsies weren't done for about two weeks. Instead, the bodies were quickly—many thought too quickly—buried, though they were exhumed about two weeks later in response to press demands, which showed the injuries to Mrs. Mills's throat, initially overlooked in the initial inquiry.

Who killed the victims? Was it one of the spouses who knew about the affair, as police suspected early on? Or could it be someone else, perhaps someone in the congregation, who objected to the minister and choir girl carrying on? Would the investigators be able to gather enough information to prove anything, given the carnival atmosphere surrounding the case and the loss of many critical clues? As the United States entered an international age with a rapacious popular press, the Hall-Mills murders entered the annals of highly publicized cases screwed up by mass media coverage—like the O. J. Simpson and JonBenét Ramsey cases continue to gain publicity today—even a decade after the original case.

Meanwhile detectives began speaking to some of the suspected principals and others to piece together what might have happened as best they could. Some of the responses and revelations were curious to say the least, and some helped further confuse the already confused investigation. Dozens of witnesses stepped forward to announce that they had heard gunshots or women screaming in the lane that night. Some locals offered theories—including that the couple had been the victims of a blackmail plot or had been shot by a do-gooder who had tried to convert them from leading a dissolute life.[33] Others proposed that they had been killed elsewhere, including a church basement, the abandoned farmhouse, or the backseat of an automobile, and then moved and posed under the crabapple tree.

Detectives became sure of one thing from their investigation—that the couple had been shot and left on the spot. They analyzed the soil and examined the blood seepage from the bodies into it—a fairly new technique at the time. The amount of blood in the soil provided the proof that they must have been killed on the spot—there was just too much blood there otherwise.

Also, the detectives immediately suspected jealousy was the motive, which made the spouses suspect, though both Jim Mills and Mrs. Hall claimed they hadn't suspected any kind of illicit affair between Hall and Mills. Given the level of town gossip, their claims of no knowledge only deepened the police suspicions. Saturday afternoon, for example, when Detective Totten contacted Mills, a meek and retiring man of forty-five, he claimed he had last seen his wife around 7:30 p.m. on Thursday, more than a day before the bodies were discovered. When he asked her where she was going, she had taunted him, "Why don't you follow me and find out?" When she didn't come home by midnight, he went to sleep. When she was still not back by 2 a.m., he went to the church, found it empty, returned home to sleep, and looked for her again in the morning. Supposedly, he ran into Mrs. Hall at the church in the morning, who said that her husband hadn't returned home either. After that, neither said anything to anyone else, including the police. Detective Totten wondered why Mills wasn't more worried. Totten also wondered when, after identifying the handwriting on the letters found around the bodies as his wife's, Mills suggested she was just a sentimental woman who had probably copied her letters from books she had read. "And I never suspected any irregular relationship between her and the rector," he declared, suggesting that though Mrs. Mills had been seeing Rev. Hall, their relationship was purely platonic. "Why, I thought more of Mr. Hall than I did of my own brother."[34] His brother, however, was surprised at Mills's lack of knowledge. How could his brother not know? The interview over, Mills admitted to reporters that his young wife had been going out of their house at odd hours for many months. "But it's all innocent," he protested.

The police didn't get around to questioning Mrs. Hall until Sunday afternoon. By then, a reporter had already called her to ask if there was anything between her husband and Mrs. Mills, after which she hung up without replying. She promptly called her wealthy cousin, Henry de La Bruyere Carpender, a prominent member of the New York Stock Exchange, and the Hall family lawyer, William E. Florence, who was also a New Jersey state senator. Both went to the site, looked at the bodies without talking to police, and quickly left. Perhaps the police weren't talking because they were still arguing over the jurisdiction of the case when Carpender and Florence arrived. Somerset prosecutor Azariah Beekman was trying to hand the case over to Middlesex County on the grounds the homes of the deceased were there and they might have been murdered there as well, though finally Somerset County got the case because the bodies were found there.

When the police finally did interview Mrs. Hall on Sunday, her lawyer was present, and she didn't mention (until asked about it) that she had gone to look for her husband at 2:30 a.m. Friday with her brother, Willie Stevens—or so she claimed. Perhaps a reason she mentioned it at this time is that the police advised her that a watchman who patrolled her exclusive neighborhood reported seeing a woman wearing a large gray coat going into the side door of her mansion around 2 a.m., and then she acknowledged that she had been that woman. She thought her husband might have gone to the church to give spiritual aid to some parishioner who might have been taken ill.[35] Early Friday morning, she said, she had called the police to ask if there had been any "casualties" reported, and they told her none had been.

She protested her husband's innocence. "I trusted Mr. Hall absolutely," she claimed, saying that she paid no attention to the "malicious gossip" she heard about the affair.[36] When she spoke to the assistant Middlesex prosecutor, John Toolan, before Somerset County finally took over the case, her response was unusual. Toolan remarked that as Mr. Hall's widow, he imagined she would "naturally be intensely interested in discovering who his murderer was, wouldn't you," and she responded in a kind of cryptic calm, "I almost feel as if I don't care. They cannot bring him back."[37] Three days after that interview, she hired a new lawyer, Timothy N. Pfeiffer, who had once been in the homicide bureau of the New York County's District Attorney Office, and she dropped Florence as her lawyer. She even hired her own private detective, Felix B. Di Martini, who had been a top New York City Police Department detective, solving a number of puzzling city murders.

For the time being, the police had nothing but their suspicions, so they turned their attention to questioning other players. One was Willie Stevens, Mrs. Hall's brother, who had the reputation of being a dim-witted bachelor with uncombed hair, thick glasses, and walrus mustache who looked a little like a myopic porcupine. Though he had a trust of $150,000 put aside for him, he lived on the dole of $40 a week and spent time trailing around the New Brunswick fire department as an honorary fireman. Initially, he claimed he had never left the house the night of the murder, though after much questioning, he acknowledged to police he had gone with Mrs. Hall to the church at around 2 a.m. Then, too, some local residents told the police that Willie was known to own a .32-caliber pistol, and some spoke ominously that he sent a suit with spots on it to be cleaned on Saturday, a few hours after news of the bodies was reported. Might it be spotted with blood? By the time the police tracked down this lead, the suit had been cleaned.

The police also briefly held the couple who found the bodies, uncovering a steamy story about them, too. As it turned out, Schneider had only separated from his wife two months earlier, though he had been seeing Pearl for two years. Soon after, the police learned that Pearl had been seduced by her own father. Schneider falsely claimed he had seen a friend named Clifford Hayes shoot Hall and Mills on the lane, thinking they were Pearl and her father, whom he and Hayes had been trailing that night. After police arrested Hayes, Schneider admitted he had made up the story because he thought Pearl and Hayes were telling stories about him. The police ended up freeing Hayes, arresting Schneider for perjury, charging Pearl's father with incest, and locking up Pearl as an incorrigible as well.[38]

Another curious suspect was Henry Stevens, another wealthy brother of Mrs. Hall who lived in Lavelette, New Jersey, and had a reputation as a hunter and marksman. Though he seemed to be hiding something—he was arrogant and uncooperative with police—he had an apparently ironclad alibi, being at a waterfront party with many other people at the time of the murders (or at least, when it seemed likely the murders occurred) sometime Thursday night. Besides, the couple had been shot at nearly point-blank range, so almost anyone could have shot them.

One of the most peculiar characters stepped into the unfolding plot—Mrs. Jane Gibson, who had been divorced twice and owned a hog farm near Phillips Lane. She looked like some kind of hefty Earth mother, with leathery skin and stringy bobbed black hair, and she wore black-rimmed glasses. She was dubbed the "Pig Lady" by the press and the public, and she told a story that, if true, helped fuel suspicion against Mrs. Hall and her brothers. According to her account, she saw or heard the killers at about 10:30 p.m. on the night of the murders when she was riding her mule to look for poachers who had been stealing corn from a field near the Phillips farm. As she rode along, she heard men and women arguing in the crabapple orchard nearby and then heard shots, after which she fled. Until the news about the bodies found under the tree came out, she didn't realize what she had seen and heard was the murder, and she came forward after she read about Hayes's arrest, because she didn't want to see an innocent man convicted. The exact details of her story varied from telling to telling, and it wasn't enough for a grand jury that considered the case to indict her when it came to a decision on November 27. The press and public loved her: She added a humorous bit of color and absurdity to a case that was already out of control.

Then there were the steamy love letters. Most were suppressed until the case went to trial, but a few were leaked early and helped raise interest. One, written in the flowery style of the day, began:

> Dearie, what a gay happy girl I am today . . . I love your dear note of last night and went to sleep happy after reading it. Of all the people that I know, no one understands me but you. But of course, I have never shown my real self to others. . . .
>
> I am looking over toward the trees by the elms and dreaming . . . I am holding my sweet babykins' face in my hand and looking deep into his heart. . . . Oh, honey, I am fiery today. Burning, flaming love. It seems ages since I saw my babykins' body and kissed every bit of you.[39]

Around the time the Pig Woman surfaced, Jim Mills found his own cache of letters from Rev. Hall to his wife and sold them to a New York newspaper through an intermediary for $500. He told the press he had been sorely betrayed by Hall after all, further stating that had he known he would have simply "stepped aside and let Hall have her. Then there would have been no murder."[40]

The web of suspicion was clearly closing in around Mrs. Hall and her brothers, particularly Willie, but the question was, would there be enough evidence to convict? Was this suspicion really justified? Or had the press and public just gone mad?

A look at the remnants of the murder scene certainly suggested a crazed public. Six weeks after the murder, the crabapple tree had been completely destroyed by eager souvenir hunters—over 1,000 of them every day. In fact, old-fashioned American entrepreneurship had turned the area into a souvenir shop. A peddler from New Brunswick obtained a lease from the owner of the property where the crabapple tree was and sold samples of earth from around the tree at twenty-five cents a bag. He also turned the farmhouse into a museum and charged admission.[41] Needless to say, in the process, justice got trampled along with the land.

Thus, it's not surprising that when a grand jury was convened and questioned the various principals, the jurors voted not to indict anyone. Shortly after that, Mrs. Hall left for a year-long vacation in Italy. Jim Mills continued to work at the church as a part-time sexton, and Mrs. Gibson returned to taking care of her hogs. For the following four years, the case went into limbo, and the murders were marked simply as "unsolved" by a frustrated police.

Four years later, on July 17, 1926, the case shot to the forefront of the newspapers again, about a month after a piano salesman, Arthur M. Riehl, filed a petition to annul his marriage to Louise Geist. Among other things, he stated in his petition that before their marriage, Louise had worked in Mr. Hall's household, had improper relationships with him, and was paid about $5,000 by the Stevens family to keep quiet about what she knew about the Hall-Mills slayings.[42]

What did she know? Philip Payne, now the managing editor of the New York *Daily Mirror*, had long suspected that the case could be solved if certain information about Rev. Hall's calling card had been presented to the grand jury back in 1922. It had previously been brought from the Phillips farm to the Somerset County prosecutor and then to the New Brunswick prosecutor, who had presented it to the grand jury. At the time, apparently no one had thought to determine whose prints were on the card, although the Middlesex County detectives had developed a print on it. Perhaps because of the early jurisdictional confusion, a Middlesex County detective, now dead, had turned over the card to Lt. Edward Schwartz with the Newark police, and he kept it in a safe through the years, though he showed it to perhaps 1,000 people on request—but apparently not to the grand jury.

Now Payne took the lead in urging New Jersey governor A. Harry Moore to reopen the case, based on Riehl's claims about what Louise knew. Then Payne borrowed the card from Schwartz, hired a fingerprint expert to check the card, and turned the card over to the Jersey City police, who passed it on to Lt. Fred Drewen. It was not the normal police procedure—breaking the usual chain of custody rule—and it became a major point of contention in the subsequent trial.[43]

In any case, with headlines in the *Daily Mirror* calling for a reopening of the case, Governor Moore, who had come from Jersey City himself, asked the Jersey City police and state troopers to check out Payne's allegations, because Somerset County officials, involved four years earlier, seemed unenthusiastic to pursue the case. The case began all over again.

On July 28, 1926, a cordon of state police surrounded Mrs. Hall's home, and two state police and two New Jersey detectives arrived with an arrest warrant charging Mrs. Hall with killing her husband. Soon after, her brothers Willie and Henry Stevens were charged as well; three months later, on October 28 and October 31, the bodies of Mrs. Mills and Rev. Hall, respectively, were exhumed once again.Though Mrs. Hall was able to get out on a $40,000 bail bond (originally $15,000 but later raised to $40,000),[44] Willie and Henry languished in jail until the November 3, 1926, trial at Somerville, which was a press celebration all over again. Over 200 newspapermen covered the trial, though only 75 could actually get in the courtroom, and about 500 spectators packed into the courtroom designed to hold only half that number.

Would the prosecution finally prevail? It certainly looked like it would. In his opening statement, Special Prosecutor Simpson regaled the jury, twelve men, mostly in their fifties and sixties, with the key lynchpins of his case—the letters found at the scene which Mrs. Hall had taken to the orchard to confront her husband with evidence of the affair; the story of Jane Gibson about seeing the defendants argue by the tree before the final shots; and the print of Willie Stevens's left index finger on the card. At the trial itself, three fingerprint experts testified about the print—among them Lt. Edward Schwartz, superintendent of the Newark police Bureau of Records, who had kept the print for four years, and Lt. Fred Drewen, the Jersey City police fingerprint specialist who fingerprinted Willie when he was arrested. Yes, they all said, the fingerprint on the back of the card was Willie's. But the defense tried to suggest that the card could have just dropped out of Hall's wallet during an ordinary robbery.

The highlight of the trial came when Mrs. Gibson took the stand. Perhaps more accurately, she was wheeled in on a hospital gurney—transferred from a hospital where she had recently undergone an operation for cancer—to testify. As a nurse helped plump the pillows and cranked up her bed a few notches, Jane Gibson lay, her head slightly elevated, looking like a chalky-white ghost. She began her testimony, speaking in a croaking voice, describing how she saw a woman and two men get out of a car near the crabapple tree and then the woman's voice shouted, "Explain those letters!" followed by a struggle between the reverend and the two men, which concluded with three quick shots.After she heard the first shot and the sound of something heavy falling, she ran for the mule. As she ran, she heard one woman say "Oh, Henry," while the other began to scream. After Gibson got home, she discovered she had lost her moccasin, and when she returned, she saw a large, white-haired woman, presumably Mrs. Hall, leaning down and fixing something.

It was damning testimony if true, and it was made all the more compelling by Gibson lying on her bed, looking the picture of death. Her own elderly mother, who sat in the first row of the spectators, kept calling out from time to time as Gibson testified, "She's a liar! She's a liar!"[45] The defense attacked Mrs. Gibson's memory as well, showing she had trouble remembering the names of her three ex-husbands or when she had been married or divorced. If she couldn't remember that, how could she remember all these details about a four-year-old murder case?

Mrs. Hall and Willie Stevens took the stand. Mrs. Hall, a large, matronly woman garbed entirely in black except for a strand of pearls around her throat and a pearl hatpin, spoke very calmly and confidently about how she had never doubted her husband's devotion, had never read the letters until a few weeks before the trial, and had even helped Mrs. Mills by driving her to the hospital for an operation. The night of the murder, she only left the house to search the church at about 2:30 a.m. because her husband had not come home. Willie told substantially the same story.

In the end, the jury came back with its not guilty verdict on December 3, 1926. After that Mrs. Hall returned to her role overseeing her husband's church and acting as the community's woman of eminence, while Willie continued to live with her in the mansion. The Stevens family sued the New York *Daily Mirror* for $3 million, though they settled the case out of court for an unrevealed amount.

The Hall-Mills murders returned to limbo and remain officially unsolved. Perhaps they might be considered one more early example of how high-profile cases often become difficult to solve because of the interference of the media, public, political pull, and money in the investigation process.

THE MURDER OF WILLIAM DESMOND TAYLOR

Hollywood, California, 1922

The most baffling murder to confront Hollywood occurred around 8 p.m. on February 1, 1922. William Desmond Taylor, a flamboyant director who worked for Paramount's Famous Players, was discovered murdered the next morning in his two-story unit in a quiet, fashionable court of eight bungalows on Alvarado Street. It was normally a quiet, tree-lined street, and many of the most popular Hollywood stars of the day lived nearby, including actor Douglas MacLean and his wife Faith, and Charlie Chaplin's good friend and leading lady Edna Purviance. That calm was shattered for good when Taylor's body was discovered by his valet, Henry Peavey, who arrived at 7:30 a.m. as usual to make breakfast for Taylor.

As he walked in, Peavey found Taylor lying on his back on the living room floor, wearing a tailored suit jacket, trousers, and shoes, with his hair neatly combed and his arms at his sides. It was as if Taylor had been positioned there, like a man on a Hollywood stage set, by whoever killed him.

After seeing the body, Peavey ran excitedly into the courtyard yelling, "Massa Taylor is dead," his body shaking with sobs. Across the court, Edna Purviance heard his cries, struggled out of bed, and immediately began phoning a few friends, including Mabel Normand and Mary Minter, to warn them that if they had anything at Taylor's they didn't want the police to find, they should get it now.[46]

As a result, by the time the police arrived, at least ten people were already on the scene. While some milled around outside the bungalow, others were in the living room, in Taylor's study, and in the upstairs bedroom, poring through his drawers, desks, and closets and burning or packing up papers so they could get rid of any anything that might seem compromising. The group included Taylor's chauffeur Harry Fellows, Henry Peavey, and others, plus Paramount executive Charles Eyton, who was getting rid of any thing that might look bad for Taylor or the studio, like letters and bootleg liquor. In some versions of the story, Mabel Normand was among the group searching for her own love letters to destroy; in other accounts, she didn't go to his house to do this until two days later—a fact that would figure in to the investigation to determine what really happened.

The police felt flabbergasted and overwhelmed, but as best they could they stopped everyone from destroying or taking away anything else and sought to secure the scene and protect any evidence from further disarray. As a result, when Mary Minter, one of Taylor's rising starlets, and her mother, Charlotte Shelby, arrived, the police wouldn't let them in. Supposedly Mary and her mother had raced to the scene so she could recover a lacy nightgown with the initials MMM and a love note she had written to Taylor, because this might harm her image as the innocent ingénue. But is that the real reason they wanted so urgently to get in? Were the articles really there? Later the gossip was that the studio executives, eager to get rid of Minter, whose last five pictures had been flops, had planted the gown and letter there themselves to compromise her and end her career.

It wasn't even clear Taylor had been murdered at first, because according to some accounts, a mysterious doctor—perhaps even Taylor's own doctor—appeared on the scene, looked at the body, and pronounced the death due to a stomach hemorrhage. The murder was soon discovered after Detective Raymond Cato arrived with the deputy coroner. When the coroner turned over the body, he noticed a stain of dried blood on the carpet and then saw the bullet holes in Taylor's jacket. The entry wound was under his left arm, and in the back of his jacket was the exit wound. The autopsy later showed that a single .38-caliber bullet had gone through his heart, killing him on the spot.[47] This discovery turned what started out as a routine death investigation into a homicide case.[48]

Very quickly, the police ruled out robbery, since they found $78 in Taylor's pocket and $1,000 in cash upstairs in plain view, and Taylor was still wearing a platinum wristwatch, a gold pocketwatch, and a diamond ring.

Meanwhile, as Taylor's body was shipped to the L.A. morgue for an autopsy, a swarm of detectives from Central Station, headed by Captain David Adams, converged on the bungalow. Two detectives went to talk to Mabel Normand, who was Taylor's last visitor on the night he was murdered, and others searched the scene and soon found the pink nightgown with Mary Minter's initials and a signed photograph of her. Also, according to some accounts, the police found some sexually explicit pictures of Taylor with various starlets, along with a stash of booze and drugs, although by other accounts, these were just stories that made the rounds, while the studio sought to cover up the real secret—that Taylor was actually a homosexual who sent Peavey out to get lovers for him.

In any case, over the next few days, as the police studied the material they had collected, talked to witnesses, and followed up on leads, they began to uncover the mysterious double life Taylor had been leading that might hold the keys to his death. This double life reflected the schizophrenia of the frenetic fast-paced life of the roaring twenties, when Hollywood, then a studio-run town, typified the glamour of life in the fast lane as many stars and wannabes sought to get to or stay on top. At the time, promiscuous sex, speakeasy booze, and con games were everywhere, and the frantic energy of the age was popularized by F. Scott Fitzgerald, whose books *Tales of the Jazz Age* and *The Beautiful and the Damned* were best-sellers that year. The American mixed drink was just becoming the rage in Europe, and a new abstractionist style of art, with artists like Paul Klee, Joan Miró, Robert Delaunay, and Wassily Kandinsky, was on the rise. This fragmented frenetic style was the perfect image for a wild and crazy age.

At the time of his death, Taylor's persona encompassed this way of life—outwardly the picture of success; inwardly, a life filled with dark secrets. Initially, the police and most of Taylor's acquaintances knew the man who captivated Hollywood, for he had become a highly successful director of big-screen silent film successes, among them the serial *The Diamond from the Sky* and the feature *Anne of Green Gables*. He lived the life of a wealthy bachelor, and he was linked romantically to several beautiful stars of the day. The most well-known were Mary Miles Minter, age twenty, who had the face of an innocent-looking bashful blonde of fifteen, and Norma Desmond, twenty-eight, an older, starting-to-fade star who had been having problems because of a growing addiction to cocaine and her late hours of sensual parties and casual sex. Ironically, Taylor was like a Boy Scout himself when it came to drugs. He was part of an effort to clean up drugs in Hollywood. He had even gone to the U.S. attorney's office to report a drug dealer, though his efforts only led to a few arrests of low-level addicts and pushers, and then faded, because drugs and decadence were too much a part of Hollywood in the 1920s.[49]

As police soon discovered, Taylor had another, more secret side. If his death had nothing to do with his efforts to inspire a drug crackdown, perhaps the killing had something to do with this secret life, or so detectives wondered.

The curiosities began to mount. The police learned that Taylor adopted his name soon after he came to Hollywood. Though he claimed to be from England, he was really born in Ireland, and his real name was William Cunningham Deane-Tanner. He had been married to a retired actress named Ethel May Harrison, with whom he co-owned and operated a successful antiques store, and had a young daughter. One day in 1908, after going to the races, he simply vanished. He took only $500, along with some clothes and personal items. Four years later, his younger brother Dennis, disappeared, leaving his own wife and two children behind.[50] For a time, Taylor looked for gold in Alaska and Colorado, briefly surfaced back in Hollywood, acted in a few films, and left to join the Canadian army.

After World War I, Taylor returned to Hollywood, reincarnated with his new name. He brought along one remnant of his past—Edward Sands, his valet for many years. This time he gained success as a film director. He made important friends and acquired a small fortune in those days—he was worth about $1.5 million in current dollars when he died.

Taylor's ex-wife tracked him down after seeing a film with him in it in his early days as an actor, and they stayed in touch sporadically by mail, with Taylor occasionally sending money to his wife and daughter and the family of his brother Dennis. Otherwise, no one in Hollywood knew the real story. Taylor's death started exposing some of his secrets.

The police were able to piece together from various witnesses what had happened the day Taylor died, trying to find any clues to his death in the day's events. It was hard to tell, because it had been an otherwise ordinary day. As usual, Henry Peavey brought him his breakfast and paper. After he read the latest news about the Fatty Arbuckle scandal—then shocking the country about the dissolute life of Hollywood and inspiring calls for a clean-up—Taylor went for a morning swim at the Los Angeles Athletic Club. He stopped at Paramount Studio for a few hours and later went to the First National Bank to redeposit $2,500 he had taken out earlier that day. This later raised questions about whether he might have been being blackmailed and decided to stand up to his blackmailers who might be behind his death. Finally, after buying two copies of Sigmund Freud's book *Inhibition, Symptom, and Desire*, he briefly met with his tax accountant, wrote a few checks, and went home.

At about 7 p.m., Taylor's longtime friend Mabel Normand arrived. She came in carrying a bag of peanuts—a habit she had acquired because she often used peanut shells to carry her cocaine—and Taylor lent her a copy of the Freud book and another by Nietzsche.[51] After seeing Normand to her chauffeured car, Taylor returned to the house, leaving the door open behind him.

Detectives believe Taylor was killed soon after that. About fifteen minutes later, around 8 p.m., in a nearby bungalow, Faith MacLean heard a loud noise and saw a shadowy figure leaving, wearing a pulled-down cap and scarf. It was a man, she thought, though he appeared to walk like a woman. Thinking the sound was just a car backfiring, MacLean said nothing about what she heard and saw until police questioned her later.

So who killed him? As police investigated, the possibilities mushroomed, like characters in a Clue game or fictional murder mystery. So many people had possible motives. Even Mabel Normand could have returned after she drove away.

Laboriously, the police explored lead after lead. An early speculation was that Taylor's former valet of many years, Edward Sands, might be the killer. The police learned he had recently stolen some of Taylor's checks and some jewelry, and charged purchases for girlfriends to Taylor's account. Then he disappeared, apparently fleeing to Europe. It turned out that at the time of the murder Sands was dead.[52]

The police also wondered if Taylor's deserted ex-wife or sister-in-law might somehow be involved. As the police soon learned, back in 1914, his ex-wife saw him in the film *Captain Alvarez* and wrote to him, after which he started sending her monthly checks for child support. Later his sister-in-law, Ada Tanner, found him after she saw his picture in the newspapers, and he began sending regular checks to help her out, too, since his brother had left her. In fact, the police were led to this part of Taylor's past by the check he wrote to Ada the day of his murder.

Was the double life Taylor was living the key to his murder? The police wondered this after detectives found a secret compartment in a locked chest in his bedroom that contained dozens of panties, bras, and nightgowns from many women, like trophies of the hunt.[53] Or, were these simply planted by the studio executives they found before they secured the crime scene to hide an even darker secret—that Taylor was, as rumored, a homosexual, which is why Peavey was arrested in Westlake Park on a morals charge shortly before the murder, trying to find some young gay men for him.[54]

What about Mary Minter or her mother, Charlotte, who managed her career like an overprotective stage mother? Early on in the investigation, detectives discovered a passionate love letter to Taylor from Minter that read, "Dearest . . . I love you . . . I love you . . . I love you," signed with about a dozen X's. Was this real or a plant? If real, could Mary perhaps be angry or jealous he didn't reciprocate her love? Could Charlotte have become concerned that Mary might run away with Taylor, as Mary hoped, thus ruining her daughter's career and her own meal ticket?

A few detectives, like Thad Brown, began to close in on who they thought were the most likely suspects, but strangely, they were removed from the case, as if someone didn't want them to solve it. But who? The powerful studios? The real murderer who had influence? Complicating the investigation even more were the hundreds of people reading the papers who eagerly confessed to the murder—over 300 people, some in Europe and South America—in the two months after Taylor's death.[55] The police had to take time to question and check out each story to determine if the person really knew anything or not. This confusion only helped conceal the real murderer and any cover-up. It was decades before the real truth finally came out.

In 1967, King Vidor, a movie director, started to investigate what really happened in the Taylor murder. By now, Hollywood was no longer the closed, protective company town controlled by the studios. A new spirit of freedom and independence was typified by the rise of popular independent films like *Bonnie and Clyde* from Arthur Penn, which brought a new spirit of rebellion to the screens. The year 1967 was also the height of the hippy rebellion and Muhammad Ali, then heavyweight champion of the world, stood up to the U.S. armed forces by refusing to be inducted. Meanwhile Twiggy, a British model, brought a new hip, scrawny, in-your-face image to the pages of trendy magazines, so different from the sweet image of innocence that Mary Minter brought to the screen in the 1920s.

Thus it seemed a fitting time for King Vidor, age seventy-one, to try to crack what was now a forty-five-year-old mystery by interviewing a cast of characters once part of the most baffling Hollywood whodunit. He found the chief of L.A. detectives Thad Brown, sixty-four and ready to retire after forty-one years on the force, eager to help him by opening the files and referring him to other cops who were still alive. Vidor's goal in conducting this investigation, as he told those he contacted, was to make a film about who really killed Taylor and why. In turn, Brown was a fervent supporter, since, as he told Vidor, his secret desire was to finally solve the case before he retired.[56] He couldn't solve the case when it opened because he or any other cop couldn't do a complete investigation at the time. They ran into too many roadblocks—too many people had been afraid to talk and when any investigator got too close, he was suddenly transferred to another job. But maybe now, Brown hoped, it could be solved. Vidor already had connections in the business as a powerful director—maybe he could get people to speak and could finally discover the truth.

To help with the investigation, Brown permitted Vidor to look at the long buried files for a few hours. Since he wouldn't have time to take detailed notes, Vidor rigged up a briefcase with a microphone and tape recorder and later reviewed a transcribed copy of everything in the files. Though this was illegal, Vidor felt it was the only way to get to the truth. At the same time, Vidor started talking to others who had known Taylor well, like New York book publisher and Hollywood historian Robert Giroux, who had many early documents about Taylor dating back to his childhood,[57] and pioneer film director Allan Dwan, who had made over 300 feature films with silent-film actresses like Gloria Swanson and Mabel Normand.

In his interviews, Vidor sought to sort through the contradictions and reveal the missing parts. He raised hard questions, like, why did the studio execs getting rid of embarrassing evidence at Taylor's bungalow leave the pink nightgown with the MMM initials? Why did the police keep looking for Sands, the former valet, when they knew he was out of the country when Taylor died? Why didn't the police question Mary Miles Minter and her mother more than they did? Why was information about the discovery of Minter's hair on Taylor's jacket and the unidentified keys found in his pockets, missing from the files, as was information that her mother owned a pistol like the one that killed Taylor?[58] It was almost as if, Vidor speculated, someone had carefully pruned the files of evidence so the police couldn't solve the case. But if so, why?

As Vidor pieced the puzzle together, the truth that began to emerge became so shocking he felt he couldn't possibly reveal it. His findings would so devastate and hurt some of the people still alive that he couldn't make the true film about the case he wanted to make now. He quietly packed his notes away, awaiting a more suitable time to proceed. Before he could pursue the project further, he died (in 1982), and his notes stayed buried among his papers, until his biographer, Sidney Kirkpatrick, found them and decided it was time to write up his quest.

Like Sherlock Holmes, Vidor had put together the pieces to discover that Charlotte Shelby had arrived around 8 p.m. that February night because she suspected that Minter, who was in love with Taylor, was about to run away with him after she overheard them talking on the phone. Always the domineering, money-mad mother, Charlotte was afraid that if Minter left she would lose her Hollywood meal ticket. That night she had locked up Minter in her room to keep her from leaving. Minter managed to escape, ran over to Taylor's, and arrived just before Normand got there around 7 p.m. As Taylor walked Normand to her car, Shelby, wearing a long coat and muffler and carrying a .38 pistol, slipped in through the open door to confront him with her suspicions. Just as she arrived, Minter came down the stairs from the bedroom. Immediately Charlotte feared her suspicions were true, so when Taylor returned, she shot him while Minter watched in horror. Then, Shelby fled, wearing her heavy coat, so she looked like the mysterious man who walked like a woman that neighbor MacLean saw running from Taylor's house.[59]

Then the cover-up began, and what Vidor discovered was even more surprising. Shelby gave the gun to her mother, Julia Miles, who took it back to Louisiana and threw it in a bayou. In fact, Mary's sister Margaret told this to one of Brown's fellow detectives, Leroy Sanderson, and district attorney Burton Fitts when they questioned her in August 1922, about six months after the murder. Fitts even found the gun. Then Sanderson was suddenly taken off the case by the district attorney who headed up the investigation at the time, Thomas Woolwine,[60] and evidence began to disappear from the file.

Why wasn't Woolwine pursuing the right suspects and hiding evidence? Vidor finally discovered what Detective Thad Brown had suspected but couldn't prove for so long—that Shelby had simply bought off each district attorney assigned to head up the investigation, starting with Woolwine who was in charge of the investigation from 1922 to 1923. Shelby had taken about $750,000 from Minter's trust fund to do this, as Vidor learned from Minter's suit against her own mother for misappropriation of funds. Initially, Woolwine got rid of some of the incriminating evidence and exonerated Shelby and Minter, and when Asa Keyes took over the investigation, she paid off him, too. Then she paid off Burton Fitts when he stepped into the job. As Sanderson told Vidor:

> Fitts had worked for Woolwine back in 1922. He knew damn well Shelby killed Taylor, but he kept his mouth shut, probably protecting his job. He did the same thing through the Asa Keyes administration. Then when he became top man himself, he wanted a little action from Shelby's bank accounts like his predecessors had been getting. So he let Shelby know he could put her behind bars, and got himself a little extra income. In exchange, he took care of the evidence for her.[61]

That's why the gun, shells, nightgown, hairs from Minter's head—every piece of hard evidence that turned up in the case—were gone. Even the checks Shelby used to pay off one of her alibi witnesses, Carl Stockdale, were missing. Her other alibi witness, Jim Smith, her night watchman, worked for Woolwine on the side. Had this evidence pointing to Charlotte Shelby and Mary Minter not disappeared, Brown believed there might have been enough to indict them, but then the physical evidence that might have been used to convict them disappeared from the file. He felt Woolwine knew they were involved in Taylor's death in some way, but did nothing.[62] Despite Brown's suspicions, he felt he couldn't do anything by himself, since Woolwine was in charge. He just kept his thoughts quietly to himself as the years went on and the Taylor case remained unsolved.

Vidor was amazed at these discoveries. When he looked at the 1937 case *Fillmore v. Shelby*, in which Margaret sued her mother for $48,000 and her Laguna Beach house for unpaid past services in 1921, 1923, and 1926, Vidor discovered another shocker. Apparently, as Margaret testified in this case, she had given false testimony during the Taylor investigation to protect her mother, and after the judge found in favor of Margaret, he referred the transcript of her testimony to Fitts, then the district attorney, who asked Charlotte for payments to keep quiet, too.[63]

If all this was true, could Minter, possibly the one living eyewitness to the shooting, confirm it? Vidor went to interview her to get this missing piece of the puzzle. Unfortunately, by 1967, Minter was in her sixties, and had become an overweight, somewhat addled woman who remembered only her original story for the press—that she was at home reading to the family when Taylor was murdered, even though Margaret said Mary had run away that night and returned saying something terrible had happened to Taylor.[64]

Vidor was disappointed because this meant he didn't have an eyewitness to support the other stories he heard indicating Shelby's guilt and the district attorneys' cover-up, especially if Fitts fought to preserve his reputation. He also realized he didn't want to make a film that might taint the lives of the people still alive.[65] The files were put away until Kirkpatrick discovered them after Vidor's death and revealed the story.

Although the story remained untold, perhaps there was some belated justice. About three years after Vidor concluded his investigation, on March 29, 1973, Fitts, then age seventy-eight, committed suicide. Ironically, he used the same kind of .38-caliber Smith and Wesson revolver used in the Taylor murder.[66] His suicide was like the death of the last ghost from the past.

Officially the Taylor murder case remains unsolved, but there is finally a solution. Or is there? Were Thad Brown's suspicions and King Vidor's conclusions correct? Kirkpatrick's account sounds compelling, and he claims it's absolutely true. If so, it's an example of painstaking interviewing, records review, and deduction in the days before sophisticated police procedures turned sleuthing into more of a science.

Or could this be just another case of compelling true to life fiction, with Vidor in the role of an American Sherlock Holmes? Kirkpatrick carefully documents all the findings while dramatizing the process of Vidor's search. But is his claim of discovery true? Even if it isn't, did he come up with the actual solution to the mystery? Or is this merely one more mysterious element in this truly baffling officially "unsolved" case?

THE CASE OF THE D'AUTREMONT BROTHERS

Siskiyou, Oregon, 1923–27

The hold-up of the number 13 train in the number 13 tunnel on October 11, 1923, was like a Keystone Kops caper committed by incompetent and bumbling train robbers if it hadn't been so bloody. Four men were killed by the blast and bullets. Not only did the robbers who got away with nothing have a run of bad luck, so did the police who were first baffled in trying to figure out who did it and then trying to find out what happened to them for four years. The case fascinated America at a time when Charles Lindbergh had become a beloved hero for the first international flight from New York to Paris. At times, the D'Autremont case competed with Lindbergh for page one headlines.

The case began on a steamy Wednesday morning, October 11, 1927, as the Southern Pacific number 13, known as the Gold Special, chugged on its route from Seattle to San Francisco. It was a time when the railroad was giving way to the motorcar, and the train, which had been at its prime hauling bullion at the height of the Northwest's gold mining days in the late nineteenth century, was like a dinosaur of a passing age. Even at the beginning of the age of aviation, the Southern Pacific was still known for its regular mail and freight runs, plus some passenger runs along the coast. Just two years earlier, one enterprising mail thief, Roy Gardiner, had stolen over $100,000 from the mail service on one such run.[67] So there was still something of the Old West mystique about the train.

That morning, the Seattle to Ashland crew turned over the train to a fresh crew from Southern Pacific's Shasta division, which included Sidney Bates, the fifty-one-year-old engineer; Marvin Seng, the twenty-three-year-old fireman; Coyle Johnson, the thirty-eight-year-old brakeman; and Elvyn Dougherty, a twenty-something mail clerk. They imagined a beautiful, comfortable run through the Siskiyou Mountains, an area of rugged beauty filled with Douglas fir and Ponderosa pine. Shortly after noon, a half-hour beyond Ashland, the train passed across the 4,500-foot summit, showing a glorious view of the timber below. Just as the train chugged north of Tunnel 13, Bates and Seng noticed two men running on the track after the train. A few moments later, the two men, one with a shotgun, the other with a Colt .45, both breathing heavily from running and wearing heavy loggers' outfits and winter coats, had caught up with the baggage car, worked their way through the train to the back of the tender, and climbed over it into the engineer's cab. One of them waved his gun, ordering Bates: "When we get in that tunnel, stop the train so the engine cab just clears the tunnel."[68] It was the beginning of the "last great American train robbery"—and it soon turned into one of the bloodiest and most bungled train robberies ever.

Within minutes the train had stopped, and the third robber, similarly dressed like a logger, ran up to the mail car with a box of dynamite and placed it against the door. Dougherty, seeing him coming, ran inside and bolted the door. The plan was to simply blow open the car door, then take the mail sacks down the track, take out any money, and escape to a car that was stowed in Eugene, Oregon. But the blast changed everything, since there had been far too much dynamite. Instead of blasting open the door, the explosion turned the mail car into a fireball and ripped through the tunnel, sending fragments of glass from the train windows flying as smoke filled the tunnel. Meanwhile, the expectation that the tunnel would muffle the sound was sadly wrong, too. The explosion could be heard several miles away at the Southern Pacific's maintenance camps in Siskiyou, Oregon, and Hilt, California, sending train rescue groups running, believing the engine had blown up. Dougherty, the mail clerk, was burned in the process, and in the confusion, the robbers shot Bates, Seng, and Johnson and fled. One shot Seng and Bates with the .45; another blasted Johnson with the shotgun when he wasn't fast enough in uncoupling the front engine car so the robbers could get away. Unfortunately, they couldn't get away; the coupling had been impossibly twisted by the blast.[69] Panicking at the killing, and with no money from the burning mail car, the robbers fled into the mountains, where they hid as the largest manhunt in U.S. history began.

Among the first on the scene were Siskiyou County Sheriff Calkins and Jackson County Sheriff Charles Terrill, who organized posses on either side of the train. Meanwhile, over a dozen railroad men armed with rifles, clubs, shovels, picks, and sledgehammers began searching the woods and gullies near the train for any trace of the robbers. Had they found them before the lawmen arrived, they would have likely formed a lynch mob. But they had no luck, and soon they were joined by dozens of citizens from town, among them ambulances and doctors.

Where were the robbers? At this point, Sheriff Terrill, who headed up the investigation since the train was still in Oregon, knew very little except that the robbers were probably rank amateurs who didn't know very much about explosives since they used far too much. Beyond that he and other lawmen estimated there could be anywhere from two to a dozen, and they were probably desperate and likely to kill again if anyone tried to get in the way of their escape.[70]

The next day, the story hit the Portland papers; by Friday, several dozen lawmen, railway men, and others were combing the woods near the tunnel. Even a few planes were in the air, searching the mountains, and both Southern Pacific and the U.S. Postal Service had posted a $7,500 reward for the killers—$2,500 from the Southern Pacific, $5,000 from the post office. Nothing turned up, though Sheriff Terrill was overwhelmed by leads and tips from citizens who began reporting sightings of possible killers everywhere.

The big problem was that initially the searchers had absolutely no idea who they were looking for. The robbers could be anyone. They got reports of drifters and anyone who looked vaguely like a suspected criminal, such as five men who drove their car into a garage shortly before the robbery and asked to have the brakes fixed. Several hunters were also stopped for questioning, and two were almost lynched by some railroad men before they were cleared for questioning.[71]

Terrill's men did turn up a few possible clues, though they didn't seem significant at the time. Besides finding a detonating machine with two batteries and wires running to the train, they found a pair of corduroy overalls and a knapsack that seemed to have been dropped near the tracks a few yards from the blown-up train. They discovered also a gun that had been recently fired, though the serial number had been scratched off, and Terrill didn't think it could be traced. Plus the robbers had left behind several gunny-sack shoe covers, soaked in creosote, which detectives imagined the robbers had used to keep the dogs from picking up their scent.[72] All and all, Terrill felt like he was searching for a few needles in a haystack, and it was anyone's guess whether the needles would even turn up. Despite the growing number of men searching the woods—up to 500 at one point—no sign of the robbers turned up, not even a clue of where they had camped, though the posses uncovered more than a dozen moonshine stills.

For a short time, the detectives thought they had found their killer. Soon after they had rounded up and released a number of suspicious-looking men they found in the nearby railroad yards, one deputy suggested maybe the batteries connected to the blasting machine came from a local garage. A team of deputies headed to a garage in a nearby town, where they found a lone mechanic with his hands and face full of grease. "That looks like the dirt on the overalls found near the train," said one excited deputy, and after they asked the man to try on the overalls, they found they fit and took him off to jail. But after questioning him for hours, they couldn't connect him to the crime, and they felt completely stumped, though they continued to hold him for a few days just in case.[73] They similarly hit a dead end after they picked up an ex-convict, Allen Hodges, who several railroad men (after they looked through a prison mug shot gallery), said had been hanging around the railroad. Two drug addicts and two hunters arrested near the scene weren't the right men either, though the addicts soon confessed to a drug store hold-up in another part of the state.[74]

What happened to the robbers? Who were they? After several days, the trail of the robbers seemed cold and the search hopeless. Meanwhile, the criminals were quietly hidden away in a cold, damp hole surrounded by fallen trees and dense brush. They had built it as a hideout, living on nuts, raisins, and beef jerky. They heard airplanes overhead from time to time, and shivered with fear every time they heard a sound, but the search parties never came close. About two weeks after the enthusiasm for the manhunt began to die down, they decided to abandon the car that had been left in Eugene, feeling it was too dangerous to try to get it, and wandered through the mountains like bedraggled tramps, hoping none of the search parties were looking for them. Amazingly, they managed to find unoccupied cabins that saved them from dying from hunger or cold, and they somehow managed to evade the law for a while.[75]

Then the police got their first breakthrough. It was an amazing feat of investigative detection, and the man who did it was the criminalist called "the Wizard of Berkeley," Edward Oscar Heinrich. He was brought into the case after Southern Pacific's Chief Special Agent, Dan O'Connell, a fifty-six-year-old detective who looked like popular movie star Pat O'Brien, stepped into the case on behalf of the railroad. By now, Terrill felt like he had reached a dead end, but O'Connell—who had previously captured mail robber Roy Gardiner whose alleged $100,000 heist had so impressed the killers who had gotten away—was determined to pursue the case. As he looked at the few items found at the tunnel, he felt the overalls and gun might be the key, though he wasn't sure exactly how, and he sent them to Heinrich, who was just starting to gain a national reputation in forensics.

Immediately, Heinrich set to work examining the garments, finding clues that O'Connell and the other investigators hadn't noticed—among them a few grains of dust and two or three tiny wood chips from the right pocket, bits of oily grime from the bib of the overalls, and some nail trimmings. The clues provided a whole new spin on the case, opening up the possibility of finding the killers. As Heinrich wrote to O'Connell in his preliminary report, cited again and again in accounts of the case:

> You're holding the wrong man. The overalls you sent me were worn by a left-handed lumberjack accustomed to working around fir trees. He is a white man between 21 and 25 years of age, not over five feet ten inches tall and he weighs about 165 pounds. He has medium light brown hair, a fair complexion, small hands and feet, and he is rather fastidious in his personal habits. Apparently he has lived and worked in the Pacific Northwest.[76]

How did Heinrich conclude all this? As he explained to O'Connell and his men, he discovered that the dirt on the overalls was not oil and grease, as the deputies had thought in arresting the mechanic, but fir pitch, and when he enlarged the grains under his microscope about 500 times, he discovered they were Douglas fir needles, peculiar to the Northwest. The neatness of the fingernail clippings led him to conclude the man was fastidious. A single strand of hair caught on a button led him to identify the color of the man's hair, and a cross-section of it led him to conclude he was a white man in his early twenties because of the shape and pith of the hair sample. The size of the overalls led him to conclusions about the man's weight.[77]

Especially significant, Heinrich found a registered mail receipt with the number 236-L. He found it in a deep, narrow pencil pocket on the bib of the overalls, which the detectives had previously overlooked. After the receipt was referred to postal inspectors, they reported this startling news: The paper was a receipt for $50 signed by Roy D'Autremont in Eugene, sent to someone in Lakewood, New Mexico.

This was the breakthrough the police needed, though they were still four years away from cracking the case. O'Connell, Terrill, and some of their men headed to Eugene, where they found Roy's father, Paul D'Autremont, who told investigators he was worried since he hadn't seen his three sons since October 1, when his younger son, Hugh, dropped off the car, told him he and his twin brothers, Roy and Ray, were going hunting and would be back in a week—but then they never showed up. He helpfully provided a detailed description of his missing sons, which closely matched that given by Heinrich. Yes, he said, Roy was in fact a lumberjack. He also gave them photographs of his sons and some clothing belonging to the three men, including a cap, red sweater, and towel belonging to Roy, which investigators sent on to Heinrich.

Though Paul D'Autremont insisted the boys must have been framed by some men who stole their clothing, Heinrich's further analysis made it even more certain the detectives had zeroed in on the right suspects. He found that a hair on Roy's towel was a perfect match with the hair he found on the button of the overalls. Hairs on the cap and sweater matched the hair on the overalls, too.

When Heinrich looked more closely at the .45 gun, taking it apart in his laboratory, he found a second serial number inside the weapon—one the detectives hadn't known was there. When detectives traced this number, it turned out to have been sold in Seattle to a man named William Elliott, which turned out to be one of the aliases Roy used. Heinrich, also an expert in handwriting, compared the signature on the mail receipt signed by Roy to that on the gun purchase receipt and found a perfect match.

Finally, the detectives learned one last bit of the puzzle in Eugene. They found a canteen and water bag in a cabin near the tunnel and were able to find an army surplus store in Eugene, where a clerk described how three men had come in to make the purchase. Detectives concluded the men must have used the cabin as their meeting point before the robbery.[78]

Thus, all of the pieces of the puzzle seemed to fit. O'Connell and Terrill were sure they had the right men. With the descriptions and pictures provided by Paul D'Autremont, the biggest nationwide manhunt in history began. The U.S. postal inspectors printed up more than 2 million circulars with their photographs and description, offering nearly $15,000 for their capture. Every police station, post office, and railroad depot around the country posted announcements about the brothers. Even the police in European countries were notified in case they fled abroad, as were maritime officials in seaports around the world. Meanwhile, newspapers all over the country printed their pictures and continued to publicize the search as it continued over the months and years. Dozens of radio stations broadcast daily descriptions of the wanted men—a new use for radio, which was just coming into its own in the mid-1920s.

Incredibly, for all this publicity and despite all of the bumbling in actually staging the robbery and murders, for the next three years, the D'Autremont brothers somehow managed to elude the armies of detectives, press, and the public searching for them. Perhaps it was a mix of luck and the fact they managed to somehow blend in and look nondescript. Initially, they continued to hide in their small hideaway in the bitter cold, because they were afraid to light a fire. After they hiked for five days to the small hamlet of Hilt, California, in the foothills, they split up, agreeing to keep in touch by mail. Ray headed to Sacramento and agreed to coordinate the communication between the brothers using general delivery, though oddly, he chose the alias of William B. Elliott—the same name Roy had previously used to buy his gun.[79] Meanwhile, Roy and Hugh headed for Yreka, California, finding a group of fisherman who took them for hobos and fed them along the way. Once there, Roy managed to find a job with a farmer in a small farming community named Grenada, and Hugh managed to enlist in the army as James C. Price. Incredibly, when the army enlisters questioned his identity, Hugh managed to persuade two men to swear they had known him while he was growing up in Pecos, Texas, and he was able to talk the enlisters into accepting him. A year later, the army shipped him to the Philippines.[80]

For a time, it seemed like the brothers were going to get away, especially as interest in the search dwindled at a time when interest in America turned to the good life. It was the height of the Jazz Age and Roaring Twenties. Despite Prohibition, booze and the excitement of the boom years was everywhere, while silent Calvin Coolidge in the White House seemed to provide a kind of steady and colorless reassurance in an "age of speakeasies, flappers, Chicago gangsters, and moral decay."[81]

From time to time, the police and post office continued the search by posting a new wave of wanted posters. No one seemed to notice the brothers, and they did what they could to remain anonymous. Ray, for instance, working in a foundry in Detroit in 1925, bleached his hair and easily blended into the anonymity of the city streets, while Roy retreated more into a kind of suspicious aloneness, increasingly feeling he was being watched or stalked when he saw the wanted posters. No one suspected them of living quietly in the Midwest. Instead, tips about them came in from all over the world, with spottings and arrests trickling in from far away places like London, Mexico City, Buenos Aires, and the Far East.[82] Ray settled down for two years using the name Elmer Goodwin after he began working for a small lumber company that made railroad ties and mine supports in a small town called Sulphur Springs in Ohio. His boss introduced him to a farmer named Bill Sprouse who had a sixteen-year old daughter named Hazel. Ray began courting her, taking hikes that summer through the rolling hills near the farm, until he popped the question, with the full support of Bill Sprouse.[83] They all thought he was such a steady worker, and by now he was. Meanwhile, his brother, who lived nearby, thought the marriage would be the perfect disguise. "They're looking for the two of us, not a married couple. It'll throw them off our trail for good."[84] Ray had to agree, though he truly loved Hazel, too. In August 1925, Ray tied the knot and for two years continued to live quietly in the nearby town of Pine Grove. In May 1926 the U.S. Post Office circulated another million circulars headlined: "$15,900 IN GOLD FOR CAPTURE OF DEAUTREMONTS," and Ray quit his job making railroad ties and began working again as a farmhand, moving around from farm to farm. In the early summer, Roy moved in with his brother and wife to help out with the rent—something that was very much needed, since Ray now had a new baby boy to care for, too.

Would the police ever be able to find Hugh D'Autremont, still in the Philippines, or the twins in Pine Grove? As 1927 rolled around, the prospects didn't look very good. The delay in figuring out who they were had hampered the investigation in the beginning—and now it seemed like the brothers had been able to get away with it.

The posters that the post office had continued to send around finally had an effect. From the Philippines, where Hugh D'Autremont was just another private named James Price, Corporal Thomas Reynolds returned from a tour of duty with Hugh's 31st Infantry Division to Alcatraz Island before being assigned to another post. He had little to do, and as he looked through stacks of wanted posters to pass the time, he noticed the photo of Hugh, which looked very familiar to him. He particularly remembered the way Hugh used to regale the company with stories about exciting adventures. After he told his commanding officer, who contacted the post office, the post office asked its agent in the Philippines to check into the matter, though there had been hundreds of reports over the past three years, so the request was initially just considered routine. A few questions and that would be that.

At first Hugh just claimed he was James Price from Texas, but when the agent kept questioning him about where he was in October 1923 and whether he was in Oregon, he finally caved in, saying, "I guess you got your man. I'm

Hugh—but I didn't kill anyone. Neither did my brothers." Then Hugh gave his story about how they had been out camping in the Siskiyou on a hunting trip for several days when four men jumped them, took their money, and tied them up. Then, he explained, they learned there had been a train hold-up. "And we knew that if we were arrested, they'd lynch us instead of giving us a fair trail, so we ran away. We were frightened. We knew no one would listen to us."[85]

Still protesting his innocence, he was shipped back to Medford, Oregon, in March 1927, to face trial, becoming something of a celebrity as he held forth for the local press about he had come back to prove his innocence. Meanwhile, his innocent, schoolboy looks helped create a favorable impression in the press, which spread support for him with headlines like: "Bantering Hugh Shivers in Jail" and "Suspect Smiles at the Crowd."[86] The presence of his shocked father protesting his innocence and fears of a kangaroo court helped, too. At times the news of the case, which went to court on May 2, 1927, rivaled the celebration of Charles Lindbergh, who captured the imagination of the public after he crossed the Atlantic to Paris.

Meanwhile, with all the news of Hugh and the missing D'Autremont brothers back in the news, an old man noticed a wanted poster at the post office in Portsmouth, Ohio, with pictures which looked vaguely familiar. After a couple of weeks, he realized that the photos of Ray and Roy looked very much like two brothers named Elmer and Clarence Goodwin he had worked with tearing down an old smokestack. He contacted the local police, who passed their information on to the postal authorities and the FBI (then called the Bureau of Investigations). After a week, Agent Edward Pomeroy, assigned to the case, had traced the brothers to Steubenville and then to where they were working in early June. Using a ploy of offering a better job to avoid the chance the brothers might flee, Pomeroy got Roy, posing as Clarence, to come to the Personnel Office and began questioning him. Just like Hugh, Roy at first held his ground, but after two hours of intensive questioning, he finally broke down, and similarly confessed they were the brothers, though he also claimed they were innocent and had run away, thinking they would be blamed. Ironically, only a few weeks before, Roy had proposed taking a vacation to Mexico after they read about the case against Hugh, but Ray had said no because he didn't want to leave Hazel. He thought they were safe because after a month of publicity about Hugh, no one had tracked them down.

Ironically, Hugh might have been found not guilty at the first trial, since the defense was able to raise questions about when the gun was purchased, and Hugh was about to give his story of being attacked by four men. But on May 11, one of the jurors died, and Hugh was tried again. Not only was the prosecution better prepared this time, but his brothers had been arrested, too, so it would be hard for Hugh to give a separate alibi. The glamour of the original case was gone.

Thus, it was soon over. The prosecution evidence was overwhelming, especially the results of the investigation done by Heinrich, which showed the purchase of the gun. The jury soon came back with a guilty verdict, and Hugh was sentenced to life imprisonment. Fearing they would hang if they were tried, Ray and Roy confessed in return for life sentences, after which Hugh and his parents dropped their own plans to appeal.

As a kind of epilogue, after twenty years in prison, Roy eventually went insane, and after going berserk one day, he was diagnosed as an advanced schizophrenic, became a borderline vegetable, and had a prefrontal lobotomy in the same hospital where Ken Kesey's novel *One Flew Over the Cuckoo's Nest* was later filmed. Ray and Hugh, on the other hand, were model prisoners. In 1958, Hugh, dying of stomach cancer, was finally paroled, and after three months working in San Francisco as a printer, he died. In 1961, Ray was given parole. Unfortunately, by then Hazel had divorced him, and at age sixty-one, he spent his last years as a part-time custodian at the University of Oregon in Eugene. He also contributed to the writing of the book *All for Nothing*, a testament to a wasted life for a crime that killed four men, ruined the three brothers' lives, and was only solved because of the careful investigation of Edward Oscar Heinrich and the continued persistence of the postal investigators after that.

Chapter 4

The 1930s

IN THE 1930s, America woke up to a kind of hangover from the excesses and speculative boom of the 1920s to the Depression. From a time of rip-roaring flappers and speakeasies, the nation bottomed out with the Wall Street Crash of 1929 into a time of economic doom and gloom, which undermined President Herbert Hoover's glowing forecasts for the future in statements such as "a chicken in every pot" and helped give Franklin D. Roosevelt a Democratic landslide in 1932, followed by years of government programs with an alphabet soup of letters to try to relieve economic misery. It was the beginnings of Social Security and Federal Emergency Relief Acts, creating a raft of new agencies, from the Public Works Administration (PWA) to the Tennessee Valley Authority. Photographers for the PWA like Dorothea Lange captured the misery on the faces of the working people that lost their jobs or their farms.

It was a time reflected in the downbeat literature and films of the decade, such as Theodore Dreiser's *An American Tragedy* (1931) and Erskine Caldwell's *Tobacco Road* (1932), turned into a long-running play on Broadway by Jack Kirkland in 1933; John Steinbeck's *Tortilla Flat* (1935) and *The Grapes of Wrath* (1939); and Mervyn LeRoy's film *I Am a Fugitive from a Chain Gang* (1932). The new development of noir detective fiction and films, such as Dashiell Hammett's *The Maltese Falcon* (1930) and *The Thin Man* (1934), and Alfred Hitchcock's *The 39 Steps* (1935) and *The Lady Vanishes* (1938), expressed this darkness. It was a time when playwright Clifford Odets aptly expressed the angst of the decade with his 1935 plays *Waiting for Lefty*, *Paradise Lost*, and *Till the Day I Die*, as did some of the popular songs of the day, like "Brother, Can You Spare a Dime?" (1932), "Stormy Weather" (1933), "Boulevard of Broken Dreams" (1933), and "I Got Plenty o' Nothing" (1935). Yet there were some stirrings of hope for a better day, such as when Dale Carnegie published *How to Win Friends and Influence People* in 1936 and in the popular songs "Pennies from Heaven" (1936), "I've Got My Love to Keep Me Warm" (1937), and "Over the Rainbow" (1939) from the Judy Garland film of that same year, *The Wizard of Oz.*

In turn, the crimes of the decade, as well as the new detection techniques aimed to solve them, reflected these times. Many of the day-to-day homicides reflected the struggles of people to survive hard economic times, such as a grocer killing a father of five when he stole a bottle of milk from the back door and a security officer killing a black teenager when he tried to steal a bag of coal from a freight train.[1] Other examples include Kenneth Neu, an unemployed nightclub singer in New York, who killed a theater owner and businessman in 1933 when the theater owner's promises of a job fell through and he tried to blackmail the businessman for money for a trip but hit him too hard and killed him. Robert Nixon killed a series of victims with a brick between 1936 and 1938 in Chicago and Los Angeles after looting their apartments and got the name the Brick Moron because of his modus operandi. Meanwhile, many of the more highly publicized murders of the day were the big bank robberies that turned deadly, as gangs of robbers stormed the banks, especially in the South and Midwest in the early years of the decade. For a time there was a certain hard-edged glamour associated with some of the more flamboyant robbers, some of whom started in the late 1920s, when times first started to get difficult—like John Dillinger, Pretty Boy Floyd, Bonnie and Clyde, and the Ma Barker gang.

As murder historian Roger Lane writes in *Murder in America*, there was a certain romance about these bank robbers ever since the days of Jesse James, and during the Depression, banks and bankers were more unpopular than ever. The latest crop of robbers became popular David-versus-Goliath and Robin Hood figures, who were cheered on by many people for representing the aspirations of the poor and desperate against a hard-hearted system.[2] Or as Lane notes: "During the early 1930s, with money hard to get, these robberies multiplied especially across the South and Midwest, seriously dividing communities, as those who had their mortgages foreclosed quietly cheered and those with life savings on deposit—in a day before federal insurance—were wiped out."[3]

However, these robbers were far more brutal and deadly than in Jesse James's day with their high-powered guns and get-away cars, and the national crackdown on them contributed to the strengthening of the FBI and its power to go after all kinds of criminals, as well as make certain types of homicides federal crimes. The FBI had started to gain power when Hoover took over in 1924 and began to expand their role in creating a national fingerprint database. Then, in 1933, the headlines-making Lindbergh baby kidnapping led Congress to pass the Lindbergh Law, making a kidnapping across state lines a federal offense. The waves of violent bank robberies in the early 1930s led the FBI to expand into this area too, and Congress helped by creating more federal crimes, including killing a federal officer, transporting stolen money or fleeing prosecution for major crimes across state lines, or robbing a national bank.[4]

This crackdown against both bank robbers and the urban gangs built by Prohibition helped turn J. Edgar Hoover into a national celebrity and the G-men into popular heroes celebrated in film and the radio-dramas on the growing new medium of radio. One of the most celebrated captures was in 1934, after Hoover declared bank robber John Dillinger Public Enemy Number 1, offered a big reward, and issued a shoot-to-kill order, leading a Chicago woman known as the Lady in Red to turn him in. As she led Dillinger into the Biograph Theater on what he thought was just another movie date, Hoover's G-men appeared at the theater and in a blaze of gunfire shot him down—or at least, they think it's him, as some legends have it that Dillinger escaped to live the rest of his life in quiet obscurity, much like Jesse James.[5] That same year, federal agents also tracked down Bonnie Parker and Clyde Barrow in rural Louisiana; they found Pretty Boy Flood near East Liverpool, Ohio, and shot him in a cornfield; they took out Baby Face Nelson in a machine gun battle in the Illinois countryside. In 1935, they scored a coup in another shoot-out in Florida with Ma Barker and her last living and free bandit son, Fred. The notorious reign of the glamorous Midwestern and Southwestern bank robbers was over.

Hoover and his federal agents went after the gangsters, primarily in New York and Chicago, capturing gang lords like Alvin "Creepy" Karpis in 1936 and Louis "Lepke" Buchalter, who had organized Murder, Inc., in 1939.[6] Meanwhile, the Internal Revenue Service helped when Al Capone was finally sentenced to prison and went to jail on tax evasion charges in 1932, because it was too hard to charge and convict him of murder.[7]

Meanwhile, a number of other developments contributed to improving investigative techniques—scientific techniques and a more centralized, professional law enforcement effort. National legislation contributed to these improvements. For one thing, in 1930, Congress passed a law authorizing the FBI to establish a Division of Identification to keep a file of all fingerprints taken in the United States. In 1932, the FBI opened up a laboratory for ballistic evidence and offered its assistance to any local police department on request. Although initially few departments made a request, and the FBI was slow in doing its analysis, over the years, the bureau increasingly provided assistance—and soon it not only offered help with ballistics but in analyzing blood, hair, soil, dust, metallic traces, and other evidence. Sometimes the FBI called on university experts around the country to help with their analysis.[8]

Another development that showed the growing professionalization of law enforcement was when the Justice Department opened the National Police Academy in 1935, through which bureau agents taught courses offered to local officers. These graduates then not only returned home to use this information to improve the divisions and departments they headed, but stayed in touch as a kind of "elite of local law enforcement officers."[9]

In turn, such developments meant that the United States was starting to take the lead in crime detection methods from England and Europe, which had provided the foundations of modern criminology in the late 1800s. There was easy sharing from country to country due to all the new technologies, from the wireless to the telephone to the beginnings of international air service, with new companies like Imperial Airways, which served 22 countries and carried 34,000 passengers and 6.3 million letters in 1932. In 1939, Pan American Airways began its regularly scheduled commercial flights between the United States and Europe on its Dixie Clipper.

One of the most significant developments had been the invention of the comparison microscope in the late 1920s, which enabled detectives to directly compare bullet markings. In the 1930s, there were further improvements in this and related technologies. One was the development of the periphery camera, which was able to photograph the whole curved surface of a bullet, so an investigator could lay the photographs of the bullet side by side to compare them. Also, a new gelatin casting technique was developed, so an investigator could make a gelatin cast of a bullet. Then he could split open the cast and spread it out flat for comparison. Still another new technique was the dermal nitrate test, which could determine if a suspect had recently fired a gun. The test was able to tell this because after a person fires a gun, a residue from the exploding cartridge remains on his or her hands. To test for this, the investigator would coat the suspect's hand with paraffin wax and then test this for nitrates.[10] Later this test turned out to be a problem because it resulted in many false positives, since an increasing number of common substances contained nitrates, such as fertilizers, but at the time it contributed to the advances in detection in the 1930s.

There was also more progress on the blood testing front. The Lattes test, developed by Dr. Leone Lattes in 1915 and described in his 1922 book *The Individuality of Blood* had established the A, B, AB, and O tests for old bloodstains. But Fritz Schiff, a Berlin serologist, felt the tests lost accuracy after a time, since all groups would lose their antibodies and could easily be mistaken for one another. He found that by adding fresh serum to the cells of old bloodstains, these cells would show a renewed attraction for each other, although he couldn't measure exactly how much. In 1931, Franz Joseph Holzer was able to do this at a murder trial, resulting in a conviction; subsequently, this test was adopted in the United States.[11]

Further refinements in blood typing came soon, so that if both the killer and the victim were from the same blood group, they could be distinguished. Not only did lab investigators learn that blood type A was made up of two strengths that could be distinguished as A1 and A2, but in the mid-1920s, Karl Landsteiner, a professor in Vienna, discovered by injecting rabbits with human blood that people could be further divided into M and N groups, so that a person could be either M or N or a combination of both. He continued to refine his methods through the 1930s by experimenting with Rhesus monkeys, until by

1940 he had discovered the Rhesus factor,[12] opening the way for further developments in the 1940s. These new methods of blood typing were called forensic serology, and increasingly the field of forensics as a whole—which included examining all sorts of biologic and inorganic traces of evidence at the scene or recovered later, including hairs, fibers, bullets, toxins, and bloodstains—became separated from its roots in medicine or the work of a pathologist. In fact, as more developments occurred in the 1930s and after, these areas of investigation became split up among many different specialists.[13] More and more, uncovering the killer in difficult crimes became a subject for criminal lab analysis. Even traces of saliva or sweat could reveal the identity of a killer.

In turn, the FBI classification system for fingerprinting came into use more heavily. Though the United States had been slow in adopting this system—for example, the New York police didn't decide to fingerprint all offenders until 1928—J. Edgar Hoover's pressure on Congress led to the creation of a Fingerprint Bureau, and soon led to the rapid accumulation of prints that could be checked when suspects were arrested anywhere in the country. By the early 1930s, Hoover had about 1 million prints, and by 1932, nearly 5,000 law enforcement agencies around the nation were working with the bureau to check prints.[14]

This was this kind of methodological investigation that helped crack many of the new types of more devious killings that occurred more frequently in the 1930s. While the most publicized homicides of the decade were the big bank robberies and the mostly unsolved killings by syndicate gangsters and organized crime figures like Vito Genovese and Vincent "Mad Dog" Coll in New York, Bugs Moran in Chicago, and Paul Ricca and Bugsy Siegel who took crime from Chicago and New York, respectively, to L.A. Many other cases involved tracking down the harder to catch lone serial killers who left few obvious clues.

One was Robert Nixon, the Chicago brick killer, who disappeared for a time into the underworld of L.A. There he survived by purse snatching and shoplifting with a new name: Thomas Crosby, though after another brick killing in L.A., he slipped back to Chicago, where he killed a couple of more times with a brick. The new national fingerprinting system made all the difference in this case. When news that the mysterious Brick Moron had struck again in Chicago, the L.A. police sent his prints taken from a killing there to the Chicago police, who picked up Nixon for questioning. After he initially tried to blame a friend, he confessed to all of the murders.[15]

Another was Gerald Thompson, a toolmaker who became a serial rapist with at least sixteen victims. He would take them to a lonely spot, usually the cemetery, and rape them in his car. He killed one who resisted and the bloodstains on his trousers and his car cushion helped convict him.[16]

There was Winnie Ruth Judd, called the Trunk Murderess, at a time when women were not only more independent as they began pouring into the workplace after the typewriter came into wider use in 1928 but more violent, reflected in the careers of Ma Barker and Bonnie Parker. In Judd's case, she was discovered in 1932 after a Southern Pacific baggage agent in Los Angeles helped her take a large trunk to her car and saw something red dripping through a crack. "It's imported deer meat," Winnie said, just before she drove off, leaving the trunk behind. But after the agent opened the trunk and found the hacked-up bodies of two women, the police were able to trace the license number of the car he had written down to find her. Though the car belonged to her brother in Phoenix, Arizona, they tracked Winnie down in Illinois, where she had gone for a tuberculosis cure.[17] This time, a new registry of records and police cooperation in different states contributed to solving a case.

But most baffling of all were the hard-to-solve cases, involving Albert Fish, who killed and cannibalized children in New York and New Jersey; Robert James, accused of killing his wives and relatives for money using snakes, spiders, and other unusual techniques from Alabama to Kansas, North Dakota, and Los Angeles; John Henry Seadlund, accused of kidnapping and killing a wealthy greeting card manufacturer in Chicago; and Bruno Richard Hauptmann, convicted of killing the Lindbergh baby in New Jersey after a two-and-a-half-year hunt—but then, did he really do it? Or was it an elaborate frame-up? The new technologies made a difference in all of these cases.

Following are some of these stories, illustrating the trends in homicide and developments in homicide investigative techniques.

THE CASE OF ALBERT FISH

New York and New Jersey, 1928–34

In the mid-1920s, residents of New York and New Jersey were mystified by a rash of disappearances and murders of young children, and the local tabloids had whipped up public concern. But the police had no clues, and the cases remained unsolved. One case from still rural Staten Island, just across the river from Manhattan, was the disappearance of Francis McDonnell in July 1924, which began when this son of a Staten Island police officer was playing stickball in the street with friends. Some of the other children observed an elderly, gray-haired man nearby, and soon after, eight-year-old Francis disappeared. His battered body was found the next day after a massive search by friends, neighbors, and the police. Over 250 officers searched for clues to the murderer, but found nothing.[18]

In February 1927, four-year-old Billy Gaffney of Brooklyn disappeared. He was playing in a hallway outside his apartment with a three-year-old friend, who later stated that a gray-haired "boogey man" had come by and taken Billy away.[19] The search and sensational newspaper headlines went on for weeks, and the New York *Daily News* expressed the growing frustration thusly: "Somewhere in New York or nearby is little Billy Gaffney—or his body."[20] But his body still didn't turn up.

Other cases were reported elsewhere. In Darien, Connecticut, a decapitated body was found; in Massapequa, Long Island, fifteen-year-old Mary Ellen O'Connor was discovered murdered.[21]

The police continued to draw a blank. In May 1928 the Grace Budd case attracted the interest of the relentless Detective William King, who was determined to discover what happened. As he investigated, he uncovered one of the most baffling and bizarre cases in the annals of homicide. The case began on May 27, 1928. The roaring twenties had given way to a more conservative period of booming prosperity, just before the stock market crash, and popular culture seemed to reflect a return to family values. The first Mickey Mouse films were introduced by Walt Disney that year, and Charlie Chaplin's popular film *The Circus* was in the theaters. America was celebrating Amelia Earhart as the first woman to fly across the Atlantic, and Al Jolson was wowing the crowds with "Sonny Boy." Fish's acts were like a parody of these values.

King, who later became the chief investigator on the Budd case, was a detective lieutenant in the Missing Persons Bureau. He was a kind of cop's cop, who looked like a tough marine drill sergeant—the sort of big-city cop portrayed in the crimebuster novels and films of the day. Formerly a locomotive fireman, he had joined the police force in 1907, dropped out briefly during World War I to fight on the front lines, and after several years of private security work rejoined the New York police department in 1926.[22]

By the time he was assigned to the Budd case in summer 1928, he was aware of the already widespread fear about the growing number of missing and murdered children. Who was doing these things? Some newspaper stories even hinted at the possibility of a mysterious kidnapping ring.

Then the Budd case hit the news. The papers picked it up soon after the Budds sent their eighteen-year-old son, Edward, to the West 20th Street stationhouse on Monday morning, June 4, to report that ten-year old Grace had gone off with an old man named Frank Howard to his niece's birthday party and never returned.

As Albert Budd and his wife, Delia, explained to the first police to arrive and later to the media as concern about Grace spread, Edward wanted to work in the country and he put an ad in the situations wanted column of the New York *World* on Sunday, May 27. It stated: "Young man, 18, wishes position in the country," followed by his name and address.[23]

On May 28, a kindly, grandfatherly looking man, who gave his name as Frank Howard (it was actually Albert Fish), knocked on the door. Albert and Delia thought he looked like a quite ordinary and respectable man in his conservative dark suit and felt hat, and he stated that he had a vegetable truck garden near Farmingdale, on Long Island, with a half-dozen milk cows, 300 chickens, and six children. They invited him in, and after they spoke briefly, he offered Edward and his friend Willie Korman, who also wanted work, $15 a week. "And I'll pick up Edward on Saturday and drive him to my farm," he said.

That Saturday, "Howard" didn't come, but he sent a telegram advising the Budds that he was in New Jersey and he couldn't make it, but he would be there on Sunday. He did, arriving around noon, carrying a jar of pot cheese and strawberries, which he said was from his farm, though he had actually bought them on the street. The Budds were taken by his thoughtfulness and treated him to a big lunch with chicken, apple pie, and other fixings.[24]

That lunch is also when Fish met Grace. She arrived from church wearing her Sunday best just as they were sitting down to lunch, and at one point, Grace sat on his lap and he stroked her head in a kindly, grandfatherly way. To the Budds, he seemed so gentle and tender. That's when Fish decided to take her instead of Edward, because she was younger and smaller; Edward and Willie were older and bigger than the kind of children Fish preferred, and he had reservations. It would be more of a struggle to overpower them when that became necessary. Of course, the Budds had no idea what Fish was thinking. They just thought Mr. Howard was such a nice man.

As their dinner ended, Fish offered to take Grace to his sister's birthday party for his niece. "I'll bring her back in a few hours, by early evening," he promised. "And then I'll drive Edward to my farm." He gave Edward and Willie $2 to go to the movies, which the Budds considered generous at the time.[25] At first, the Budds hesitated at letting Grace go, but after Fish described how much fun the party would be with lots of children and games, Grace begged to attend, and they finally said all right. After all, they thought, Fish seemed like such a kind, generous man, who looked like a perfectly safe grandfather, and he was going to employ their son.

"So where does your sister live?" Mrs. Budd asked and Fish quickly gave an address: "137th Street and Columbus." Then, as he left with Grace, he assured the Budds he would take good care of their daughter.[26]

He never came back, and the next morning, the Budds sent Edward over to the West Street stationhouse to report this to the police. Lt. Samuel Dribben arrived at the Budd's house a short time later, and after Mr. Budd recounted his story about how Grace had gone off with Mr. Howard, he recalled how before he left Howard had picked up the copy of the telegram he had previously sent. At once, Dribben suspected foul play, since he knew this was a fictitious address—Columbus ended at 110th Street. He imagined that Howard had taken the telegram copy not to leave any clues.

As he did his best to comfort the Budds, saying the police would try to find Grace and bring her home quickly, two other detectives began checking the neighborhood rooming houses. Meanwhile, a third detective took Edward and his friend back to the stationhouse to look through a book with pictures of so-called rogues. The following day, another detective headed to the Motor Vehicles Bureau to see if Howard's name and address were in the records, and still another went to the Western Union office to try to trace the telegram Fish had sent about his arrival.

But nothing turned up. Even a search of the Budds' neighborhood in the Chelsea district of New York turned up nothing. Though officers searched cellars, rooftops, alleyways, lots, lodging houses, movie theaters, subway stations, and garages, they came up empty.[27] Likewise, when several detectives went to Farmingdale—in both Long Island and New Jersey—to find Howard's farm, they found nothing either—because, of course, "Frank Howard" and the farm didn't exist.

Meanwhile, as the police search went on, the media had a field day, giving even more publicity to this case than to the previous child disappearances and murders. Starting June 5, the news of Grace Budd's disappearance was trumpeted in the New York papers and was soon picked up nationally. In part, the attention was due to the concern raised by the previous cases. There was also something compelling about the picture of Grace Budd looking innocent in her white silk communion dress, light gray coat with fur collar and cuffs, gray silk hat, and white pearls, with a rose on her lapel. Her image of innocence betrayed captured the nation, much like the image of JonBenét Ramsey dancing on stage in her beauty pageant costumes captures public attention today.

As in other widely publicized cases, the newspaper coverage, as well as a thousand circulars sent to police departments all over the United States and Canada, brought in all sorts of leads, as well as dozens of crank letters to the Budds, such as one writer who described how he had given Grace a good home.[28] In turn, Dribben had to check all these leads out, with the help of about two dozen detectives from the precinct or from the Bureau of Missing Persons.

There were spottings in Pennsylvania, Long Island, and upstate New York, as well as around the city. After one detective found the pushcart where Fish had bought his pot cheese, using the handwritten forty-cent price on the wrapping paper as a clue, the detectives searched the nearby area in East Harlem. But they turned up nothing. They had more success with the telegram, however. Though Fish had taken the telegram with him, a detective from Missing Persons found a copy of the original Western Union blank that Fish used for writing his telegram.[29] Though the clue provided no helpful lead at the time, since Howard did not exist, the handwriting on the form later helped show that Howard was really Fish.

Unfortunately, after a two-week massive manhunt, the investigation turned into a complete blank, and Dribben even told reporters that this was the "most baffling" case he had ever dealt with.[30] While the newspapers and crank letters turned up plenty of false leads, in time they provided key information that would help Lt. William King, who inherited the case from Dribben, crack the case.

King's involvement began in late summer 1928, when he was one of several detectives assigned to look for a suspect named Dr. Albert Corthell. Corthell's name had turned up when a prison farm warden in Florida, J. S. Blitch, looked at an NYPD flyer describing the old man who went off with Grace. He thought the description sounded like a former inmate who was in his early fifties, used various aliases, and had spent much of his adult life in prison.[31] Unfortunately, Mrs. Budd had the habit of misidentifying suspects, and after she saw Corthell's photo at police headquarters, she said she was sure this was Frank Howard. So King and the other detectives headed to the Midwest to try to find him. Though

Corthell wasn't the mysterious Mr. Howard, the search helped motivate King to keep up the quest for Budd's kidnapper, since the police didn't yet know that Grace Budd had been murdered. So King stayed with the case and kept it alive over the next few years despite all the dead ends and false leads. In fact, the Budd case became literally a "personal obsession," as one chronicler of the case observed.[32]

King went on numerous goose chases, though he kept hoping each time he would finally hit pay dirt. One hopeful lead came in early 1930 when the Budds got an anonymous packet in the mail and Mrs. Budd thought the handwriting of the address from New Hampshire looked like Grace's. But after he traced the address to a young navy man, Herbert Sherry, King found he had nothing to do with the case. A graphologist reported that the handwriting wasn't Grace Budd's in the first place.[33] Still, King was determined not to quit.

A few months later, in June 1930, a fifty-year-old woman from Florida reported that her bridegroom of eight days, Charles Howard, had disappeared with nearly $4,000 in cash. Thinking he was Corthell using yet another alias, King flew off to Florida to track him down. Alas, after he found the elusive bridegroom, he not only turned out to be a real Charles Howard with an airtight alibi, but Mrs. Budd identified him as Frank Howard, too.[34]

In September 1930, Mrs. Budd identified still another man named Charles Edward Pope as Howard, after Pope's estranged wife told police she thought he was Grace Budd's kidnapper. His wife came forward because, she told King, she suddenly recalled a 1928 incident in which her ex sent her a telegram to meet him. When she did, he was with a little girl and asked her to care for the girl while he was on a business trip. At the time, she refused, but now she remembered the incident. Pope did in fact look like a virtual double for Fish, and again, Mrs. Budd was sure he was Howard. But Pope showed he had been living quietly with his elderly sister until his spiteful ex-wife turned him in. So that lead went nowhere, too.[35] Then, when King finally located Corthell in December, after Corthell tried to cash a $15,000 check belonging to someone else in St. Louis and was arrested, Mrs. Budd said, "That's Howard!" too.[36]

Thus, it's no wonder that by the end of 1930 King felt increasingly frustrated. After two years, he had logged in over 50,000 miles traveling all over the country searching for the wrong people, and he felt no closer to solving the Budd case. There seemed to be no leads left, though he still felt a dogged sense of commitment.

Ironically, during this time—in 1928 and again in 1930—the real killer, Albert Fish, did have a few run-ins with the police, but they were minor offenses that ended up in local records. On two occasions, Fish spent a brief period in a mental hospital but was released. Just a harmless eccentric, concluded the psychiatrists who saw him.

Paradoxically, three of Fish's arrests occurred in the summer of 1928, shortly after he had kidnapped Grace Budd. But they were only for petty larcenies, so the police scouring New York for "Howard" never made the connection.

Then, Fish slipped through the cracks again after he was arrested in 1930 for sending one of his many strange, raving letters to a professional housekeeper. He sent it after he saw her name in the New York *World*'s situations wanted section. As he often did in his letters, he rambled on about how he was a successful Hollywood producer, and he was willing to offer a large sum if the housekeeper would only perform various sadomasochistic services for himself and his teenage son, "Bobby," like hitting him with a paddle and letting him drink her urine. Though Fish used "Robert Fiske" as a pseudonym, he neglectfully included his return address, and the police tracked him down. A court social worker referred him to the Bellevue mental hospital, where he spent thirty days under observation. Staff members found him so quiet, cooperative, and seemingly ordinary during this period, according to a report by head psychiatrist Dr. Means S. Gregory, that they recommended letting him go. After reviewing his case, a judge simply put him on probation and turned him over to his daughter, Anna Collins.[37] Again, like a slippery eel, Fish got away.

Meanwhile, King had no idea how close Fish really was. From time to time, he glanced at the file in his still active but unsolved case files, feeling deeply frustrated yet determined to see the case through. Otherwise, the case largely went into a limbo for the next four years.

Finally, a break came due to three main factors—a revived media scare about kidnapping cases triggered by the Lindbergh trial, Fish's penchant for writing obscene letters, and the ramblings of a lone cockroach. Yes, a cockroach. It was a fitting symbol that finally helped bring Fish down.

The case came back to life when the national attention turned to kidnapping again because of the discovery of what was believed to be the remains of the Lindbergh baby in the New Jersey woods. It's not clear if these really were the Lindbergh baby's remains; they might have belonged to an unidentified orphan. But at the time, the kidnapping and the later discovery of the dead baby shocked the nation and inspired a fear that anyone's child was in danger. As one *New York Times* headline proclaimed shortly after the Lindbergh baby disappeared in March 1932: "Kidnapping: A Rising Menace to the Nation." Among the illustrations of four recent victims was the picture of Grace Budd.[38]

Though the story didn't produce any immediate results for King, it contributed to a continuing public awareness about the Budd case. At the same time, it led Fish to think and dream about Grace, which later came out at his trial. Fish's son, Albert Jr., who had been living with him since 1929 in Manhattan, described how Fish would wake up at night sweating and screaming from these dreams, and then, as if in atonement for what he had done, he would strip off his clothes and paddle himself or stick needles in his body.[39] It was a strange mix of guilt and sexual excitement, which was reflected in other practices in which he engaged, since he had a life-long fascination with experiencing and giving pain.

As Fish continued his sick fantasies and King remained committed to solving the case, a newspaper article set in motion events that would finally bring them together. This occurred on June 4, 1994—over six years after Grace was originally kidnapped—when the *New York Daily Mirror* ran an article and series of photographs about the arrival of the U.S. Navy fleet in New York. It was a gala occasion, highlighted by a twelve-mile procession of warships and aircraft carriers through the New York City harbor, and one photograph captured two young sailors and their dates watching the festivities. When Adele Miller, a Brooklyn housewife, saw the photo, she was instantly sure that one of the girls, who was wearing a long white dress and full-brimmed hat, was Grace Budd grown up into a teenager. Miller had been following the Budd saga over the years, and she had kept up with the Budds' address through the news, so she sent them a clipping of the photo.[40]

Immediately, Mrs. Budd called King, convinced that, yes, this must be Grace. But once more, her eagerness proved wrong, for after the newspapers printed her story and the photo, the real girl with the sailor appeared. It seemed like one more hope dashed. But not quite, because the story caught Fish's attention, and he clipped it out, along with the Budds' new address. A few months later, still tormented by his memories as news of the Budd case continued to appear from time to time, he sent a letter with strange ravings and assurances to Mrs. Budd. King had indirectly contributed to Fish's decision to send this letter, because he helped keep the story alive in the New York press by planting phony news items, such as one in a November 2, 1934, Walter Winchell column. In it, Winchell, then the top Broadway columnist, reported that the Department of Missing Persons now had an informant—a "cokic" on Randall's Island who knew about the crime, and police expected to break the case in four weeks.[41]

Whatever the particular trigger, the continued prodding paid off when Fish's letter to Mrs. Budd arrived November 12. She turned it over to Lt. King right away, and though Fish didn't sign his name, King could tell immediately it wasn't just another piece of crank mail. Though the writing was crazed, rambling, illogical, and filled with strange references, such as to the famine in China and the price of meat there, it included some accurate details. One was the reference to the pot cheese and strawberries Fish had brought to the Budds six years before. Also, the letter mentioned a real address where the writer claimed to be living in 1928 that was near where the police had conducted their fruitless search.

To check his hunch, King dug out a copy of the handwritten message Fish had drafted six years before at the Western Union office for his telegram to the Budds, and bingo—it was a match. As King placed the two handwriting samples side by side, he saw the same letter formations and flourishes. He hoped excitedly that this might finally be the break he needed to solve the case.

As he read the letter, it literally opened the door to Fish's crazed mind at work and provided some details about just what happened that day he took Grace. As Fish wrote,

> My dear Mrs. Budd . . . In 1894 a friend of mine shipped as a deck hand on the steamer Tacoma, Captain John Davis. They sailed from San Francisco for Hong

> Kong, China. On arriving there, he and two others went ashore and got drunk. When they returned, the boat was gone. At that time there was a famine in China. *Meat of any form* was from $1 to 3 a pound. So great was the suffering among the very poor, that all children under 12 were sent to the butchers to cut up and sold for food in order to keep others from starving. A boy or girl under 12 was not safe in the streets.[42]

Then he described how this captain stayed so long, that his friend "acquired a taste for human flesh," and after he returned to New York, he stole two boys, took them home, "stripped them naked, tied them in a closet" and several times a day spanked them "to make their meat fresh and tender." After describing how his friend killed, cooked, and ate the boys, he spoke about how he was inspired by the example to taste human flesh himself. That's what he had planned to do when he called on the Budds in 1928, bringing pot cheese and strawberries for lunch, and when "Grace sat in my lap and kissed me, I made up my mind to eat her."

He went on to explain exactly how he did it.

> On the pretense of taking her to a party. You said yes she could go. I took her to an empty house in Westchester I had already picked out. When we got there, I told her to remain outside. She picked wild flowers. I went upstairs and stripped all my clothes off. I knew if I did not I would get her blood on them. When all was ready I went to the window and called her. Then I hid in a closet until she was in the room. When she saw me all naked she began to cry and tried to run down stairs. I grabbed her and she said she would tell her mama. First I stripped her naked. How she did kick—bite and scratch. I choked her to death then cut her in small pieces so I could take my meat to my rooms, cook and eat it. How sweet and tender her little ass was roasted in the oven. It took me 9 days to eat her entire body.[43]

Finally, as if this would be some comfort, he ended his letter on this reassuring note: "I did not fuck her tho I could of had I wished. She died a virgin."

Although the letter described exactly what happened, the key to finding Fish was not the letter itself but the envelope it came in, which provided the important clue. Though there was no address or signature, the rear envelope flap had a monogram design and the initials PCBA. Though Fish apparently tried to scratch out the emblem with a heavy pencil, King soon discovered that the initials stood for the New York Private Chauffeur's Benevolent Association at 627 Lexington Avenue, and he rushed over to see if anyone knew the mysterious Mr. Howard. No one did, and a search of their records turned up nothing.

King asked if any member knew of someone who had removed stationery from the office. No one immediately came forward, but the next day, a part-time janitor and errand boy, Lee Sicowski, approached King and confessed that he had taken a few sheets of stationery and envelopes six months earlier.[44]

But Sicowksi hadn't sent the letter. King theorized that perhaps someone living at the rooming house where Sicowski lived might have taken one of his envelopes, and he went to the rooming house to check. Again, it seemed like he had hit a dead end. There was no Frank Howard listed in the register, and no one recognized King's description of the small gray-haired man.

Desperate, King went to talk to Sicowski again. Was there any way someone might have gotten this stationery? This time, Sicowski remembered that he had lived in a different rooming house at 200 East 52nd Street. He even remembered the room number—room 7 or 11, according to varying accounts.[45] Excited at the new possibility, King headed to the address with his flyers describing the Budd kidnapping. Success! The landlady, Freida Schneider, recalled how a few days after Sicowski moved out, a man who fit the description on the flyer moved in. He was in his sixties, had a thin gray moustache, was very quiet, and stayed in his room for long periods.[46] In fact, only a few days earlier, he had moved out.

King grimaced to think he might have just missed the elusive Mr. Howard after coming so close, if it was in fact the right person. To be sure, King checked the register, and when he compared the signature with handwriting on the letter to the Budds, he knew he had a match. Even more important, now he finally had a name. The thin gray man had recorded his own real name—Albert Fish.

Where was he now? Schneider offered King another ray of hope. Even though Fish had left, she explained that he had a son who worked for the Civilian Conservation Corps in North Carolina, and his son contributed to his support by sending him his $25 paycheck every month. Fish had even asked her to cash several checks for him. Fish was expecting at least one more check and had asked her to hold it for him. "He's supposed to be back for it in about a week," she said.

Taking no chances, King took a room in the house and set up a twenty-four-hour stakeout, calling on several detectives to take over different shifts. At the same time, he asked the CCC finance officer to advise him when he was mailing out the next checks, and he asked the city postal inspector to advise him as soon as any letter was sent to Fish. Finally, on December 5, the letter with the check arrived, though it took another week for Fish to appear.

King was ready. Once he was alerted that Fish had arrived on December 13, he sped to the room where Fish was quietly drinking tea. As King approached, Fish reached in his pocket and pulled out a razor blade, perhaps knowing the game was up and about to kill himself. But King quickly grabbed Fish's wrist, and he dropped the blade. Ecstatic, King hustled him off to headquarters for questioning and then to jail. After six long years, he had finally gotten his man.

After Fish's arrest, the rest of the investigation was relatively easy, though it was increasingly horrific. Once in custody, Fish confessed and confessed and confessed, first to King and then to a growing army of detectives in New York City and other jurisdictions. He also confessed to psychologists and psychiatrists, to the press, and then at his trial.

At once, Fish admitted he was the mysterious Frank Howard, and he explained how he was initially going to take Edward and his friend but decided to take Grace when he saw her, just as he described in his letter to the Budds. He described how, carrying a small bundle with a cleaver, saw, and knife, he had taken her on the subway to the Bronx. From there, they took the Central Railroad to Westchester County to an empty two-story house, called Wisteria Cottage by the locals. It was up a small hill and hidden away from the view of neighboring houses by several hundred yards of the surrounding woods. Fish described how he led Grace to the house, lured her inside, butchered her, and then ate her over a nine-day period, feeling a sense of sexual excitement as he did.[47]

The next day, Fish led King and several other Missing Persons Bureau detectives to the cottage, where they found the first evidence of Grace's body—some bones and her severed skull. It was like a macabre real estate tour, as Fish pointed out various sites where he had committed the crime. The trip provided enough evidence to establish the corpus delicti, and the detectives notified the Westchester authorities about their grisly find. Over the next few days, a team of detectives dug up the property to locate the rest of Budd's skeleton and other evidence.

Meanwhile, as the hunt for evidence continued, Fish talked and talked, while the press had a field day for weeks reporting the details. Soon he had confessed to other mysterious disappearances, including the Gaffney, McDonnell, and O'Connor cases, and he explained how he had strange interests and felt driven by strong sexual urges ever since he was young. He was especially fascinated by pain, and he described the many different ways he inflicted pain on himself. He did everything from paddling himself with a hard paddle to inserting a piece of cloth doused in gasoline in his rectum and lighting it to feel the searing flames. He even had engaged in an act of contrition for the Budd killing by shoving five sewing needles up behind his testicles. A doctor not only confirmed this but discovered that Fish had inserted twenty-seven needles into his pelvic region and left them there.[48]

In the end, there was more than enough evidence to convict Fish of Grace Budd's murder at trial in March 1935 in Westchester County. The only real issue was whether he was insane. His lawyer, Jack Dempsey, did his best to get the jury to spare Fish's life by finding him insane, leading to a commitment to a mental hospital for life. In the end, the jury found him sane, and the judge sentenced him to death. One juror later told a reporter the jurors had concluded Fish was insane—though he knew what he was doing and knew that it was wrong—but they felt he should be executed anyway.[49] On January 16, 1936, Albert Fish was executed.

As for the cockroach that contributed to his undoing? Well, that's how Fish found the stationery he used that gave him away. He saw the cockroach run by him in the rooming house on 52nd Street, and when he got up to chase it away and try to kill it, it ran by the shelf where Sicowski had left the envelopes when he moved out. In a very real sense, a tiny New York cockroach helped bring Fish down.

THE CASE OF ROBERT JAMES

Los Angeles, 1935–36

When L.A. detectives arrived that Monday night of August 5, 1935, it seemed like just an unfortunate drowning of a young twenty-seven-year-old woman, Mary Busch James. They arrived at a pink stucco house with brightly striped awnings that was surrounded by shrubbery and a grove of pepper, bamboo, and eucalyptus trees in La Canada, a suburb of Los Angeles. It was an area that had grown up in the L.A. boom of the 1920s, when go-go flappers and wannabe movie stars had come to a thriving area that grew up as the Hollywood film industry took off. In the 1930s, it shared the same tired worries of the Depression years, which just seemed to linger on. In a way, the suburban cheeriness of the brightly colored homes gave a lie to the economic turmoil that lay underneath the surface.

At the door, Bob James, a very upset husband, greeted them and led them to the backyard garden, where a small fish pond was surrounded by rocks. Several small goldfish darted around in the clear water, in and out of the carpet of pink and white water lilies that floated in the pond. In the center, a bearded cement gnome with crossed legs sat with a pipe in its mouth, like a kind of all-seeing protector of the pond.

Detectives and the doctor who arrived with them saw the body. Mary, dressed in bright red silk pajamas, had fallen face down, with her legs splayed outward across the edge of the pond, her head plunged into the water. Bob sobbed out his story. "The baby . . . Mary got dizzy spells . . . She loved to watch the goldfish."[50]

As detectives pieced together the story, Mary had worked together with James in his beauty parlor and barbershop in downtown L.A. But Sunday night, she hadn't felt well and James had put her in a taxi and sent her home. On Monday morning, she was still feeling poorly and stayed home, so James worked alone, and that night he had invited two friends—Viola Lueck, an old friend of Mary's, and Jim Pemberton, Viola's boyfriend—to join him for dinner. When they arrived at around 8:15 p.m., James was surprised that the house was completely dark and Mary didn't come running to the door to meet them. Inside, they looked for her for a few minutes—checking the living room, the bathroom, the bedroom, and the gleaming kitchen that looked like it hadn't been used that day. But no one was home. James had gotten a flashlight, and lighting the way, they went outside into the garden. "And that's where I found her," James sobbed to officers. "And Jim called the police."

He was obviously upset, detectives noticed, as he explained, almost in a daze now, how he couldn't understand how his wife was suddenly dead. As he described it, she had seemed so happy when they kissed goodbye at 7:30 that morning. They were going to have a baby. She seemed so happy about it. The only thing that troubled her was a little nausea due to her condition. After he left the house, he was at the shop all day, except for about ten minutes around noon, a story later supported by Viola, Jim, and personnel at the shop. They even said he phoned her while they stood nearby to arrange plans for their dinner that night. She would prepare the vegetables, and he would buy the meat and they would have steaks. But now, James sobbed, his beloved wife was dead.

Detectives duly noted his story and apparently distraught condition. They also carefully looked at the body and searched through the house to try to better understand exactly what happened. Presumably, if she had a dizzy spell or other accident, she had fallen forward into the water and perhaps might have hit her head on the stones around the pool as she fell. With no one around to help her, she had drowned.

But is that how it happened? As the detectives and the doctor looked at the body, they saw no head injury. They noticed that her right leg was curiously swollen up to twice its normal size and had a strange purplish cast up to the knee. Also, there was a quarter-inch cut in her big toe. She must have been cut by a sharp instrument or perhaps an insect or snake bit her. The coroner later determined she must have been bitten by a snake.

As they searched the house, the police found a note that Mary had apparently written to her sister, and James confirmed it looked like her writing. The note was like an explanation of her current condition. As it stated, in part: "Dear Sis. Just a line to let you know I am pretty sick. My leg is all swollen; something bit me while I was watering the flowers this morning. This is my old blue Monday, but Daddy will be home tonight, and he takes good care of me. Be sure and write me soon."[51]

Odd, the detectives thought. One found a collection of black widow spiders in the garage. Why were they there, in that dark corner, he wondered, and he spoke to the other detectives about his suspicions. Somehow Mary's swollen leg, her toe gash, and now the spiders made her death seem suspicious. The police spoke to a neighbor named Dinsley who was retired from the English army and he said he had seen a woman walking alone around the garden near the pool that morning. In the end, at the coroner's inquest, the question of just how Mary James had died remained a puzzle, and after the coroner reluctantly ruled it accidental, she was buried.

Perhaps that might have been the end of the story. But James filed his claim for the insurance money—about $20,000 in two policies—and the insurance companies conducted their usual investigation. What the investigator found was anything but routine. For one thing, Robert and Mary James hadn't been legally married at the time he paid the first and only premium, though they married later. Also, the investigator thought it unusual that Mary was so heavily insured, far beyond what would be the normal insurance of someone with the lower income of the couple. The investigator also thought it was strangely coincidental that James's last wife, Winona, had died by accident and been heavily insured, too. She had died by drowning in a bathtub, complicated by injuries received in an earlier car accident, and he had collected $14,000. An unfortunate accident, the coroner had ruled, but suspicious nevertheless. One insurance company refused to pay the new claim and was subsequently vindicated when James tried to sue and the company won in court; the other bargained him down. It argued there were some defects in the policy, and James finally settled for $3,500.[52]

Seemingly James moved on with his life. He bought a small bungalow in southwest L.A. and moved in with his niece Lois and began seeing other women. Life seemed good. He hadn't gotten as much as he hoped from the insurance settlement. He began to think about marrying his niece and insuring her. He returned to his barbershop, imagining the future possibilities.

In the meantime, the insurance investigator whose suspicions were aroused tipped off Detective Captain Jack Southard, the chief investigator at the district attorney's office. There the matter remained until March 1936, seven months after Mary's death. That's when Chief Deputy District Attorney Eugene Williams decided to take a closer look at the case. A team of detectives working under his direction had just finished a big murder investigation leading to the conviction of a woman who had killed her husband eight years before, and they now had some time for another case. Williams decided to act on the investigator's tip. He felt the James case reeked of suspicion, because James had insured both his wives for unusually high amounts and then both had died in apparent accidents. Or as Williams put it in his account of the case, "We felt it was unlikely that within three years after one such fortunate accident for James, a similar accident equally fortunate for him, should happen to another wife, likewise heavily insured."[53]

Williams began the investigation. After looking at James's insurance records more closely, he discovered that in both cases he had initiated the insurance applications himself and then had gotten the cheapest insurance he could that would pay double for an accidental death. After he paid a single quarterly premium, both wives had died.

So what happened to the first wife? Was that really an accident or might that be murder, too? To check, Williams sent a detective to Colorado to learn more about just how Winona had died. The results proved to be truly shocking.

As the story came out, in the summer of 1932, soon after James had gotten Winona to change a longtime $1,000 insurance policy, making him the beneficiary instead of her sister, he had taken out the additional policies with double payments for an accidental death, and he had taken her on a honeymoon trip. They drove up into the Colorado Mountains near Pikes Peak and were enjoying the scenery when their car suddenly went out of control while his wife was driving, James reported, and then he leaped from the car. She must be dead, he reported, explaining that the car had fallen about 150 feet. "And you jumped?" the Pikes Peak road superintendent had asked, wondering why James was wearing a well-pressed, untorn and unmarked suit.[54] "Why, yes," James reassured him, as the superintendent eyed him suspiciously.

At the site, officials discovered the car had been stopped from falling to the bottom hundreds of feet down by a huge boulder, and lying beside it was Winona, who was unconscious but not dead. They immediately brought her to a hospital in Colorado Springs, where surgeons were able to save her life, though she didn't remember what had happened. As Winona was still healing from the accident, James took her to a remote cabin in Manitou. This was in a summer resort area and it was now fall, so the area was generally unoccupied. To help the couple survive, James borrowed some money from Winona's father and on her $1,000 insurance policy.

One day, he took the stage to the nearby town of Colorado Springs, where he reported on Winona's conditions to the hotel proprietor and others he saw that day. He described how he was worried about her because "her head was still bad" and he mentioned how "she was having dizzy spells."[55] When he returned to Manitou from his trip, he stopped at the small grocery store and asked the delivery boy to take him and some groceries to his cabin, since he was tired from the trip. It was the first time he had ever done this, and when the boy, at his request, carried the groceries into the house and began putting them on the sink board, James suddenly appeared looking very upset. "Come look," he said, and the boy followed him into the bathroom, where Winona's nude body was lying on its back in a tub of warm soapy water, her feet hanging out over the end of the tub. She was dead from drowning. As Williams describes it, her position was such that it was almost impossible for her to have gotten into that position and have drowned without help.[56] But no one seemed interested in digging deeper, so there was no official investigation. James simply collected $14,000 for her accidental death, and then he went on a spending spree. According to Williams, "He bought himself a new Pierce Arrow convertible coupe. He bought a lot of clothes and expensive luggage. He took a trip back to Birmingham. He bought presents for his sisters and other relatives."[57]

Birmingham is where he met his eighteen-year-old niece Lois, daughter of a barber who had married one of his older sisters and originally sent James to barber school and gave him a job. He took Lois to L.A. with him, sent her to beauty school, and from time to time she worked as a manicurist in his barber shop. Williams discovered James was again living with Lois after his second wife's death.

Williams decided to set up a twenty-four-hour surveillance of James and his niece, and he sent out a team of detectives to watch the house. They rented the furnished house next door, installed microphones attached to a dictograph, and began recording everything for the next month. Though they never heard a word about Mary James's death, they discovered enough to arrest James for other reasons, since he was having sexual relations with his niece (besides seeing several other women), and incest was a felony under California law. At this point, Williams gave up learning any more about Mary James's murder, but asked the investigators to arrest James the next time he engaged in incest with his niece, and they did on April 19, 1936.

James had nothing to admit about Mary's murder after extensive questioning, but Williams decided to try the press card. Maybe he could find someone who knew something and would talk. The L.A. papers played up the story, reporting on not only James's prodigious sex life but the unusual parallels in the unexpected accidental deaths of his two wives.

This time, someone did come forward—a liquor store owner who told a reporter of the L.A. *Herald Express* a rather bizarre tale about a customer named Hope. Hope came into his store close to having a delirium tremens attack and began babbling about how he had gone around the country buying and testing rattlesnakes and how a pregnant woman had been bitten by these snakes, but she didn't die of the bites. Instead, she had drowned in a bathtub and her body was dumped in a fishpond. At the time, the store owner had thought his tale just an alcoholic delusion and had asked him to leave after giving him a bottle of wine so he could avoid the DTs. After reading the story about James, the tale from months before sounded oddly familiar.

But who was Hope? All the shop owner recalled was that he owned a rather distinctive car. After hearing this strange saga, the reporter contacted Williams. The one lead was the car, and one of Williams's investigators contacted the California Motor Vehicles Department, which looked through all the car registrations of everyone named Hope in the state of California. At the time, this was a laborious process that had to be done by hand. Within hours, the DMV turned over the records of every car owner named Hope, and investigators found that Hope had once owned that type of car—though now he owned another—and that gave them an address, which led them to Mrs. Hope. "He's a short-order cook at a hamburger stand in Hermosa Beach," she told investigators.

Within an hour, the investigators had arrested Hope for questioning, and within another hour he was at the DA's office, face to face with Williams. At first, though, he seemed unwilling to talk, only acknowledging that he knew about the drowning of Mary James but saying nothing about the snakes. After a night in jail, officers took him to the scene of the crime at James's pink stucco cottage in La Canada, and after they took him into the bathroom, he suddenly went white and pasty and broke down, pouring out his weird, gruesome story.

As he explained, in June 1935, he had gone into James's barbershop and asked James if he could give him a haircut on credit, since he was broke. "Sure," James agreed, and then, as he cut his hair he asked Hope, "Do you know anything about rattlesnakes?" When Hope wondered why, James told him about an opportunity to make a $100. "I have a friend whose wife has been bothering him and he wants a couple of snakes to bite her."[58]

At first, Hope thought James was kidding, but James said if he could find a couple of deadly snakes, he could make $100. Hope agreed to take him up on it, and he began searching around. He found some from men exhibiting snakes at carnival side shows in Long Beach and Ocean Park. Unfortunately, the first two sets of snakes Hope brought to James's house weren't deadly enough: James tried them out with some chickens and then a rabbit. They didn't kill the chickens, and when James put the third snake in with a rabbit, the next morning the rabbit was fine, but the snake was dead.

Finally, after a third attempt, Hope found a snake dealer named Snake Joe

Houtenbrink who sold him two Colorado rattlesnakes. This time, when James put them in a cage with two live chickens, they killed the chickens in minutes. "Then he paid me the $100," Hope said.

Williams could scarcely believe the bizarre tale he was hearing, and as the Chief Deputy DA in L.A., he had heard plenty. Hope's story became even more bizarre. As Hope explained, though Mary was very eager to have a baby, over the weeks James had persuaded her to have an abortion, and he convinced her that Hope was a doctor or medical student who could do this. Since abortions were illegal, they would do it at home in their kitchen. So there would be no noise and she wouldn't be able to see the man who did it, they would strap her on the kitchen table, blindfold her, and seal her lips with adhesive tape.[59]

Incredibly, Mary agreed, and on August 4, the day before she turned up dead in the fish pool, she clambered onto the kitchen table, and James strapped her down and sealed her eyes and mouth with tape. Then, he gave her several glasses of whiskey as anesthesia, and told Hope he was going to use the rattlesnakes to kill his wife. He even told Hope he would split the insurance money with him for his help. When Hope expressed some reluctance, James told him he was already deep in the plot, since he had been "going all over Southern California buying rattlesnakes."[60] So Hope went along with the deal.

Carrying one of the snake boxes with a sliding glass door, Hope followed James from the garage into the kitchen and put the box near Mary's foot. James then grabbed her foot and stuck it into the box, where the snake quickly stuck its head up and bit her, making the quarter-inch gash on her toe. The deed done, Hope took the snakes back to Snake Joe, sold them back for half price, threw the empty boxes in a field, and drove back to James's house. Meanwhile, as James tidied up the house, Mary presumably lay on the table writhing in agony as her leg swelled up to twice normal size and a long purplish gash of dying cells spread from her leg through her body. Sometime during this period, James persuaded her to write the scrawled letter that the detectives had found at their house after her body turned up in the pond.

By late Sunday night, as James and Hope sat in the garage drinking whiskey, Mary still wasn't dead. "The damned snake didn't work," he said, and when Hope suggested calling a doctor, he squelched the idea quickly. She'd tell and they'd hang, he said. So finally, after a few more drinks, James decided to drown her, just as he had Winona. As Hope continued to sit in the garage drinking, James carried Mary's limp but still living body into the bathtub and pushed her in, so her head went under, and her feet hung over the rim. Around dawn, he asked Hope to help carry her out to the fishpond, and he did. Supposedly, Hope hesitated after they got her into the back yard, and James dragged her the rest of the way and pushed her in, face down, so she looked like she had tripped and fallen in.

After that, James drove Hope to his home in Los Angeles and gave him the assorted evidence of the crime—the towels, clothes, blankets, and pieces of rope and tape—to get rid of, and he burned most of them in an incinerator. But the blankets were almost new, so he took them to a dry cleaner and kept them. James never saw Hope again.

At first, when confronted with this story after he had been in jail for eleven days on the incest charges, James said he had nothing to say. After officers took him back to the house where he had killed Mary, after he saw the officers take more pictures, and after he was asked about Winona's death, he finally realized that the police believed Hope's story. He decided to talk, thinking maybe he could blame Hope for the actual murder. "All right, I'll talk," he said, and over a steak dinner in a nearby café, he told three officers his story, though he claimed that it was Hope's idea to use the rattlesnakes and that Hope had probably killed her during the abortion.

In the end, the evidence against him was overwhelming. With Hope as their star witness, in return for pleading guilty to first-degree murder and a life sentence, the prosecution presented their case. They also had the help of one of James's many lovers, who testified that he had offered her $2,000 if she would swear that she had seen Mary alive in the barbershop on the day of her death.[61]

The trial was short, and the jury quickly came back with its first-degree murder verdict. James was sentenced to hang, though he fought the sentence with six years of appeals. In the end, though California had replaced the gallows with the gas chamber, James was in fact hung—the last person to be executed this way in California.

THE CASE OF JOHN HENRY SEADLUND

Chicago, 1937

The kidnapping of seventy-two-year-old Chicago greeting card businessman Charles Ross turned into one of the FBI's biggest manhunts under the Lindbergh Law. It was a time when kidnappings for ransom had become a problem, due both to the lingering effects of the Depression and to copycat criminals inspired by the vast publicity given the Lindbergh case, resulting in the trial and execution of Bruno Hauptmann in 1935. Now that the FBI had successfully gone after the major bank robbers, sometimes with the assistance of local law enforcement and the IRS, and had cut down gangsters, a new focus became cracking down on kidnappings.

The problem was definitely serious, especially because many victims were killed even after the ransom was paid. Thus, when Hoover learned of the vicious kidnapping of Charles Ross, while he was driving with his secretary in Franklin Park, Illinois, he was determined to do everything he could to find Ross and his abductors and launched a full-scale hunt.

Ross's frightened secretary, Florence Freihage, told the Chicago police what happened shortly after the kidnapping, before the FBI got involved, and then repeated her story to FBI agents. As she described it, the two had just finished dining at the luxurious Fargo Hotel Restaurant in Sycamore, Illinois, a

Chicago suburb, and were leisurely driving along quiet Wolf Road southwest of Franklin Park when it happened. As Freihage explained, "We were driving along when this other car zoomed ahead of us, cut us off, and forced us off the road. Then, these two men got out and approached our car with their guns drawn." She was terrified, not sure what the two men intended, though they were originally just planning a robbery because Ross's expensive-looking car made them think the passengers would have money. As the men forced open the door, Ross observed philosophically, "I've often thought about being kidnapped," and suddenly, that's what they decided to do.

Before then, John Henry Seadlund, the leader, had been just a small-time petty crook who had drifted around the country taking occasional jobs as a day laborer, since he was seventeen in the mid-1920s. During the Depression, even these occasional jobs were hard to come by, so Seadlund used petty crimes, like holding up an Illinois gas station or a store in Minnesota, to pay the way. In early 1937, he met his partner, James Atwood Gray, who came from Kentucky, and was also a petty thief, seeking more success with bigger crimes. Together, they had robbed a few homes and rolled a few drunks, and they felt that stopping cars with wealthy people in them might be another source of money. That's how they happened to choose Ross's car to stop that night.

It was a crime for money at a time when Americans were still struggling to get out of the long Depression, despite the alphabet soup of social programs passed under the watch of President Franklin Roosevelt. Many of the popular songs of the day were focused around getting work, such as "It's Nice Work If You Can Get It" or "Whistle While You Work" from Disney's popular picture *Snow White and the Seven Dwarfs*. Many books or plays were focused around this theme too, like Clifford Odets's *Golden Boy* about a boxer who longs to become a violinist or the more serious works by Walter Lippmann (*The Good Society*) and Seebohm Rowntree (*The Human Needs of Labour*). There was a great deal of labor turmoil due to poor working conditions—about a half million Americans were involved in sit-down strikes between September 1936 and May 1937 according to U.S. government statistics, and even the Wall Street stock market decline that year signaled a serious economic recession. So times were still bad, despite the stirrings of war abroad, as when Italy withdrew from the League of Nations and joined the Anti-Comintern Pact, when Mussolini visited Libya and Berlin; when Poland refused to agree to return Danzig to Germany; and when Lord Halifax visited Hitler, beginning Britain's policy of appeasement that led Germany to become even bolder.

Like characters in William Wyler's popular 1937 film *Dead End*, many would-be robbers and kidnappers were searching for a shot at a better life, if not a way to simply survive the current hard times. Thus, when Ross mused about being the victim of a kidnapper, the two robbers jumped at the suggestion. One man, later determined to be Seadlund, ordered Ross to get out of the car. "And he told me to stay where I was," Freihage continued. Then, with Ross in their car, they sped away.

Scared, frantic, watching their car disappear with her boss, Ms. Freihage moved over into the driver's seat, restarted the car, and drove to the first filling station she found. There she rushed over to the phone, hysterically calling the police and sobbing out her story. "Mr. Ross, my employer was just kidnapped," she sobbed.

Soon after, the police called Mrs. Ross, who lived a luxurious home on Commonwealth Avenue in Chicago. It was an area of large, serene mansions near the lake. As Mrs. Ross heard the police recount what Ms. Freihage had told them, she became excited and hysterical, too, explaining, "My husband has a slight heart ailment. If he's kidnapped, he can't live very long. His doctors say he must have constant attention."[62]

For several days, the police heard nothing, and in the meantime, they contacted the FBI, since the kidnappers might have taken Mr. Ross anywhere, and under the new Lindbergh Law, the FBI would have jurisdiction. Hoover assigned Special Agent Earl Connelly to personally handle the case. "Just wait to hear something from the kidnappers," he advised Mrs. Ross. Meanwhile, she worried. Was her husband alive or dead? Could he last without the necessary medical attention? Would the kidnappers try to help him if his heart started giving him problems?

Finally, on September 30, a friend of Ross's, Harvey Brackett, living in Williams Bay, Wisconsin, received a letter written in Ross's hand, which stated: "I am held for ransom. I have stated I am worth $100,000. Try and raise $50,000."[63] Apparently, the kidnappers had taken Seadlund to Wisconsin after he said he had a friend there who could act as an intermediary in trying to negotiate and collect the ransom money. So the kidnappers had taken him there and then sent the letter to Brackett. Brackett, in turn, forwarded the note to Mrs. Ross in Chicago, who contacted Connelly, who came right over to look at the note.

"Yes, it looks genuine," he agreed, since Mrs. Ross recognized the handwriting. He advised her to turn over the money. His hope was that this would at least bring Mr. Ross back, and then the FBI had a plan to find the kidnappers by marking the money. It was a new approach the bureau had recently started using in kidnapping cases by using a special dye on the money that could be identified later. In the Lindbergh case, the money had been identified by keeping a list of numbers on the ransom bills.

"I'll try to get the money," Mrs. Ross advised Brackett. "Tell me what to do now."

Within a day, a second note arrived, which was also in Ross's handwriting. Mrs. Ross was relieved as she read the note with instructions on how to proceed to turn the money over. The kidnappers wanted $50,000, but Mrs. Ross hoped they might settle for less, perhaps because she didn't trust the FBI to be able to get all the money back or perhaps because she wanted to be a sharp negotiator like her husband in an industry where manufacturers tried to pay as little as they could for suppliers. In her ad, placed in a Chicago paper, she told the kidnappers she was willing to offer $25,000. Or as the ad cryptically disguised the amount offered in a supposed car for sale ad: "For Sale: 1934 Dodge Sedan. $250. William Gegenworth, 5043 South Western Avenue."[64]

Unfortunately, the offer to bargain wasn't acceptable, and a day later, Mrs. Ross received a typed note demanding the full $50,000 and asking her lawyers to "contact a motorcycle shop," which the kidnappers had selected at random. "Then find a driver" and tell him it's "for a dangerous mission,"[65] the note instructed.

"Go do it," Mrs. Ross told her lawyer, and he made the necessary arrangements. A young motorcyclist, George Kukovac, would take on the assignment when it finally came.

However, the typed note was a matter of concern. If Ross didn't write the note, as he had the two previous ones, did this mean he might now be dead? Mrs. Ross hoped that wasn't the case. As if to reassure her, another note requesting the $50,000 arrived at her house with a picture of her husband, who was standing in the woods holding a Chicago newspaper dated October 2, 1937. Now there were additional instructions on just how the motorcyclist should look, where to go, and what to do. The picture gave her a feeling of anxious hope as she took the $50,000 in marked bills and placed them in an envelope.

Her lawyer gave Kukovac the $50,000 and told him exactly what to do. To begin with, he had to paint his cycle white and dress completely in white, so the kidnappers would know he was the one delivering the ransom money. Then, following the detailed orders in the letter, he began his journey.

He headed toward Rockford, Illinois, following an unusual stop-and-start pattern. Did this mean he was being followed as he rode along to make sure he was exactly following instructions? Kukovac didn't know. He just knew he absolutely had to follow every direction to the letter. Someone's life could depend on it.

As he approached Rockford, he heard a car slowing down behind him, and then, as it came close, it blinked its light three times. It was the signal Kukovac had been told to expect in the letter, and as instructed, without looking back, he unzipped the package with the ransom money and dropped it on the side of the road. Still without looking back, he continued. As he disappeared from view, the car stopped and the kidnapper picked up the money. For now, the FBI and police were nowhere around, because any sign of their presence on this quiet road would have certainly alerted the kidnappers and destroyed any chance of getting Charles Ross back alive.

A few days later, Mrs. Ross received another note from the mysterious kidnapper stating that he would bring Mr. Ross back to Chicago "if I collect and if I have an opportunity to get rid of the bills by that time."

When Mrs. Ross turned the note over to Agent Connelly, he looked at her grim-faced, knowing the letter was just a ploy to buy time. Unfortunately, he realized, it meant that the kidnapper realized that the bills had been marked and it would take several months or more to get rid of them. He would have to spend them carefully, in places where they wouldn't be readily checked and the authorities alerted. He couldn't just take them to a bank and make a deposit. Grimly, as gently as he could, he shared his concerns with Mrs. Ross, and she realized she would probably never see her husband alive again.

The FBI and Connelly still hoped to find the kidnapper and hopefully save Ross's life. Finally, they got two key breaks. First, the FBI had discovered a fingerprint on the first typed ransom note. Whether or not Ross was still alive at this point, the kidnapper had apparently typed the letter, leaving his print, and now the FBI with its growing collection of fingerprints—about a million by 1932 and many more by 1937—found a record of the print on file. It was that of John Henry Seadlund, who had already acquired a record dating back to 1927, when he tried to burglarize a restaurant and was caught on the scene. He was quickly shipped off to jail and sentenced to serve a short term, but after a brief stay, he escaped. At least the FBI knew who they were looking for—a man of twenty-seven who was born in rural Minnesota, about five feet nine inches tall, with brown eyes and brown hair.

Then the FBI got its other major lead. The typeface of the typed ransom notes showed that they had been written on a new typewriter. Presuming the note had been written in the Chicago area, since the picture of Mr. Ross in the woods showed a Chicago newspaper, the FBI sent a team of agents to check all the typewriter shops in Chicago to learn if any had recently sold a new typewriter and to whom. Over 150 agents went shop to shop, and finally they found one that had been sold to a curly-haired man in his twenties. "He bought a new portable typewriter," said the clerk. It sounded like a hit, and they used this description to track the buyer down to an address at a cheap rooming house. "It sounds like a man with curly brown hair named Peter Anders who stayed here for several days, but he moved a few days before and left no forwarding address," the desk clerk said. The FBI agents checked the room for prints, and in a few more days, they learned they had a match with the one on the note.

Now the big question was, where was Seadlund? After several weeks, it appeared he, along with his partner, and Mr. Ross, who was probably dead by now, had vanished from sight. With FBI agents on the alert, the marked bills began to turn up everywhere. There were reports of bills in major East Coast, Southern, and West Coast cities, among them New York, Philadelphia, Washington, Atlanta, Miami, Palm Beach, Cincinnati, Cleveland, and Toledo. The detectives noticed a curious pattern. Most of the bills could be traced back to race tracks in these cities, and when they plotted out the dates and locations with pins on a map, they realized that the trail of bills now appeared to be heading West, since the latest reports came from Arkansas and then from Denver.

Could the agents use this information to find Seadlund? Where might he go next? They reasoned that if he followed the races and was going West, he might be heading for the widely publicized races at the Santa Anita race track in Los Angeles in mid-January. If so, the FBI would be ready. Naturally, they played their chase very close to the vest and didn't let the press know about their plans. Hoover himself flew to L.A. and assigned an agent with a list of the serial numbers on the marked bills to each betting window.

On the morning of January 14, as the races were about to begin, the agents were on alert at every window. They looked like just another assistant betting clerk helping count the money. A curly-haired young man stepped up to the $10 window looking like just another bettor and handed over his $10. The agent at the window saw it was one of the listed numbers. Quietly, he signaled this to the other agents who were standing nearby looking like ordinary bettors, too.

In moments, they surrounded Seadlund, and he quietly walked off with the agents and quickly admitted his guilt. "Yes, I killed Ross, and I killed my partner James Gray," he admitted, explaining that he had held Ross captive in a cave in Wisconsin. While they were holding Ross, Seadlund and Gray had gotten involved in a fight over the ransom, and when Ross tried to intervene, Seadlund had critically injured both men. "I killed them to spare them from further suffering," he claimed.[66] Then he took the agents to a spot in Spooner, Wisconsin, where he had buried both bodies, and the agents dug them up. They also quickly recovered $47,345 of the ransom money. "I was lucky at the track," Seadlund explained, and as it turned out, Seadlund had won as much as he had lost there, since he really did know his horses. Once he had a bankroll to get him started, he did fairly well.[67]

After that, the case was over in just two months. There was nothing to prove; he simply pled guilty, and the federal judge sentenced him to die in the electric chair at the jail in Cook County, Illinois. After he had confessed he had asked the agents, "Will I get hanged or fried?"[68] At the time, J. Edgar Hoover referred to him as "the most vicious cold-blooded killer I ever knew," and when Seadlund died, he had nothing to say, no words of regret.

But Connelly, Hoover, and the FBI felt good that they had been able to solve the kidnapping fairly quickly, after they had taken so much criticism for their long delay in solving the Lindbergh case—and even afterward there was much dispute over whether they really did solve it. But at least Seadlund was a win for the FBI and their national fingerprint database that helped break the case.

Chapter 5

The 1940s

THE 1940S INCLUDED the war years, and they shaped the pattern of murder, too. For one thing, there was less of it, as noted by murder historian Roger Lane, in that the murder rate as measured by the Bureau of Vital Statistics dropped during wartime, as it did during previous wars. Though the rate went up briefly in 1946–47, when the servicemen came home, it kept declining through the 1940s and 1950s. There was none of the widespread violence that characterized the 1920s and 1930s.[1] Rather, the 1940s marked the emergence of more organized—and less violent—crime, in which urban gangsters formed into loose cooperatives and territorial arrangements, eliminating the violent, bloodthirsty competition of the previous decades.[2]

In turn, the media paid less attention to murder cases generally, with a few notable exceptions, since the focus of the country was on World War II and recovering from it. At the same time, the war brought about one of the biggest U.S. economic booms in history, since most of Europe was a theater of war. The Allies in Europe—most notably Britain and France—turned to American factories for production of weapons beginning around fall 1939. Germany invaded Poland on September 1 and Britain and France declared war two days later. Soon after that, the U.S. economy boomed, as the country at first remained neutral. When American men went off to war, women—characterized as "Rosie the Riveter"—went to work.

Meanwhile, the newspapers and movie newsreels were filled with the latest events of war, and crime news took a back seat. Most of the big gangs of the 1920s and 1930s, fueled by Prohibition and hard times, had been broken up, with the leaders either dead or in jail, and gangsters and bank robbers lost their roaring twenties and Depression allure. Now the world was in a struggle for survival, and these were serious times. At the height of the war, nearly 11 million Americans went into uniform.[3] For a few years after the United States dropped atomic bombs on Hiroshima and Nagasaki in August 1945, and war ended with the surrender of Germany and Japan, the focus was on the victorious aftermath—celebrating the return of the soldiers and adjusting to a postwar world.

The popular culture of the times reflected this attention to war. The decade started off with literature like Graham Greene's *The Power and the Glory* (1940), Ernest Hemingway's novel *For Whom the Bell Tolls* (1940), Lillian Hellman's *Watch on the Rhine* (1940), and Arthur Koestler's *Darkness at Noon* (1940). By 1941, there were serious popular books like William L. Shirer's *Berlin Diary* and Winston Churchill's *Blood, Sweat, and Tears*. At the same time F. Scott's Fitzgerald's *The Last Tycoon* was the last gasp of a passing age.

In 1941, 1942, and 1943, the popular films and songs of the times had picked up the interest in war, with films like *49th Parallel,* directed by Michael Powell (1941), and *Casablanca* starring Humphrey Bogart (1942), and songs like "White Cliffs of Dover" and "Praise the Lord and Pass the Ammunition" (1942) and "Comin' in on a Wing and Prayer" (1943). There was some nostalgia for simpler times in books, like Betty Smith's *A Tree Grows in Brooklyn* (1943), and in plays like James Van Druten's *I Remember Mama* (1944), set in San Francisco, which celebrated the power of family togetherness in a time of disruptions due to war. Other songs of the day tried to reflect a hopeful optimism, such as "Oh What a Beautiful Mornin'" from the hit musical play of 1943—Rodgers and Hammerstein's *Oklahoma!*, and "Ac-Cent-Tchu-Ate the Positive" in 1944. It was also a time of uncertainty, reflected in the beginnings of sugar and gasoline rationing in 1942, followed by rationing of shoes, meat, cheese, and all canned foods in 1943.

With victory came other books, plays, films, and songs both celebrating success and pondering the meaning and value of war. For example, in 1946, Arthur Miller's play *All My Sons* (1947) and John Hersey's novel *Hiroshima* (1946) expressed these recriminations, and John Gunther's *Inside U.S.A.* celebrated a powerful new America. Popular songs celebrated love and happiness, such as "Zip-a-Dee-Doo-Dah" (1946), "Almost Like Being in Love" (1947), "All I Want for Christmas Are My Two Front Teeth" (1948), and "Buttons and Bows" (1947), and a flurry of songs from Rodgers and Hammerstein's 1949 musical of faraway paradise, *South Pacific*: "Some Enchanted Evening" and "A Wonderful Guy."

The war years were a time of incredible progress in science and technology spurred by the war effort and then the shift of factories geared up for war to consumer products. Some of these developments contributed to the improvement in investigative techniques. Among the most notable developments were the first electron microscope in 1940; the first "electronic brain" or automatic computer developed in the United States; the first magnetic recording tape, invented in 1942; the invention of xerography by Chester Carlson in 1946; and the development of the transistor in 1947. That was also the first year that a U.S. airplane flew at supersonic speeds, and Thor Heyerdahl sailed on a raft from Peru to Polynesia in 101 days; 1948 brought the first long-playing (LP) record invented by U.S. inventor Peter Goldmark. Through the decade there were all sorts of other inventions in medicine, rocketry, aeronautics, molecular science, human physiology. There was a growing fascination with the ideas of Sigmund Freud about the workings of the human mind; after the war, psychiatrists discovered that a new drug—sodium pentothal—might help shell-shock victims uncover their buried memories and talk about previously suppressed experiences.[4] It was truly the beginning of the scientific and technological age in America—and these new inventions helped make crime fighting even more scientific.

The war years also gave a boost to the FBI and its development of more sophisticated investigation techniques. Besides the scientific developments, the war effort contributed to making the U.S. government more centralized than ever and its people more united, too—first in war and then in victory.[5] In the late 1940s, as fear began to rise over the growing strength of communist Russia and the fear of soviet spying in the United States, the Red Scare helped to strengthen the FBI as well.

The war years helped strengthen the homicide divisions in the local police departments, too. As described by Roger Lane in *Murder in America*, by the end of the war, in police departments all over the country, "after decades of advances, the homicide squad was . . . at the top of the police department's ladder of prestige, commanding the services not only of experienced detectives but also of specialists in handwriting, fingerprinting, photography, and ballistics, among others."[6] Typically, too, an expert forensic pathologist worked with the coroner to carefully analyze the body tissues and more accurately determine the cause of death. All over the country, homicide was treated far more seriously than in previous years. The romantic glow of the killer outlaw was gone. Murderers were more likely to be convicted and charged with more serious offenses.[7]

In fact, instead of gangsters and bank robbers being colorful folk heroes, cops and G-men became the new heroes, featured in the newly popular radio dramas of the day. The decade marked the beginning of crime dramas like *Dragnet* featuring the gravelly voice of Jack Webb as the LAPD detective who solved every case by asking for "just the facts," and *Junior G-men*, featuring FBI agents as all-powerful crime busters.

There was a clear need for these new techniques, since during the war years a new type of killer became more common—the serial or sex killer. These were killers like William Heirens and Raymond Fernandez, who felt driven by sexual urges and other compulsions to kill, and others who simply snapped and killed at random, such as Howard Unruh, an ex-GI who was regarded as the first of the "crazy gunman" or "spree killers."

Some of the new psychological techniques were used to understand these killings. For example, after psychiatrists began using sodium pentothal with shell-shock victims, those in the crime field saw that this drug, popularly called a "truth serum," might be used to get criminal suspects to talk freely and truthfully, making them unable to lie. In 1946, investigators used it for the first time in a criminal case—by getting William Heirens to talk.[8] Still, it was controversial, because many psychiatrists questioned how reliable the drug was, and many lawyers and jurists questioned whether using it was constitutional, leading the Illinois Supreme Court to rule that it was a violation of the right against self-incrimination in the Fifth Amendment to use this drug on someone without permission. However, in its place, the polygraph machine, developed in the 1930s, came into more common use beginning in 1947. Though its results were not completely certain and it was viewed with skepticism by many—as it still is today—most states starting permitted the results to be used in court as expert evidence if both the prosecution and defense agreed in advance.[9]

Likewise, psychiatrists began to play a role in understanding the spree killers, like Unruh. In Unruh's case, after he returned from the war to his home in Camden, New Jersey, he enrolled at the university and spent his spare time studying the Bible. Over the next few years, he became more paranoid and increasingly directed his hatred at some of his neighbors, who he felt didn't treat him with proper respect. He began collecting high-powered weapons. On September 6, 1949, he lost control after a local prankster took off a gate he had installed in the fence in his garden. He took off with two loaded pistols, and over a quarter of an hour, he killed thirteen people with rapid fire and returned home to barricade himself in his bedroom. Within minutes the police surrounded his house. After they persuaded him to surrender, the psychiatrists stepped in, eventually finding him insane, and he was sent to a mental institution.[10]

Psychiatrists also played a role in understanding Raymond Fernandez, one of the Lonely Hearts killers along with Martha Beck. In contrast to the earlier generation of killers who used matrimonial ads to lure victims because they were interested in their money, Fernandez was an insatiable seducer of women, driven by his out-of-control sex drive. He suffered a heavy blow to his head from a falling hatch when he was on board a ship in the service. After that he turned into a sex maniac, whereas before he had been "a normal law-abiding citizen."[11]

This new pattern of sex, serial, and sadistic killers was part of a growing worldwide epidemic, perhaps because the war and the greater mobility in society with new technologies contributed to a growing sense of social upheaval. At the same time, there was more sharing of techniques and information in police departments in different countries, as well as between national crime-fighting organizations like the FBI and Scotland Yard. For example, in the 1940s, England was confronted by London's left-handed wartime Ripper Murderer, who killed three women in five days and was discovered by the serial number on his air force service gasmask; another famous case was that of sexual psychopath Neville Heath. In 1948, there was the capture of sex maniac Peter Griffiths who snatched a baby out of a hospital cot, leaving one fingerprint, and was captured after Scotland Yard fingerprinted every man and boy in the city of Blackburn—about 50,000 individuals. And in 1949, Scotland Yard captured human vampire John George Haigh.[12] So America's burgeoning number of serial, sex, and sadistic killers was part of a growing international trend.

There were killers (or would-be killers) who were simply angry at society as a whole. For example, one man who wasn't uncovered until the 1950s, George Metesky—later called the Mad Bomber—planted his first bomb on November 16, 1940, and included with it a note reading in block capitals: "CON EDISON CROOKS—THIS IS FOR YOU!" The bomb, which was found on a window ledge of the New York Con Edison company, didn't explode, and the police felt the bomber was angry at the company and didn't take the threat very seriously at the time. Between 1941 and 1946, a series of other unexploded bombs were discovered, and the bomber sent sixteen additional angry letters to newspapers, hotels, department stores, or Con Edison before he took a break for four years. It was the beginnings of a case that terrorized Manhattan and baffled the police in the 1950s—and it reflects the growing trend for rage against society or its institutions.

Brian Marriner, in his book on the development of forensic science, describes the emergence of this new type of killer as part of a third phase in the history of murder. In the first phase, killers primarily killed for an economic motive or for survival. With the increased prosperity of society, the second phase was characterized by the domestic murders committed by killers or alleged killers like Lizzie Borden, who kill because of problems in a relationship, to safeguard their own security, or to maintain their current middle- or upper-class lifestyle. In the third phase was the rise of the sex murderer, in which "the killer hungers for sex as the old-time killers hungered for money."[13] Though this is obviously a simplification, since killers kill for all sorts of motives, it reflects the growing influence of the desire for sex, power, and a general anger at society as a whole. As Marriner characterizes it, the new type of criminal might be called "Reactive Man." As he describes it:

> In simple terms, Reactive Man refuses to accept life as he finds it. The old-style criminal wanted to steal an apple from the orchard; Reactive Man wants to burn the orchard down. He is the scavenger, the looter living in the wreck of a civilization. Freedom—the problem of what to do with it—is his disease. Boredom is his natural state. He feels stifled, trapped, viewing violence as the only means of escaping from the straitjacket. He is the complete criminal, his existence is a chain reaction which can only end with his death or imprisonment for life.[14]

In effect, this new criminal is the modern sociopath who feels no restraints or limits on his behavior. He is without conscience, free to do or take what he wants, including another human life. We see much more of this in the 1970s, 1980s, and 1990s. But the beginnings seem to be in the 1940s, particularly the postwar years. Marriner continues:

> Reactive Man . . . reacts against what he feels to be the restraints and repressions of our society. He is never in the wrong, he is never sorry. He is breeding fast—faster than we can build cages to house him. He is the stranger among us, never of us . . . Rebel. Psychopath. Terrorist. All are shorthand symbols for a state of mind. And that is hate. Freud said that if a baby had the power, it would destroy the world from the frustration of its infantile desires. Perhaps Reactive Man is simply immature. Certainly he feels superior to the rest of us.[15]

The new technologies contributed to tracking these killers down. Among them were the discovery of DNA as the basic building block of life. Scientists began to realize that there was some kind of secret code, similar to the dots and dashes of the Morse code that contributed to making each individual unique. They began the search to break this code,[16] which became an important technique in the 1990s.

Fingerprinting also became more extensive and developed. Palm prints were now used in crime fighting. In England, for example, the first murder conviction due to a palm print occurred in 1942, when a print was found at the shop of a seventy-four-year-old pawnbroker, Leonard Moules, who was killed when two robbers came to his shop. That technique spread to the United States.

Another increasingly important technique after the war was the use of the spectrophotometer, which measures the intensities of light of different wavelengths and is used to analyze fibers. This is done by passing a beam of light through the fiber, such as one left by a suspect brushing against a doorknob, and looking at the spectrum. The scientist can tell the chemical composition of the fiber by looking at the different absorption lines—and can also tell when fibers found at the scene of a crime match other fibers by comparing their patterns. This technique works by examining the absorption bands that show what chemicals have been used to create the material. Substances can be identified even more precisely because they also absorb the infrared and ultraviolet light that lies beyond the visible light at either end of the spectrum. However, salt is invisible to infrared rays, which pass straight through it, so in infrared spectrophotometry, investigators add salt to the sample. Then they pass light through the sample; the resulting light that emerged is *minus* the rays absorbed by the chemicals and this spectrum, which takes the form of a series of waves and valleys on a graph, will show what is missing.[17] Scientists can use this process along with a spectroscope, in which they vaporize a sample between two electrodes and analyze the spectrum of light given off by the burning substance, to determine just what traces of dye, mud, tobacco, coal dust, or other substances were on the body of a victim. This way they could more precisely identify certain types of substances, such as what traces of paint came from a car involved in a hit-and-run accident.[18]

More generally, such new techniques were used to solve day-to-day crimes like robbery and burglary, such as a series of safe robberies that occurred in New York in 1944. In these burglaries, the thieves used an oxyacetylene torch to burn their way into bank safes—a much more sophisticated and targeted device than explosives, usually nitroglycerin, used in the D'Autremont brothers' day. The men wore gloves so there were no fingerprints, and the police were especially puzzled by the way they had broken through the heavy solid doors of the bank. After trailing two men spotted near the bank and tying them to one burglary, the police still needed evidence to show they committed the others, and they found it using the spectroscope. They did this after the police found expensive safe-breaking equipment in one man's garage in Astoria, Long Island, and the lead detective noticed some metal filings on the floor. After he turned them over to the laboratory for analysis, the investigators used a microscope to determine that the floor sweepings included metal filings, as well as asbestos, which were a likely indication these materials came from a safe, because safes then were typically fire-proofed with asbestos. The investigators used a spectroscope to perform a technique called emission spectroscopy, in which they compared these samples with a safe that had been taken and abandoned from a previous burglary in a nearby city. In this technique, investigators placed a sample between two carbon electrodes and struck a spark between them; as the light from the burning sample was split into a spectrum, investigators could see the emission lines on a graph that were unique for each sample—"as distinctive as a fingerprint," so they could tell that the filings and asbestos found in the Astoria garage matched perfectly the filings and asbestos from the safe.[19] Similarly, homicide investigators could use this technique in comparing minute bits of evidence left at the scene by a killer with materials found on his person or in his home.

Such sophisticated techniques became more necessary in the 1940s and thereafter, because, increasingly, homicide investigators were confronted by a new type of killer who wasn't motivated by the usual money, greed, or conflicts arising out of a personal relationship. Some of these killers used more unusual or sophisticated methods of killing, including cutting up, burning, and burying bodies of their victims. Such killers became more common in the following decades, but some of the accounts from the crime compilations of the 1950s show what detectives were now up against in the United States as well as in other European countries.

Following is a brief sampling to illustrate.[20]

- In 1940, Wilhelm Johanssen, a man who previously worked as a janitor in the morgue of New York's Mount Sinai Hospital and developed a fascination with dead bodies, was arrested for killing a prostitute by strangling her with a belt. Later it was discovered he had committed two previous murders because he just liked to kill.
- In 1941, fifteen-year-old Raymond L. Woodward Jr. was arrested for torturing and murdering a sixteen-year-old girl, Constance Arlene Shipp, in a rambling parsonage across from her home. He kept her alive and

tortured her for at least twenty-two days, and when police found the body, there were twenty-two cuts, blows, and knife thrusts, before he finally killed her with a heavy blow to the head.

- In 1942, a religious fanatic, Donald Fearn, who was married and had several children, enticed a young woman named Alice Porter to an empty church outside Pueblo, Colorado, where he tortured, raped, and finally killed her. After he was tracked down, he was found insane and sent to a prison for the criminally insane.
- In 1943, Robert Lee Folkes, a cook on a train, slashed the throat of Martha James, a woman on a sleeper train traveling from California to Oregon, apparently after he saw a woman in the dining galley, found her attractive, and learned where she was sleeping. He went to her sleeper car. After James woke up, screamed, and tried to throw him out, Folkes killed her. Later, when detectives traced the murder to a member of the crew and then to Folkes, they discovered he had a criminal record that included several sexual assaults on women, including one where he tried to rip the rings off the woman's fingers.
- In a 1945 unsolved case, the mutilated and decapitated body of forty-seven-year-old Mrs. Lydia Thompson, the wife of a Detroit car dealer, was found in the woods near Pontiac, Michigan. Her husband was tried for the murder, on the grounds that he killed her to marry his secretary. However, there wasn't enough evidence, and he was found not guilty and released.

The 1940s brought an increase in more sexually motivated and brutal crime, and most baffling and bizarre were the killings by Heirens, who burglarized for a sexual turn-on; by Fernandez and Beck, the Lonely Hearts killers, who killed because of Fernandez's insatiable sex drive; and by the killer of Elizabeth Short, known as the Black Dahlia, whose cut-in-half torso was found in a lot in Los Angeles. Following are their stories, which illustrate the trends and new developments in investigative techniques.

THE MURDER OF ELIZABETH SHORT

Hollywood, 1947–49

The Black Dahlia case was like the O. J. Simpson trial in the 1940s in Los Angeles—a beautiful woman found horribly mutilated and dead, a media circus, and an officially unsolved case. Unfortunately, before the investigators could close the net on the prime suspect, who was believed to have committed another horrible bathtub murder, the suspect died in a mysterious hotel fire. That opened the door to continued speculation, including the claims of a woman in the 1990s who has been on *Oprah* and other shows claiming that with her therapist's help she remembers that her own father was the killer, although the LAPD discounts her story.

The case began on a cool gray morning in Los Angeles on January 15, 1947, when America was still recovering from the war years. Soldiers, sailors, and marines recently released from the war were still basking in a glow of glory; Tennessee Williams's steamy play *A Streetcar Named Desire* was presenting a new image of respectable but lusty women; and Mickey Spillane was glamorizing the underside of life in the hard-boiled thriller *I, the Jury*. In this milieu, Elizabeth (Beth) Short, a twenty-two-year-old wannabe actress, gained fame in death as the Black Dahlia.

For Sgt. Harry Hansen and the other LAPD detectives who followed the case, the first notification came shortly after 10:30 a.m. Betty Bersinger, a young housewife with her three-year-old daughter on her way to a shoe repair shop, called and frantically described someone lying in the weeds in a lot at 39th and Norton. Within minutes, the first officers were on the scene, and what they saw was a shock—a stabbed, mutilated woman.

Her naked body was dumped in the lot near a cement sack, and as the detectives described it, she had numerous slash marks on her face, breasts, and lower torso. But what was most gruesome is that her torso had been cut through at the waist, and both parts had been aligned with about ten inches between them. Her body had also been carefully washed, so the blood had drained away and the corpse now looked almost lily white. There were other odd signs, as if the killer wanted to leave his signature on the body—her legs were spread wide apart and a gouged-out piece of skin from her left thigh was stuffed into her rectum. There were some bruises from a severe beating, as well as rope marks on her wrists, neck, and ankles, suggesting she had been tied, perhaps hog-tied, before her body was dissected.

Although the police and the coroner were able to keep some of the more detailed findings (like the heart on the piece of skin) confidential, unfortunately the press arrived within minutes of the police. Ironically, Hansen, a twenty-year LAPD veteran who supervised most L.A. homicides, had written a police handbook on preserving evidence and protecting crime scenes—but this case made a quick mockery of what he had written. As often is the case in high-profile murders, the ensuing tabloid headlines not only resulted in numerous inaccuracies in what was printed but interfered with the investigation. For example, the detectives first on the scene had noted some spots of watery blood on the cement sack and a heel print on the sidewalk. But within a half-hour, by the time Hansen and his partner, Finis Brown, arrived, reporters from newspapers were already there, trampling the print, as well as leaving their own imprints on the scene in the form of cigarette butts and used flashbulbs. The scene was reminiscent of the chaos that interfered with the 1930s Lindbergh baby investigation and the Taylor and Hall-Mills case in the 1920s. It was as if the pursuit of the public's right to know actually made it more difficult to know the truth and solve the crime. Over the next months, the major newspapers—the *Los Angeles Herald* and *LA Times*—were in a race to print the latest headline story, and other papers and radio stations around the country echoed the story from there.

After Hansen called for back-up to document and photograph the crime scene and arranged for a full autopsy, about 250 detectives and patrol officers spent the first day fanning out around the neighborhood, stopping passersby and ringing doorbells to ask if anyone saw anything. But as was to be a continuing problem in the case, no one knew anything or had any useful information. Though the light morning dew on the grass under the body helped pinpoint that she was dumped there sometime before early dawn, about 6 a.m., little else was known except that the killer had been handy at using a butcher knife or small saw and had the foresight to carefully clean the body of clues. Even the woman's face had been so carved up that it was impossible to use her photo to help identify her.

Thus the investigation started with some very basic police work, initially led by Captain Jack Donahue and then turned over to Hansen, who had a reputation as a play-it-by-the-rules kind of cop, not one to be swayed by the demands of the press. As *LA Examiner* editor James Richardson once described it, "You had to play the game the way Harry saw it, or you didn't play it with Harry."[21]

One of Donahue's first investigative thrusts was locating and talking to all known sex offenders in the city to check their alibis. At the time, there was no organized sex registry. Instead, a team of detectives were sent to look through the files of a police psychiatrist, Dr. Paul DeRiver, who had spoken to every offender who had been jailed for the past ten years. Eventually, these files proved to be another dead end. But it was a place to start.

Meanwhile, a second and more promising thrust was trying to identify the body from the fingerprints. Because the victim had never been arrested for a crime in Los Angeles, she had no prints on file there. But there was a chance her prints were in the FBI's collection of 104 million prints in Washington, D.C. At the time, the usual procedure was to airmail the prints to the FBI. However, because this was midwinter and storms could easily delay or even ground flights, Donahue was concerned that it could be several days or even a week to learn the victim's identity.

There was a new technology that made a quick reply possible—a photo wiring service with equipment used by the *LA Examiner*. Assistant Managing Editor Warden Woolard invited the police to wire the prints that way, with one small catch. The *Examiner* wanted a scoop on the other papers. It was the first time that fingerprints would be sent by wire anywhere—but Donahue agreed to speed up the process, and the *Examiner* got its scoop. As soon as the International New Photowire service opened at 4 a.m., a sheet of prints was sent over the wire. The first prints were too blurry to classify, but an FBI agent suggested that the *Examiner* enlarge the prints. After they wired individual 8 × 10 enlargements of each print, within a few minutes the unidentified victim had a name—Elizabeth Short. Her prints were on file because four years earlier she had filed a civilian job application at the Lompoc army base near Santa Barbara, California.

The detectives now had additional information to go on—that Short was born in Hyde Park, Massachusetts, in 1924. With Hansen in charge, the cops went about contacting her parents and other people who knew her, as well as getting leads from the press and a curious public. Soon the detectives were able to put together a profile of who Short was and began searching her past for clues to somebody she knew who might have killed her. As it turned out, her short history did eventually provide a path to the prime suspect—though he died before the police were able to make their case.

The information the detectives got about Beth provided even more mystery. She seemed to be a woman without roots, who moved around without much direction or money in the last months of her life. After the family fell on hard times after the 1929 crash, her father, Cleo, who had a failing construction business, abandoned the family. Meanwhile, her mother, Phoebe, tried to keep the family—which included four other girls besides Beth—together. It was a struggle, and Beth grew up in a family that was often on welfare, and her mother worked hard as a store clerk and at other jobs to survive.

Early on, Beth developed a fascination with movies, which eventually drew her to Los Angeles, hoping for a movie career. But she never had the stamina or dedication to make a go of anything. Additionally, she suffered from two conditions that in retrospect contributed to her difficulties and death. Though she became strikingly beautiful, by her late childhood she developed a sickly, asthmatic condition, which often left her weak and gasping for breath. As was later revealed in the autopsy, she had an undeveloped vagina, which made it impossible for her to have normal sexual relations. Thus, Beth was a beautiful, doll-like tease—a fragile moth dancing around the flames of an underworld of drifters in postwar America.

By the time she was sixteen in 1940, Beth knew she wanted to get out of Massachusetts, and she started her pattern of drifting from one place to another. Initially, she spent winters in Florida, working as a waitress, which seemed to improve her health, and after America was sucked into World War II following the bombing of Pearl Harbor, she was attracted to men in the military, starting with the pilots she saw at the army air corps base at Miami. In 1942, she briefly made contact with her father who was working at the Mare Naval Base in Vallejo, California. He sent her bus fare for her trip to California. But after six months, the arrangement didn't work, mainly because Cleo considered Beth lazy, felt she was always asking him for spending money, and he didn't like her running around with sailors from the base.

So Beth moved on, drifting to southern California, alighting briefly in Long Beach, Lompoc, San Diego, and Los Angeles. In 1943, she worked briefly at Camp Cooke, an armored division training base in Lompoc, where she was voted the "Camp Cutie"; she was arrested with a group of soldiers and girls and charged with underage drinking and sent back to Massachusetts. After another brief stay in Florida, she headed back to California.

Significantly, one of the women she hung around with for a time was Georgette Bauerdorf, who turned up dead in a bathtub in October 1944. Like Beth, Georgette was drawn to barhopping on the Sunset Strip and partying with servicemen; there were some parallels between the two murders, in that Georgette was found nude from the waist down with a towel or cloth stuffed in her mouth, which was used to strangle her, after which she was raped. The police found hundreds of different prints of soldiers and servicemen in her house. Her friends also reported that Georgette had dated a very tall soldier, but after seeing him several times, she was frightened of him and refused to go out with him again. Though the case was still unsolved at the time of Beth's murder, Hansen and other detectives eventually began to connect the dots and came to conclude that this mysterious tall serviceman was likely the killer of both women. It would take a lot of digging before all this theorizing came together. In the meantime, this tall serviceman, assuming he was Beth's killer, roamed free.

For a brief three-month period, Beth did some nude posing for an artist; she drifted back to Florida in 1945, where she fell hard for an airman, Major Matt Gordon, whom she hoped to marry. After she joined him in Long Beach while he was on leave, spending time in a hotel room with him, he left again, not ready for marriage, perhaps because Beth's flirtations with other men led him to think she was being unfaithful. He died soon after he left her to fly out on assignment, and Beth told others they were engaged or already married.

Sometime after Gordon left, she acquired the nickname the Black Dahlia because of a movie called *The Blue Dahlia* with Alan Ladd and Veronica Lake. After the film's release, two soldiers started kiddingly calling her "the Black Dahlia" at a local drugstore because she frequently came in wearing black lacy clothes and had jet black hair. When the tabloid reporters following her murder heard this story, they picked up the name and spread it nationally—giving Beth the national fame she could never achieve as an actress.

After Long Beach, it was back to postwar Hollywood, where Beth drifted aimlessly, as part of an underworld of wannabes. They were, as described by crime writers Marvin Wolf and Katherine Mader, a group of "phony producers, pious pornographers, schemers, opportunists, petty chiselers, hustlers, and crooked cops."[22] Beth lived like a street hustler, moving around frequently, including brief stays with middle-aged theater owner Mark Hansen and several young women in a flat on Cherokee Street. She spent most of her days sleeping late, her nights at different bars like the Shanghai Dance Club on Hollywood Boulevard, or going out with different men. She often asked for handouts—from meals and drinks to clothing and a little cash.

It was a period of growing desperation, and the L.A. detectives tracked down the people who knew her in her last months. These contacts described her as a woman who was afraid of something or someone. Some of them reported that she complained about a jealous boyfriend, and one shoe salesman who gave her shoes in exchange for oral sex reported once seeing her with a part-time photographer and musician who was selling stag movies and girlie photographs. The police had him under surveillance, and he was later arrested and went to prison.

In December 1946, Beth decided to try to pull herself together by moving to San Diego. She told a friend she had met a navy officer, Les Warren, who was talking of helping her find a job at the Naval Hospital and possibly getting engaged. After she went to San Diego to meet him at a café, he never showed up, and she checked her bags in the bus depot and spent the night in the Aztec Theater. That's where the cashier and usher Dorothy French found her, seeming to be very lost, and took her in for the night. It turned into a stay for a month, but instead of trying to find a job, as French told the police, Beth spent much of time going out on dates, sleeping late, and writing letters. When the police tracked down and reviewed the letters, they found many were to a former air force pilot now working for a commercial airline, Gordan Frickling. Again and again, Beth asked him for money or expressed her love for a future relationship, though Gordon was not encouraging, writing that he couldn't "be optimistic about a future together."[23]

Eventually, by the time the Frenches were ready for her to leave, Beth decided to return to L.A. herself, and she got a ride from Robert Manley, nick-named Red. It was January 8—a week before she turned up dead. She had met Manley a few days earlier while she was standing on a street corner, and he offered her a lift. For a time, the police considered him a key suspect because he was the last known acquaintance to spend time with Beth before her body was found. But after several hours of interrogation and corroborating what he told them, the police were convinced that after spending a brief night with her in a motel on the way to Los Angeles, he dropped her off at the Biltmore Hotel at about 6:30 p.m., where she claimed she was going to meet a sister from Berkeley. Just before he left her at the hotel, Manley took her to the Greyhound Bus depot on 6th Street, where she checked her bags. As several hotel staffers reported, Beth waited around the lobby for about three hours, made a few phone calls, and waited some more. Apparently, whoever she was waiting for never called or came, and the doorman finally saw her leave at about 10 p.m., heading south on Olive toward 6th. He was the last known person to see her alive until her body turned up in the lot.

As in many newsworthy cases, complicating the investigation from the beginning was the eager involvement of the press and the public. In the immediate confusion at the lot, the police lost some important clues, because the police photographers and lab failed to take photographs or make casts of several key bits of evidence before they were scuffed over by the throngs at the scene—the tire tracks, a heel print, and a few sprinkles of blood on the sidewalk.

Another problem was that for several weeks after the crime, the press ran shrill headlines about each new development. Although the reporters sometimes helped the police by tracking down many of Beth's elusive contacts, they also confused the investigation by interviewing many of Beth's acquaintances before the police got to them. At the same time, as news about the Black Dahlia murder spread, some people who came forward supplied useful clues; but dozens of others provided false leads and even false confessions. Unfortunately, the police had to check them all out, because until they did, they couldn't know which leads and informants were dead ends and which might be promising.

Even the first sketch by a police artist contributed to the confusion, when he created a touched-up photo of how Beth might look without her facial wounds. As detectives hit the streets in the surrounding area with 200 photos to show to see if anyone knew her, the first edition of the paper with the photo also hit the streets. Almost immediately, a barrage of calls began as anxious parents and husbands called in to report missing daughters and wives. Again, none of them were Beth.

Once Beth's true identity was known from the fingerprints wired to the FBI, anxious reporters were on the phones seeking information, often beating the police to the source, though sometimes they passed useful information on to the police. For example, on Saturday, January 25, ten days after the body was discovered, one of the most helpful leads was a package sent to the Los Angeles *Examiner* and other newspapers that was shared with the police. The letter and contents, which were doused in gasoline to remove any fingerprints or identifying clues, included a collection of Beth's belongings that provided all sorts of leads. Besides her birth certificate and Social Security card, the package included a claim check from the Greyhound depot from which Beth's luggage had already been recovered, several photos of pilots, and a newspaper wedding announcement for Matt Gordon, whom Beth had loved so much, but the name of the bride was crossed out, presumably because Beth wanted to be there herself. Significantly, the package also included a diary full of names and numbers, though one page was ripped out. The mysterious sender also wrote on the package: "Letter to follow"—but the letter never came.

Who sent the package? Was it the killer? Or perhaps someone who knew Beth but didn't want to get involved? Although the press reported that despite the gasoline cover-up, a dozen or so clear prints had been lifted from the parcel and its contents and had been sent to Washington, apparently the prints got smudged in the mail and couldn't be analyzed. It was one more failed possible opportunity.

Harry Hansen and Finis Brown theorized the package was probably from her killer because it had been cleaned carefully with gasoline, much like the killer had carefully cleaned up the corpse.[24] Then, too, they thought the missing page(s) of her diary seemed significant—perhaps the killer's name was on that very page. Even if the killer had been able to conceal his identity so far, the names and photos in her diary provided more leads. Among others, it led the police to Mark Hansen, who had rented a room to Beth and tantalized her with dreams of stardom; to Matt Gordon, who was now dead, having been killed on a flight in 1945; and to Robert Manley. But all were cleared. Hansen and Manley both had alibis showing they were somewhere else at the time of Beth's death, and Gordon was simply dead.

Meanwhile, the police managed to hold back a few critical pieces of information from Beth's autopsy report so they could use this to screen out any would-be confessors. In particular, these secrets bits of evidence included the pieces of skin from Beth's thigh with the initials "BD" that had been stuffed in her rectum and the report of the blockage of her vaginal area due to her vagina not being fully formed. They also found pieces of feces stuffed in her mouth.

This information provided an important clue as to why Beth might have been killed. As Hansen observed in his postmortem discussions with the deputy coroner, chief surgeon, Captain Donahue, and Finis Brown, the fact that Beth wasn't "able to have satisfactory intercourse" might be especially telling, since not being able to do so could have made her partner very mad.[25] In Hansen's view, Beth was a gorgeous female who looked like a woman in every physical way but didn't have all the right equipment. It was an explosive combination, he figured, and he urged the coroner and chief surgeon to keep these details out of the postmortem transcript, so only the real killer would know them. This way, he could know whether any information he was getting came from the real killer.

Because the absence of blood made it clear that the body had been carefully washed and dumped, the police began canvassing the neighborhoods around the city to see if Beth had been hidden in a basement, attic, or some small apartment. They went door to door to homes, stores, and bars, showing pictures and asking if anyone saw anything suspicious or heard any unusual noises, such as screams in the night, water running, or someone digging a hole in the backyard. Whether people saw nothing or weren't saying, the door-to-door search produced nothing. No one heard or saw anything. The police began checking storm drains, as well.

The police allowed much of the false speculation circulated by the press to continue. It was their way to conceal the truth and eliminate false leads. For example, many reports suggested that Beth had been tortured for hours before she was finally killed because of all the slashes on her face and body. But the police knew better, because the postmortem showed she had died fairly quickly from hemorrhage and shock due to blows on the head.[26]

Eventually, over 750 investigators from the LAPD and other police departments were working on the case, including 60 vice detectives, 400 sheriff's deputies, and 250 members of the California State Highway Patrol. Although the police did flesh out the picture of who Beth was and how she had been drifting about, and found some of the downtown clubs where she hung out, like the Dugout, Rhapsody, and Loyal Cafe, they never turned up any information about where she was from the time Manley dropped her off at the Biltmore to when she turned up on the lot. They did come up with some information about her that especially intrigued Hansen, because it contributed to the picture of a girl who teased but then didn't put out. As Gilmore reports, one stripper told the cops that Beth was a loner who "liked to get guys worked up over her, but she'd leave them hanging dry."[27]

As to where Beth was and with whom during that fateful week, there was nothing. Even the police efforts to interview previous sex offenders turned up a complete blank. The press kept national excitement going by printing the latest tidbit, including a leak that seriously bothered Hansen—a leak from the deputy coroner's office that Beth couldn't have sex with men. This leak sent some cops and reporters in the wrong direction of checking into the possibility that Beth was a lesbian and investigating lesbian bars. Hansen worried that he'd lose his secret information that only the killer knew. That's why, two days later, Hansen convinced Donahue to let him have the records coded so only he and Donahue would know the truth. After Donahue agreed, he got a policewoman from the academy to do this.[28]

Secret information was sorely needed because after two weeks of hysteria, as the *LA Daily News* reported on February 1, the Black Dahlia case had run "into a Stone Wall."[29] Despite all the hoopla and all the police and reporters checking, all the leads had turned up nothing. Donahue told the press he believed the murder site was "a remote building or shack in a thinly populated district on the fringes of Los Angeles,"[30] because the police had swept through the city itself so intensively without finding anyone who saw or heard anything. After February 1, a contingent of detectives briefly checked all the eating places outside the city to see if anyone saw any suspicious persons getting meals between January 9 and 14. But after that, efforts went nowhere, and the investigation largely went cold.

In the 1980s, with a new generation of detectives in charge, a serious lead suddenly appeared in the form of an informant with information that only the real killer might have known. At the time, the case files had been turned over to a John St. John; Harry Hansen had retired.[31] However, the police found the information sufficiently credible that they were ready to make an arrest, but then the suspect died in a fire. In the 1990s, there was another flurry of public interest in the case when a woman came forward claiming she remembered how her father had been the Black Dahlia killer, although the police discounted her claims, because they found discrepancies in what she said and the information they had in their own files. The woman, Janice Knowlton, fared much better with the press.

Each claim presents a story of who killed Elizabeth Short and how. They each represent a kind of tantalizing epilogue to the case that may provide a final conclusion. Officially, the Black Dahlia case remains unsolved, but the mystery surrounding Beth's missing week has provided an opportunity for at least three different scenarios of what happened.

The apparently more credible police version is described by John Gilmore in *Severed*. Gilmore provides no specific dates, but it would seem that sometime in the 1980s, a man paid an informant to go to the homicide division and tell a story about what happened. After speaking to Detective Marvin Enquist and playing a nine-minute tape with the man's story, the informant met with St. John, who had taken over the mostly inactive case for about a year, and his partner, Kirk Mellecker. Allegedly, the informant, who knew nothing more and wanted to stay out of the picture himself, had been told the story and gotten the tape from a man using the name of Arnold Smith. In his story, Smith described how Beth had been imprisoned and killed at a house at 31st and San Pedro, not far from the infamous lot at 39th and Norton.

As the man explained, he had met Smith a few years earlier at a party. They began talking about the days when the Hollywood Freeway was being built and hundreds of old houses were torn down in the 1940s. Smith described how a man he knew named Morrison used to pick up girls downtown and got a kick out of choking them and fantasized about hog-tying a waitress and screwing her. Eventually, Smith said, one night he picked up Beth when she didn't have any other place to go, took her back to his hotel, slept beside her, though not with her, since she didn't want to and said he would be disappointed anyway. A few days later, Smith claimed, he ran into Morrison, who told him about running into Beth and taking her to a ramshackle house with rented rooms owned by a Chinaman on East 31st by San Pablo. Supposedly Morrison gave her some beer, wouldn't let her leave, hit her, locked the door, and hit her some more. Finally, he got a knife and rope from the back porch and tied her up like he had once imagined hog-tying a waitress. He tried to scare her with the knife and became angry when she resisted, so he started slashing her. After he went too far, he realized he had to kill her. That's when he decided to cut her up and clean up the body in a bathtub. After he wrapped the body in the curtains and a tablecloth, he put it in the trunk of his car, dropped it in the lot, and shoved all of her cut-up clothes and pocketbook into a storm drain.

Is this what really happened? Reportedly, the detectives tried to find out where Smith was from the informant. After checking his information and police files, they concluded that Smith had really made up the name Al Morrison as a smoke screen, because no confirming information about Morrison was ever found. So why tell at all? Because, they concluded, Smith felt a need to talk about what had happened, perhaps more as a way of satisfying his ego, rather than really confessing.[32] Supposedly, St. John believed the story because Smith knew details that no one else would know besides the detectives and coroner, such as Beth's inability to have sex.[33] After discussing this story with other detectives while still trying to find Smith, St. John learned how a similar suspect was wanted for questioning in connection with the Georgette Bauerdorf murder, and that "Arnold Smith" was one of many aliases used by Jack Anderson Wilson, a tall, thin, alcoholic with a limp and five-page rap sheet dating back to 1943. It was a connection L.A. County Sheriff Detective Joel Lesnick was making himself after reviewing various unsolved homicides with the LAPD.

All the red flags making Smith a suspect were there—he had been arrested for sodomy and hung around skid-row gay bars and female impersonators, and the bathtub scenario in his story shared many elements with the Bauerdorf bathtub murder, including the rag stuffed in her mouth. Plus, alcohol would help trigger the overkill in both cases. Meanwhile, other homicide detectives working unsolved cases had discovered from an informant that Bauerdorf and Short had known each other. They had not only worked at the same USO canteen at one time, but Bauderdorf had mentioned Short in her diary.

Another compelling factor was that a doctor who had reviewed the transcript of the Smith interview—Dr. John Money, director of Psychohormonal Research at Johns Hopkins School of Medicine—concluded that Smith fit the profile of a lust murderer, who might take time to get to know his victim before killing her, concluding that Smith was very likely Short's killer. In fact, Smith reportedly told the informant that the place where the body was dumped was shaped like a woman's pussy—a fact consulting expert Forensic Psychologist Paul Cassinelli found illuminating. It was as if Smith, knowing Short had an undeveloped vagina or "blank place," left her in an empty lot that was halfway between where he lived and where he worked briefly as a sign hanger. In slashing her pubic area after death, he cut an opening to symbolically correct the problem.[34]

So was Wilson, alias Smith, now perhaps in his sixties, the mysterious Black Dahlia killer? St. John set up a meeting with Smith, saying he wanted to discuss what he knew about Morrison's connection with gangland figures. It was a pretext to get Smith talking. Just before the meeting, an undercover detective working with the LAPD Narcotics Division actually met Smith, describing him as a "tall, gaunt, older man."[35]

Thus, St. John finally felt he had the solution to the long unsolved Short case in his grasp as he prepared to meet with his suspect. The meeting was set for San Francisco at the Holland Hotel on 7th Street, where Wilson had been living for about four years, much of it in an alcoholic daze. A few days after St. John spoke with him by phone, Wilson died in a fire. Apparently, in a drunken stupor, he had dropped a cigarette, which ignited his room. Was it an accident or was arson involved? Did Wilson perhaps commit suicide now that the noose linking him to this long ago murder was tightening? There was no way to tell since the room was so badly burned. St. John tried to tie him to Short's murder, and Lesnick believed if St. John had been able to talk to Wilson and arrest him, Wilson would have confessed to both murders.

Once Wilson died, the crime would have to remain unsolved. Though the district attorney's office reviewed Short's case file after Wilson's body was cremated, it could only conclude that an "intensive inquiry would be recommended," due to the circumstantial evidence linking Wilson to the murder. Without an opportunity to interview the now deceased main suspect, there was no way to ask about their theories and suspicions, much less try him for the crime.[36]

So is that the solution, though the case can never be officially solved? Perhaps. But the mystery of Short's missing week has also provided an opportunity for others to fill in the gaps with their explanations of what might have happened.

Novelist James Ellroy, for example, published *The Black Dahlia* in 1987, in which he created the story of two fictional LAPD detectives, Bucky Bleichert and Lee Blanchard, who were fascinated with the case. As they track down what really happened, through their eyes Ellroy suggests that Short's journey through the underbelly of postwar Hollywood led her to look for an abortionist after she became pregnant. Unfortunately, a Scottish immigrant associate of the abortionist, Georgie Tilden, turns out to be a sexual deviant who has a history of cutting up dead animals. He takes Short to one of the abandoned homes he owns, which is shortly to be torn down for the Hollywood Freeway. There, with his girlfriend, he tortures her for two days; after she dies, he cuts the body in two and washes the halves in a stream outside the shack before dumping it at the lot.[37]

In 1992, a recovered memory twisted up a new confession. Janice Knowlton, a professional singer and publicist, came out with a story that riveted America, and it was later published in *Daddy Was the Black Dahlia Killer.* As she informed a fascinated nation in the press and on talk shows, she remembered how her father, George Knowlton, actually killed Short and got Jan to help him do it. Apparently, she claimed, the memories began to come back to her in the late 1980s after she sought treatment for unexplained depression, anxiety, and panic attacks she started experiencing in 1981. These became worse after her pet dog was euthanized after surgery to remove a tumor.[38] Something about seeing that incision haunted her. After she started having physical problems and began taking steroids and antidepressants to overcome the effects of a hysterectomy, her health and business rapidly declined while doctors and therapists seemed unable to do anything.

She went into treatment with Jim Frey in 1989, and the memories gradually began to come back. By November 1989, she was convinced that her father had committed several murders. Perhaps with the help of a suggestion from her sister, Prudence, who had recently read some of the Ellroy novel, Janice came to believe that her father, who had a reputation for going to bars and seeing other woman, had killed Elizabeth Short, too. Her subsequent dreams and memories convinced her.

As she remembered more details, she proceeded to investigate various records, including news reports, to corroborate her memories. As she recalled, when she was ten, living in Westminster on the outskirts of L.A., her father had been seeing Short on the side and got her pregnant. While he was trying to arrange an abortion, Short stayed in a detached garage out back and had a miscarriage. He became angry that Short was ready to take off and leave the dead fetus with him to take care of, and he was also angry that his wife saw her and the fetus back there. He decided to tie Short up to punish her, and he called on Janice to help him. After two days, when he was ready to cut the ropes to set her free, Beth's gasp of fear set him off, leading him to slash her face. Fearing she might tell what happened, he decided to kill her, and with Janice watching, he hit her on the head, cut her up, and took her body to the Seal

Beach pier. But when the body wouldn't sink in the water, he took it to a shed by the picnic area used for cleaning fish and cut it up into smaller pieces. After he washed it off in a shower stall at the Culver City Moose and Legion Hall, he asked Janice to fix Short's hair, and he took the body to the lot. He warned Janice to say nothing to anybody, and she hid the memories away.[39]

But are the memories accurate? John St. John didn't seem to think so, because he brushed Knowlton off when she called him at the end of 1989, as did the robbery-homicide commander, Captain W. O. Gartland, saying there was no connection between her father and this case.[40] But while the police remained skeptical and advised her that the records were sealed, Knowlton sought support and corroboration from the American public, so she began her round of appearances on major talk shows, including *AM/LA*, *Larry King Live*, *People Are Talking*, and *Hard Copy*. She also gained some at least consistent confirmation from siblings who described her father's violent temper, sadistic punishments, cruelty to animals, drinking binges, and adulterous affairs. She even arranged for a brief archaeological dig at her old Westminster home and accused St. John and the police of trying to avoid seriously looking into her report.

Perhaps so. But if the dead Wilson was the presumed killer, and the evidence in the files shows Short couldn't have intercourse (much less become pregnant), why should they believe her memories? Knowlton herself obviously does.

In any case, Knowlton's memories have added another layer of mystery to an already strange case. Who really knows? Was Wilson really the killer? Or, as Knowlton believes, could it have been someone else? The initial investigation and hoopla surrounding the case made everything so muddled, it's virtually impossible to know.

THE CASE OF MARTHA BECK AND RAYMOND FERNANDEZ

Pensacola, Florida; Grand Rapids, Michigan; New York City, 1948–49

What came to be known as the Lonely Hearts killings began in New York soon after Christmas 1948 with what seemed to be just another missing person case. Mrs. Janet Fay's stepdaughter Mary called the police and reported Janet missing. At the time, New York and the rest of the country had entered a period of peace and prosperity after the war, and a feeling of success and victory was in the air. The U.S. team had just won the Davis Cup tennis matches against Australia; another U.S. team was the high scorer in the Olympic Games held in London. Also, the United States had successfully tested new rocket missiles in New Mexico that had climbed 78 miles at the rate of 3,000 miles per hour. At the same time, the postwar period brought about a new attention to sexual feelings—along with the growing interest in all sorts of consumer goods and personal pleasures. Cheap Japanese goods flooded the market for new gimmicks, and this was also the year Alfred Kinsey brought out his breakthrough book *Sexual Behavior in the Human Male*—which reflected just how sexually active American men were in all sorts of ways, many which hadn't been before recognized in a more conservative-minded America before the war. Then, too, this return to normality after the war brought about a growing market for lovelorn services and publications to bring together people of all ages who were lonely and seeking love.

That's what Janet Fay, a sixty-six-year-old widow living in Albany wanted, too. In fact, the year before Mary called the police to report her missing, Janet had already been swindled by a lonely hearts suitor who had taken some of her money and left. Thus, Mary was worried when she got an excited letter, purportedly from her stepmother, claiming she had finally met the most wonderful man of her dreams. The style and content of the letter sounded like Mrs. Fay could have written it; yet the letter was carefully typed with no mistakes, and Mary knew Mrs. Fay had never typed a letter in her life. The letter enthused in part:

> Dear Mary,
>
> I am all excited and having the time of my life. I never felt as happy before. I soon will be Mrs. Martin and will go to Florida.
>
> Mary, I am about to ask you a great favor. I would like you to call on the American Express Agency and have them ship my trunks and boxes that I have there to me. The address is on the various stickers I am enclosing in the letter . . .
>
> I am so happy and contented, for Charles is so good and nice to me and also his family. They have done everything to make me feel comfortable and at home.[41]

After Mary called the police, there was little they could do. There was no evidence of any crime unless Mrs. Fay continued to remain missing. If she did leave the state, any crime might be in another jurisdiction. Thus, Mary's call went into the police file as a suspicious circumstance for the time being, and they didn't begin investigating until several months later when Mrs. Fay still hadn't turned up.

It was six months before the police would begin to discover what happened to Mrs. Fay and the other Lonely Hearts victims. In Fay's case, she had been impressed by a "very gentlemanly" letter she received from "Charles Martin," who impressed her because he was a Catholic and spoke about his strong spiritual beliefs. After an exchange of several letters, she invited him to meet her, and he arrived in Albany on December 30, 1948, with a heavy-set woman he introduced as his sister. A couple of days after they met, after Charles explained that his wallet had been stolen on New Year's day, Mrs. Fay had taken the Martins into her home, with Charles sleeping on the couch, while his sister slept in her bed. A day or two later, believing they would soon get married, Mrs. Fay took most of her savings out of the bank—about $6,000, $2,500 of it in cash. The Martins took her to a rented flat on Long Island, where Charles convinced her to sign several sheets of notepaper with the word *surprise* written in pencil on them, supposedly to be sent to friends and relatives to coyly hint at the news that would later let them know about their impending marriage. After that, she was beaten to death with a hammer, her body was placed in a trunk, and it was buried in the cellar of a house in Queens. But for a while, Mrs. Fay was simply another missing person.

This was the beginning of a strange killing spree by two oddly matched lovebirds whose story captured the nation and attracted a cadre of psychiatrists and scientific experts to address questions of love, sexual deviance, and sanity, never before raised in a criminal trial. In fact, the case represented something of a shift in the growing awareness of and public fascination with conscienceless serial killers who killed out of powerful sexual drives, as well as other motives. In the 1930s, the Albert Fish case had been seen as something of an aberration; for the first time psychiatric testimony for and against insanity by a few experts played a major role in a criminal case. Now, even more, psychiatric considerations fascinated the public—and the case turned into a kind of legal true confessions—paralleling the growing popular interest in sex, love, and the true confession and romance magazines that appealed to women in the postwar years. It was an explosive mixture—warped love and sex leading to insanity, leading to murder. Or was it really insane? That was the big question as police—and later psychiatrists—began to piece together the mystery of the Beck and Fernandez case, which led to about 45,000 pages of trial testimony and months of steamy prose in the press.

Ironically, before he met Martha Beck in 1948, Raymond Fernandez, a Spanish American born in Hawaii, was just a two-bit Romeo in his mid-thirties, advertising to meet women in several correspondence clubs and matrimonial bureaus. When they responded, he would wine and dine them, promising marriage, but only after getting their money. Before going to the altar, he would conveniently disappear.

Oddly enough, Fernandez's matrimony for money idea had its roots shortly after World War II, when he had worked for British intelligence in Spain and received awards for his courage. Before the war, he had been a fairly ordinary and productive person, with just one arrest as a boy for stealing chickens from a neighbor. He worked on his uncle's prosperous farm in Spain; married a Spanish woman with whom he had four children; decided to strike out on his own by finding employment in New York; and then spent some time wandering between Spain and New York working as a gardener, paperhanger, plasterer, and stevedore.[42]

After the war, while he was working as a seaman on an oil tanker, in December 1945, he was struck on the head by a falling hatch, which led to a deep scar on his forehead and, as was later discovered, an injury to his brain tissue as well. After he was released from the hospital a few months later, his whole personality began to change. Before he had been a very shy man, even afraid of women. He suddenly found a powerful sex drive stir within him that led him to crime. It started just after he left the hospital—he took up with prostitutes who ply the beaches of Aruba, was robbed of all his money, and was arrested trying to take some government sheets and towels through customs when he arrived in Mobile, Alabama. After he was sent to the federal penitentiary at Tallahassee, Florida for a year, he learned about voodoo and black magic from the West Indians serving time with him. He became convinced he had supernatural powers and the ability to hypnotize from a distance.[43]

After he was released and went to live with some relatives in Brooklyn, Fernandez decided to use these newly found powers to get women to fall in love with him. Instead of bringing his wife and children over from Spain as he once planned, he began communicating with women through lonely hearts clubs. To add to the illusion of himself as the debonair Latin lover, he bought a slick black toupee to cover up the deep scar on his forehead. He began meeting the women he wrote to—mostly older and not particularly attractive women in their fifties and sixties. With them he engaged in a kind of wild, frenzied love and was soon carrying on affairs with several women at the same time.[44] Psychiatrists later suggested that his brain injury had damaged his frontal lobe, causing him to lose the normal functions of self-control and conscience. Fernandez was like a man possessed as he went around charming these lonely, love-starved women. At first he only did so for sex and enjoying the sense of being able to hypnotize these women with his flowery speech and Latin charm. Then he found that he could get money from them. He stopped trying to find work and began consciously seeking out women to not only satisfy his sex drive but get money.[45]

In at least one case, his charm turned deadly—though at the time, no one knew it. It happened in October 1947. He had met Jane Thompson in early 1947 through a lonely hearts club—she was a cook who was separated from her husband and lived with her mother in a large Upper West Side New York apartment, where they rented out a few rooms to boarders. Soon after he met her, he left his relatives and moved in with her. In October, traveling as a married couple, he took her on a "honeymoon" trip to La Linea, Spain, where his wife and children still lived. Mrs. Thompson paid the bill. Bizarrely, he introduced Mrs. Thompson to his real wife, though he introduced her as Señora Robles (her maiden name). For about a week, this odd triangle continued, until Fernandez and Thompson had a big argument in their hotel room on the evening of November 7. Fernandez stormed out, presumably to visit his real wife. In the morning, the maid found Mrs. Thompson dead in the room, but when the local physician examined her, he attributed her death to a heart failure during an attack of acute gastroenteritis, and Fernandez acted seriously broken up by her death. Though the American consular officials became aware that he and Mrs. Thompson weren't really married and were traveling under false pretenses, the authorities only questioned him briefly and decided there was nothing suspicious about Thompson's death.

A few weeks later Fernandez sailed back to New York. Meanwhile, an English woman who had become friends with Mrs. Thompson on board wondered about her death and wrote the U.S. consulate in Spain. But the officials there didn't pay serious attention to her letters, thinking they were written by a crank. For the next few months, they only investigated haphazardly—just another unfortunate tourist death. Meanwhile, on his return to New York, Fernandez played the role of the bereaved husband, and he showed Mrs. Thompson's widowed mother, Mrs. Pearl Wilson, a paper signed by Thompson that deeded the apartment and all the furniture in it to him, along with a will leaving him all her property. He magnanimously offered to let Mrs. Wilson stay in the apartment, and he once again resumed what had become his profession and passion—meeting lonely hearts club women.[46] That's how he met Martha Beck, who answered one of his ads. Their strange sexual passion and chemistry became an even more deadly mix.

While Fernandez was leaving his trail of lonely hearts, Martha Beck was dealing with her own sexual demons. When Fernandez first wrote to her, Martha was a twenty-seven-year-old nurse working as a superintendent at a home for disabled children, but she looked much older because she was grossly obese, weighing about 300 pounds, with heavy pendulous breasts, thick hips, and flabby rolls of fat over her stomach. She had been overweight and dumpy ever since childhood, leaving her very much a lonely outsider who didn't fit in. In elementary school and as a teen, she was teased mercilessly by other students. In adolescence, the problem became even worse, because she was forcibly and violently raped repeatedly at thirteen by her own brother, and, as later discovered, she had a glandular condition that not only led her to become fat but gave her a powerful sex drive. This drive was hard to satisfy, because her appearance sent most men running quickly away from her. From early childhood, she was given to spending long, lonely hours by herself brooding and fantasizing. She was eager to please anyone so she could feel loved and wanted—like a beggar seeking for meager handouts of love.[47] Worse, at one point she thought she was pregnant by her own brother, and when she shared her fears with her mother, her mother accused her of having sinned and being bad—a feeling of worthlessness and evil that stayed with her throughout her life.

Martha even had trouble getting a nursing job, despite her good marks in the Pensacola School of Nursing in Florida, because of her appearance. After experiencing rejection after rejection, she ended up taking a job with a local mortician, who hired her to wash, embalm, and prepare female corpses for burial.[48] In time, the hated job helped make her callous and unfeeling, while she found an emotional retreat in the true confession and romance magazines of the day. Magazines like *True Story*, *True Romance*, and *True Confessions,* helped her vent her imagination to the erotic and emotional desires she had trouble experiencing in real life.[49]

A few experiences helped unbalance her even more. After she went briefly to northern California and got a job at a hospital at a military base, she took to hanging out in bus stations and railroad depots, picking up men. She took up with a Vallejo bus driver and found herself pregnant, and she pressed for marriage. After he reluctantly agreed, he tried to commit suicide a few days later by driving his bus to a deserted wharf and jumping into the water, though he was pulled to safety. The incident led to a traumatic break, in which she was briefly admitted to Mission Emergency Hospital in San Francisco suffering from hysteria and amnesia. After a month or so of living at loose ends, she fled back to Pensacola, still pregnant and unmarried.[50]

To cushion the blow, she created a fantasy husband named Joseph Edward Carmen, a lieutenant commander in the U.S. Navy, and she showed off a diamond engagement ring and golden wedding band, describing their loving relationship ecstatically. Shortly before the birth of her child, she reported being devastated by his death in action in the Pacific. Whether people believed her or not, her show of grief helped silence the doubters. Soon after she gave birth, she found a job in the hospital where she had her child. She met and married Alfred Beck, a bus driver she met at the local station. Beck never intended to marry her, but she became pregnant. He spent most of his time away from home, and a divorce soon followed.[51]

Again, Martha was lonely, but with two young children. At least work supplied some measure of stability, since soon after her son was born, she began working at the Pensacola Crippled Children's home, where she got the reputation of being a neat, conscientious, willing worker, and was promoted after six months to be superintendent. She still tried to live a life of occasional friends and parties, though one former classmate kept poking fun of her at parties like he did in their school days. A few days after she went to a party at a nearby apartment, which this acquaintance also attended, he sent her name to the Mother Dinene's Family Club for Lonely Hearts.[52]

At first, Martha cried hysterically as she read the words of the advertisement that appeared in her mailbox: "Are you lonely and shy? Then join Mother Dinene's Family Club for Lonely Hearts." She felt the prankster who sent it was surely sneering and making fun of her as the fat, homely loser once again. After a long night of crying herself to sleep, in the morning she decided to try it anyway. The ad included testimonials of mostly middle-aged and elderly women describing how they had gained happiness by marrying a desirable husband found through the service. If they could find husbands, maybe she, only in her twenties, could, too; the cost was only $5. What more did she have to lose? She mailed off her $5, and she met Raymond Fernandez when he responded to her ad. Neither of their lives would be the same, and the story of their strange, puzzling relationship soon transfixed America, as well as mystified psychiatrists and the police.

Ironically, their relationship nearly didn't get off the ground. Beck sent in her description in November 1947, describing herself as being told she was "witty, vivacious, and oozed personality."[53] A few days later she got a letter from Fernandez. For about a month, they corresponded, and Fernandez's letters became increasingly lyrical and emotional. He spoke about being guided to her by a "psychic power" and spoke about how their souls had "been in love since the dawn of creation," and Beck herself was soon head-over-heels infatuated with this lusty, lyrical Spaniard. On December 22, he wrote saying he had to come see her, and at first Beck was frightened that when he arrived their relationships would be all over, since she hadn't told him of her heavy weight, her children, or her divorce. It was unbearable to think she might be rejected once again. Before she could write back, Fernandez sent her a telegram letting her know that he would be arriving in Pensacola on December 28.

When he did, Beck was duly impressed, because he looked every bit the tall, thin, sensuous, and prosperous Latin lover with his slicked black hair and well-pressed suit. In fact, he resembled her current movie picture heartthrob, Charles Boyer, who had the same kind of dark eyes and brooding languorous look. For his part, Fernandez was actually taken aback by Beck's grossly obese appearance, though he didn't let her know it. After Beck treated him to a fancy meal at her apartment and introduced him to her two children, they spent a wildly passionate night together, which cemented Beck's love for him. After another day and night of erotic passion, Beck sobbed out her undying devotion and desire to be with him forever.

This was the last thing Fernandez wanted, particularly as he realized that Beck had no money, so he explained that he had to return to New York and did so. Beck was devastated, and for the next couple of weeks, she sent him daily letters expressing her undying love, while telling her friends and relatives that she would soon be married again. At first, Fernandez didn't answer; when he finally did, he firmly told her she had misunderstood his feelings and it was all over, that it was best they not see each other again. But Beck was determined. She made a suicide attempt with gas, and after the woman next door smelled it and the police revived her, she or her friend forwarded the suicide note she had written to Fernandez. Afraid of the possibility of any police inquiries resulting from her attempt, he wrote back describing his sorrow, begging her forgiveness, and inviting her to stay with him for a week or two in New York.

It was all the encouragement Beck needed. Immediately, she got a leave from work and took the train to New York, where she moved into Mrs. Thompson's old room at the apartment Fernandez still shared with Mrs. Wilson and several roomers. As best she could, she expressed her love for him by preparing meals, doing household chores, and occasionally enjoying a few nights of sex. After two weeks, he took her to the station to return to Florida, thinking their relationship was over. But when Beck returned, she discovered that she had been fired from her job, and again she packed her bags and went back to New York, this time taking the children, and appeared on Fernandez's doorstep.

Fernandez felt powerless to resist. Trying to make the best of a bad situation, he explained how he had been earning his living by swindling the women he met through lovelorn ads, and then either he or Beck suggested that she might be able to help him by posing as his sister. But she had to get rid of her children; they were simply an inconvenience. Finally, she agreed and worked out arrangement to send them back to her mother in Pensacola.

For the next eleven months, Fernandez and Beck became partners, traveling around the United States meeting middle-aged and elderly lonely women through lonely hearts clubs. Typically, they would spend a few days at the hopeful woman's house; Fernandez would offer the prospect of marriage. He might sleep with the woman during this time. After the woman had given him money or property, they would disappear and go on to the next victim. At times, Beck was a little jealous about Fernandez sleeping with the latest conquest, and they would have words. But mostly the partnership proved successful and profitable. Sometime during this period, Fernandez actually fell in love with Beck. In some strange way, they fulfilled each other's needs for love and sex.

In August 1948, their love-for-money partnership included murder, too, though their first murder raised no suspicion—much like what happened after Mrs. Thompson's death in Spain.

It began after Fernandez impregnated one New York woman he had started corresponding with and then met, but she had no money. He and Beck decided it was time to leave New York. After selling the lease for the apartment he had fraudulently taken over from Mrs. Thompson (he had previously gotten Mrs. Wilson to leave), he and Martha headed off to visit the next victim in Greene Forest, Arkansas, Mrs. Myrtle Young. After a whirlwind courtship led to marriage August 14, Fernandez took his new bride to a rooming house in Chicago, and for three days, a jealous Beck slept in the same bed with Myrtle to keep Fernandez from sleeping with her. By the third day, when Myrtle began to protest about this strange arrangement, Fernandez or Beck fed her a heavy dose of barbiturates. She woke from being unconscious for over twenty-four hours, and they took her to the bus station and put her on a bus back to Arkansas, keeping $4,000 of her money and her car. By the time Myrtle arrived in Little Rock, she was half comatose and was carried off the bus to a hospital, where she died the following day. Oddly, the doctor recorded her death as due to a "cerebral hemorrhage and liver inflammation." No one then suspected any wrongdoing, so there was no further investigation at the time.

After several more meetings with women in New England came the meeting with Mrs. Fay in Albany, who was killed and buried in a trunk in the Queens apartment. Thinking it best to move on before the authorities came checking, Fernandez found another prospect, Delphine Downing, a forty-one-year-old widow with a two-year-old child, among his lonely hearts correspondence, about his hundredth at this point. The two headed off to Grand Rapids, Michigan. The letter, addressed to Fernandez's frequent alias, Charles Martin, read in part:

> Dear Charles,
>
> Thank you for your thoughtful Christmas greetings.
>
> Christmas is so busy with its hustle and bustle and the lull afterwards is such a letdown. It gives me an empty lonely feeling . . .
>
> Rainelle got a tricycle from some friends and she is sitting on it now and really making a noise. Do you like children's carols? I hope you do.[54]

Fernandez wrote back, telling her he adored children and was on his way. As usual, after they met, Delphine found Fernandez charming, and she found his "sister" full of fun. To dissuade neighbors in this prosperous, middle-class suburb from gossiping, Delphine put out the story that Martha was the nurse who had delivered Rainelle in the hospital, and that they had become such good friends that she had invited Martha and her brother to come for a visit. The usual plans for the marriage went forward. Soon Fernandez had become sexually intimate with Delphine, and although Beck was steaming with jealousy, she kept her true feelings hidden. As plans for their upcoming marriage in New York went forward, Delphine began turning her various properties into cash.

The plan almost collapsed when Delphine saw Fernandez in the bathroom without his toupee and saw the long, ugly scar on his forehead. Accusing him of deceiving her, she threatened not to go through with the marriage. She expressed her displeasure about Fernandez's sister, who was always around. Somehow, Fernandez managed to charm her. She decided to go through with the marriage.

Meanwhile, the police in Albany were looking for Mrs. Fay and were still mystified as to where she might be. The new tenants at the house Fernandez and Beck had rented in Queens had no idea about the body buried under the cement in their basement.

Shortly before the planned wedding, while Delphine was sleeping under a sedative Beck had given her to calm her nerves, her daughter, Rainelle, began to cry. Beck began choking her to keep her quiet before Fernandez pulled the child away to stop her, and Rainelle calmed down. There were still angry red marks on Rainelle's throat, and both were afraid that when Delphine woke up she would see this and perhaps not only call off the marriage but go to the police. "We'll have to keep her quiet," Fernandez said, and finding the service pistol of Delphine's late husband in the next room, he took it back to the bedroom, and before she could wake up, he shot Delphine in the head. While Beck destroyed the bloodstained pillows and other signs of the crime, Fernandez buried Delphine's body in the basement, covering the hole with fresh cement. Briefly, Fernandez and Beck considered taking the child back to New York with them. They told neighbors that Delphine was called away on an emergency trip to see a sick relative and they were staying in the house to take care of the child. But the next day, when the little girl kept crying and seemed afraid of them, Beck took the child to the basement and held her head under a washtub filled with water. They buried her in a second cement-covered grave in the basement by her mother.

By 4 p.m. they were done, and when some neighbors dropped by to see Delphine, they had another explanation: they were going to purchase some household goods from Delphine. Tired from their exertions, they went to see a film at a nearby movie theater. As they enjoyed the movie, several neighbors, suspicious at the sudden disappearance of Delphine and Rainelle and unconvinced by the explanation Fernandez and Beck gave, called the police. When they returned, two police officers were waiting for them and asked if they might search the house—they already had a search warrant to do so, according to various accounts.[55] In either case, Fernandez and Beck invited them to do so, perhaps feeling confident they had cleaned up all signs of the murders well.

In short order, the police officers found the newly cemented patches in the cellar and took Fernandez and Beck off to jail. Both began quickly confessing, as if actually proud of what they had been able to do for so long without being caught. Fernandez began describing at length his history of wooing a stream of women, and Beck confirmed whatever he said. The police who questioned them were amazed by their stories, but just listened so as not to turn off the flow of admissions, and then gave them each written confessions to sign. Contrary to regular practices, they were not questioned separately. It seemed as if Fernandez was only too eager to boast of his conquests, while Beck was willing to echo whatever he said, perhaps because of her love for him and desire to please. Perhaps they spoke so freely because they had clearly been caught with the evidence against them—"You got me dead to rights," Fernandez reportedly said, just before his confession began pouring out. Then, too, perhaps they felt safe they wouldn't be put to death in Michigan, which had no death penalty.

After the news of their arrest and crimes broke in stories all over the country the next day, their stay in Michigan was shortened. With their admissions about the Fay killing in Queens, investigators went back and found the body in the basement. After a bitter national outcry calling for their deaths and a brief legal struggle between New York and Michigan, the two were shipped to New York to be tried for the murder. New York *did* have the death penalty.

The tabloids had a field day, reporting on the strange relationship between Fernandez and Beck. How could this lonely hearts lothario have ever hooked up with such a "fat," "unattractive," "flabby" woman? How could these two evil degenerates have committed such cold-blooded killings?[56]

The only major question remaining was whether Fernandez and Beck could escape the death penalty by pleading insanity. An incensed and outraged public wanted their heads, but their defense, with the help of a team of psychiatrists, argued that they suffered from a special form of insanity called *folie à deux* in France. Under this theory, two people can be individually sane, but their relationship can inspire each other to madness.[57]

Would the defense work? It was the only legal strategy that might, because any other defense was undermined by Fernandez and Beck having the same legal counsel, Herbert Rosenberg, a lawyer in Manhattan. Though he was hired with the help of Beck's family, the court assigned Fernandez, who pleaded indigence, the same counsel—a decision that undermined any separate defense. After all, any mitigating factor favoring one defendant would harm the defense of the other and vice versa.

The case became not only the most highly publicized one of the times but the most hotly contested because of the insanity defense. Fernandez and Beck were examined by dozens of investigators, including doctors, psychiatrists, probation officers, representatives from the district attorney's office, and others;

the court record grew to over 45,000 pages as the battle over their sanity went on. At times, the defense tried to argue that Fernandez suffered from a lack of conscience because of his earlier head injury and Beck had become a psychopathic personality because of her infatuation with Fernandez and her belief that she had been hypnotized.[58]

Meanwhile, the trial turned into a kind of 1940s circus. As one reporter of events writes:

> Everyone got into the act. Lawyers on both sides used flowery, overdramatic language. Witnesses seemed determined to steal the show with startling revelations. Psychiatrists issued statements bound to make newspaper headlines. . . . Even the defendants at times seemed to be playing for the grandstand instead of fighting for their lives.[59]

At the same time, the trial turned into a test of psychiatry, which was then still considered an "embryo science."[60] It raised questions like whether Beck at the time of Mrs. Fay's killing was the victim of a "compulsive, irresistible and obsessive act," as Dr. Richard H. Hoffman, the chief psychiatrist for the defense, testified. Or were both Fernandez and Beck completely sane, as the state psychiatrist, Dr. Perry M. Lichtenstein firmly intoned?

In the end, after forty-four days of trial, the jury found both guilty of murder in the first degree. The crimes were too shocking, and they found both too morally degenerate to show them any sympathy. Both were sentenced to death and taken to Sing Sing Prison, where they were housed in opposite wings of the prison. After a series of appeals, they were electrocuted on March 8, 1951. Through it all, until the very end, they continued to correspond, expressing their love for one another, though at one point, Beck became angry when she heard rumors that Fernandez had been saying "vulgar and insulting things" about her to other prisoners. She wrote in one letter:

> You are a double-crossing, two-timing skunk. . . . It's nice to learn what a terrible murderous person I am, while you are such a misunderstood, white-haired boy, caught in the clutches of a female vampire. It was also nice to know that all of the love letters you wrote "from your heart" were written with a hand shaking with laughter at me for being such a gullible fool to believe them.[61]

A few days later, she reconsidered, writing back in a passionate letter that "this doesn't mean I don't love you."

Still sharing the strange love that had led them to murder, seventeen months after the trial, both went to the electric chair. As Fernandez was strapped in, the story goes that he "pulled up his trousers to preserve the crease," always the charming lothario obsessed with his image. Twelve minutes later, Beck was strapped in. According to observers, just before the mask was put over her head, she seemed to smile slightly with a lopsided grin, perhaps because she had died with her lover.

THE CASE OF WILLIAM HEIRENS

Chicago, 1945–46

The mysterious sex killings that terrorized the city of Chicago in the mid-1940s started with a series of burglaries of homes on Chicago's North Side, near Lake Michigan. At the time, it was an area of towering apartment buildings and hotels and a mix of expensive brick homes and fading wooden slat houses, plus a potpourri of churches, night clubs, and stores. At first police recorded these as ordinary unsolved burglaries, though from time to time there were reports of a "phantom" burglar, who was seen, usually by janitors, running away quickly through the alleys behind buildings or leaping up and down fire escapes. By the time the police got there, the phantom was long gone.

On June 3, 1945, the police got a report of a burglary that turned to murder. The United States had recently celebrated the end of World War II with V-E Day on May 8. There was a feeling of victory and renewed hope for the future in the air. The popularity of the boxer of the year, Rocky Graziano, helped unite people around a scrappy figure of strength and power. Denizens of Chicago were feeling especially good because their city's baseball team had reached the top of the National League and played in the World Series, though they were ultimately defeated by Detroit. It was also a year when bebop and swing had come into fashion, the happy musical *Carousel* by Rodgers and Hammerstein was drawing the crowds, and the wry cartoon humor of James Thurber poked fun at the foibles of city dwellers. Yet there was an undercurrent of people who felt alienated and in pain, somehow unable to adjust to the anonymity and stresses of urban living, such as in Billy Wilder's popular film of that year, *The Lost Weekend*, about a man who spends a weekend getting drunk to still his pain.

When the police, led by Captain Frank Reynolds, arrived in the early afternoon of June 3 at the fifth-floor apartment of Josephine Alice Ross on North Kenmore Avenue, they were shocked by the bizarre evidence they discovered that showed this was not just a burglar who killed while trying to get away. They arrived shortly after Mrs. Ross's seventeen-year-old daughter, Jacqueline, came home for lunch at 1 p.m. from the neighborhood shop where she had been at work and called the police, hysterically describing how she had returned to find the family's pet bull terrier whimpering under a couch and her mother's body in the bedroom.

The police saw signs that some strangely perverse killer, not just a surprised burglar, was at work. Mrs. Ross's nude body was stretched out on her bed, with a nylon stocking and red skirt tied around her throat. After they removed these, the officers discovered she had been stabbed again and again in her face and neck, one stab going deep into her jugular vein, so she bled to death. Even more unusual was that some of the cuts were covered with strips of adhesive; there was a lack of blood on the body itself, though the bed was soaked with it. They found the tub in the bathroom partially filled with water mixed with blood.

Apparently, the killer had gone to the trouble of washing blood from the body. The report of the coroner's physician came back, stating that the woman had died around 10:30 a.m. but the adhesive tape hadn't been put on her cuts until after she had stopped bleeding, about an hour and a half later. It was an indication that the killer had stayed in the apartment for about two hours after the woman died. The coroner's physician said there had been no sexual attack or abuse of the body.[62] Even the burglary itself didn't make much sense, because when Jacqueline and her sister, who also lived with their mother, checked through the apartment, nothing seemed to be missing, except perhaps a small amount of money from her purse—perhaps about $12 as later reported in various accounts.

As the police put the story of what happened together, they got only fragmentary clues of this mysterious killer. Another fifth-floor neighbor, Mrs. Bernice Folkman, reported that shortly after 10 a.m., as she returned from a shopping trip, she noticed a young man without a hat walking toward the Ross apartment. "He was wearing a white sweater, dark trousers, and wore his dark hair brushed back in a pompadour," she said. The building janitor described seeing a hatless man wearing a sweater jump off the fire escape about noon, just after he heard the clang of the escape ladder dropping down and went to look. Thinking he was just a tenant or delivery man using the fire escape as a short-cut to the rear parking lot, he didn't pursue the man.[63]

The lack of clues from fingerprint experts who carefully checked the apartment was equally disheartening. They found that all of the furniture, doors, and even the wall baseboards had been wiped clean. They didn't even find fingerprints of family members. Obviously, this was a well-organized, careful killer, and perhaps part of the reason he had stayed in the apartment so long was to clean up. Yet the clean up of the body was unusual. Though the victim hadn't been raped, the clean up hinted at some sexual overtones to the killing.

For now, the police had no leads and no place to go next. The case remained an open, puzzling crime in their files.

In October came two more puzzling attacks. One was on October 1, when nineteen-year-old Veronica Hudzinksi was sitting at her desk in her apartment at North Winthrop Avenue. Suddenly she heard a tapping noise on her window, and as she got up to pull up the shades, she heard two shots, and one hit her in the shoulder. After the police arrived, they found a revolver wrapped up in a crude mask made from a rubber shower curtain directly underneath her window. There were no prints, and Veronica had no idea why anyone might want to shoot her. The police felt stymied again.

On October 5, Lieutenant Evelyn Peterson, a former army nurse who lived with her sister in a penthouse apartment on Drexel Avenue near the University of Chicago, was attacked. Early in the morning, as she was waking up, she discovered a prowler who had dropped into her apartment through a trap door. Moments later, he hit her with a thick metal bar, knocking her unconscious. When she woke up, she discovered that her arms were bound with the electric wire from a lamp cord. After she worked herself loose, she found that the man had taken $150 from her purse. Moments later, a young man appeared at her door, saw her bloody face, and offered to call a doctor for her. When he was unable to reach one, he saw the apartment manager on the way out and said that the woman in the penthouse was ill and needed attention. He quickly left; soon after, Peterson was taken to the hospital with a fractured skull. Though the young man had vanished, the police had their first solid clue. The man had wiped away his prints, but he left the partial thumbprint in the apartment.[64] By itself, the print was impossible to trace, because without a known suspect's prints for comparison, the police would have to manually check the print against over 1,250,000 prints in Chicago police headquarters. Further investigation would have to wait.

December 5 brought another strange shooting, when Mrs. Marian Caldwell was sitting in the kitchen of her home on Sherwin Avenue. Suddenly, she told police, a bullet crashed through the window and grazed her as it whizzed by before lodging in a baseboard. By checking the angle of the shot, the police judged that it had plummeted at a downward angle and was probably fired from a roof across the street.

On December 10, a maid ran screaming from the sixth-floor studio apartment of thirty-year-old Frances Brown, an ex-WAV who worked as a secretary at a business machine company and lived at the residential Pinecrest Hotel on Pine Grove Avenue. "There's a body in the bathroom!" the maid gasped, as she ran to the desk in the lobby, and a few minutes later, Captain Reynolds and his men were at Brown's apartment. As they entered, they discovered this chilling message written in four lines in bright red lipstick on the beige living room wall:

For Heaven's
sake catch me
before I kill more.
I cannot control myself

They noticed that the top line was slightly over six feet from the floor, and the writing was uneven, with some letters as small as three inches and others six inches high. Some letters were printed as capitals, others were in script.[65] They found the lipstick used on the table—it had been Miss Brown's.

Officers continued on into the bathroom, where they discovered the nude body of the slim, petite brunette bent over the rim of the bathtub, her head hanging into the tub. Loosely around her neck, the killer had placed the top of her pajamas. When they removed the pajama top, they discovered a long bread knife protruding from her neck. It had been driven into her neck just below her left ear with such force that the blade went entirely through her throat and projected out the other side. They also noticed that she had been shot twice, once in the right side of her head and once in her right arm. They also discovered a deep cut between her right thumb and index finger, indicating that she must have struggled with her killer for the possession of the knife before she died.[66]

This curious pattern reminded Captain Reynolds of the Ross case. As in that case, the killer had washed the blood from the body; several wet and bloody towels lay nearby on the floor. The police also noticed that the living room, which doubled as a bedroom, was in a shambles. All of the drawers had been ransacked, and the contents were thrown everywhere. Even the bedding from the studio couch was on the floor, and a trail of blood led from the bloodstained sheets to the bathroom.[67]

A group of homicide detectives were soon on the scene, including Lieutenant Philip Breitzke and chief of detectives Walter G. Storms. As they began their investigation, they noticed several faint scratches and smudges on the sill of one of the living room windows, which was closed but not latched. When they looked out, they saw a fire escape landing about three feet above and to the side of the window. They surmised the killer had jumped from the fire escape onto the window ledge and, had he missed the ledge, he would have hurtled down six stories to the cement in the yard below. They marveled at his agility, since to get to the fire escape, he would have to scale an eight-foot fence.

The detectives spread out through the building to question other tenants and employees. Eventually, from the report of the coroner's physician, the accounts of one guest who heard shots fired around 4 a.m., and others who variously saw Miss Brown's apartment door closed and open, they determined that Brown had probably been killed around 4 a.m. Then the killer had remained in the apartment for about two hours, though he had not raped or abused her sexually. Oddly, despite the ransacked upheaval of the apartment, the killer had not taken anything of value according to Brown's roommate, Viola Butler, who had been away for the night.

The detectives also found that the killer had tried to wipe off all the fingerprints. But this time, he had overlooked one—a blood-smudged print of his right index finger on the left jamb of the bathroom door.

At this point, Reynolds and Storms realized there was probably a single killer behind the unsolved killings of Mrs. Ross and Miss Brown because they shared certain similarities—the nude bodies had been washed; they had knife wounds in the neck; and the killer seemed to spend about two hours in the apartment after he killed his victims. The police thought there might be some connection with the vicious beating of Miss Peterson as well. Despite the daunting task of checking fingerprints, one officer—Sergeant Thomas Laffey—was assigned the job. It meant reviewing every card on file, each of which contained ten prints (one for each finger) and comparing the prints on each finger—meaning potentially 12.5 million comparisons to find a match.[68] But with unsolved killings that were apparently the work of a crazed killer, Laffey was urged to start. As Storms had told his men: "We're working against time. He's killed twice, and will keep on killing until we catch him."[69] Laffey began his thankless task. But day after day, nothing. The investigation seemed stalled.

Then came the Suzanne Degnan case on January 7, 1946. Suzanne, a six-year-old girl from Chicago's North Side, was kidnapped from her bed. Her father, James Degnan, recently appointed to the price control board executive office for Chicago's District Office of Price Administration, discovered his daughter missing when he walked down the hall to her room at the rear of their downstairs apartment about a block from Lake Michigan, a mile from where Mrs. Ross had been murdered. Their apartment was in an attractive cream-colored mansion surrounded by a sloping lawn and hedges setting it off from the street in what was considered an elegant Chicago suburb, the fashionable Edgewater district.[70]

Mr. Degnan went back to wake her because it was the first day of school after the Christmas holiday. He wanted to be sure to get her to her first-grade class at the Sacred Heart Academy on time. As he walked in, he saw she was not in her bed and the window was wide open, although he had pulled it down so it was just open a few inches when he put her to bed the night before. He noticed that the bedcover was neatly folded back, though Suzanne never did this—and her bedroom slippers were side by side on the rug, arranged precisely, so unlike her.

With growing concern, he began searching under the bed, in the closet, and in the bathroom. With his wife, he searched every room in their apartment. Then they called the police. Within minutes, two detectives cruising the neighborhood were there, and as one entered Suzanne's room, he noticed a piece of oil-stained paper on the floor. When he opened it, he saw this crudely lettered penciled note: "Get $20,000 ready & waite for word. Do not notify FBI or police. Bills in 5's and 10's." On the reverse side of the paper, the writer had scrawled, "Burn this for her safty."

In moments, the detectives called in a kidnap report. Soon top law enforcement officials in the city arrived, including the recently appointed Police Commissioner John C. Prendergast, and State Attorney William J. Tuohy. Storms was on the job, too.

Though Degnan didn't have the money asked for by the kidnapper, he told police detectives he would try to borrow it from friends and relatives. Meanwhile, officials arranged for him to make a radio broadcast directly from his house in which he begged the kidnapper not to harm Suzanne while he tried to get the money. "Please don't hurt her. She's only a little girl," he begged, his voice cracking. Officials recorded his plea as he spoke, and copies were supplied to local radio stations, which replayed the plea at frequent intervals during the day and night. There was no further response from the kidnapper.

In the meantime, detectives began looking for clues throughout the day. They soon learned that a barking dog had awakened one of the upstairs residents, Louis Flynn, and the family maid, Ethel Hargrove, who heard the Flynns' two boxer dogs barking around 12:30 a.m. The maid had also heard what sounded like Suzanne's voice saying, "I don't want to get up. I'm sleepy." Thinking it was Suzanne's voice that woke the dogs, she went back to sleep. A few other neighbors reported waking up to their own dogs barking around 2:30 a.m., and they heard footsteps in the area between their house and the Degnans' home.

Another clue was a ladder with one rung missing, which detectives found in the rear alley near the garage. They tried propping it against the wall under Suzanne's window, and found it reached about a foot below the sill.

Storms soon had a picture of just how the kidnapper apparently got in through the window using the ladder. He was struck by the time delay between the 12:30 a.m. entry and 2:30 a.m. departure—two hours, just like in the Ross and Brown cases. He felt sure there was some connection.

When Storms looked at the ransom note, he felt even more certain. He recalled the strange lipstick message on Brown's living room wall, and he noticed that the e's in both messages were identical—like the e's on a typewriter. He asked Sergeant Laffey, who was working on the massive fingerprint project, to check the note for prints. Despite the oil apparently used to clear off any prints, a single print was raised. But when he compared it with the print in Brown's apartment, he couldn't make a match, because the prints came from different fingers. There was no way to tell if they were left by the same person. At least, if they could identify a suspect, the prints could show if the same person did both crimes. And what about the Peterson case, Laffey wondered? When he checked the print on the ransom note with that, he found they matched.

With this information, Storms was sure the kidnapper and double-killer were the same person. He suspected that meant the Degnan child was already dead, so there was not much hope waiting for the kidnapper to call. But why the ransom note? Storms wasn't sure, but just in case his hunch was wrong, he arranged for special telephones to be installed in the Degnan apartment and assigned detectives to answer them to trace any calls that might come in from the kidnapper. Many calls did begin to come in as news of the kidnapping hit the papers. One came in from a man who claimed he had Suzanne and arranged to bring a lock of her hair and piece of her pajamas to a 9 p.m. rendezvous, giving the Degnans hope. But he never showed up, and it soon turned out he was just another crank caller.

Meanwhile, as the wait for a possible call from the kidnapper went on, Storms sent men out to search for Suzanne's body if, as he feared, she was already dead. They began checking the nearby streets, looking through garbage cans, rubbish heaps, and opening sewers. It was a grim, depressing task, and Storms kept information about the search from the Degnans, letting them hope for the best.

Unfortunately, though, his men soon discovered the worst. Two detectives passing by the opening of a sewer about a block from the Degnans' home noticed that the rim of the iron lid seemed loose. After prying it off, they flashed a light into the sewer. They discovered the head of Suzanne Degnan floating in the water. After searching other nearby sewers, they found almost all of her body (except her arms) scattered around in different sewers, as if the killer had deposited remains within a four-block radius of the Degnan house. The arms turned up six weeks later, when two engineers testing transformers, looked down into an open sewer and saw the arms.

The search for Suzanne's killer began in earnest, as the citizens of Chicago went into a near panic, thinking that an unknown pathological killer was on the loose.

One witness, a former marine parked in his car with his girlfriend near the Degnan home, helped provide further confirmation that the killer was the same dark-haired hatless young man seen near earlier burglaries and killings. As he described it, around 2:30 a.m. such a man passed by his car carrying a shopping bag—and because parts of Suzanne's body had been found in a shopping bag, it seemed likely this was the suspect.[71] "And I think I can recognize him again since he stepped directly under a street-light near my car," said the former marine.

Other clues helped investigators piece together how the crime was committed. After a careful search of the area around the Degnan house, investigators found a small piece of wire twisted into a loop, and one of the investigators noticed three blonde hairs on it. Then he noticed that the handkerchief wrapped around the wire had a laundry mark: 3168—S. Sherman, and another handkerchief nearby was embossed with the initials *S.S.* After technicians at the police laboratory studied the find, one noted that in the army, the laundry was marked with the last four digits of a soldier's serial number, followed by his first initial and last name. A detective headed to Washington to get a list of all soldiers with this last name and then trace them down—a huge task, because the list turned up almost 1,500 men. Meanwhile, the careful autopsy helped pinpoint Suzanne's time and location of death. It probably occurred around 12:30 to 1 a.m., said autopsy surgeons, and they suggested that the wire might have been used to strangle her. The autopsy also suggested her body might have been cut up by a surgeon's scalpel or other very sharp knife. However, though it appeared to be washed after this cutting, the investigators found traces of coal dust in her hair and on the soles of her feet, leading them to believe her body had been cut up in a basement. To check this theory, a team of detectives fanned out to check the cellars of all houses in the surrounding neighborhood. Late that afternoon found a likely location. A block from the Degnan home on Winthrop Avenue, they went into the laundry room at a four-story apartment building, and in one of the tubs, detectives noticed several faint smears of blood. One opened the drain trap and found bits of flesh and blonde hair. Several tenants in the building heard the sounds of someone running water late at night, too—between 2:30 and 3:30 in the morning. After a detective moved a new shipment of coal that had arrived that morning, they found bloodstains on the floor. One tenant said a shopping bag was missing from his locker, which had been forced open.[72]

Storms felt encouraged. It was laborious, tedious work checking out various leads. The building janitor, who worked in several other buildings in the area, was brought in for questioning, but after hours of interrogation he was released. So were twelve former soldiers with the name S. Sherman who lived in the Midwest. Army officials found the owner of the handkerchiefs and flew him back to Chicago, at the request of the police, though he was in the Pacific when Suzanne was murdered. "Yes, they're mine," he acknowledged. He described how a former buddy who had lived in Chicago might have taken the handkerchiefs by mistake, and after the friend was tracked down, he acknowledged the handkerchiefs had been in his luggage. But they had been stolen in a burglary about a month earlier, which he had reported to police, and in fact he had listed the handkerchiefs on the list of stolen items. Besides, he had an alibi for the night of the kidnapping. Storms pondered the burglary. Maybe the mysterious burglar had taken these handkerchiefs and subsequently used them in the Degnan killing.

Detectives turned up another tantalizing clue suggesting the killer had been a burglar. A resident of a neighboring building, Harry Gold, returned from a vacation in Florida and reported that his apartment had been ransacked. When officers came over to investigate his report, they noticed his apartment windows overlooked Suzanne's room. Was that how the burglar got the idea to kidnap the little girl, especially if he noticed the nearby ladder? Detectives added that theory to their growing collection of evidence and theories about the case.

They still had no viable suspect—though the tips and crank callers and letter writers were multiplying because of all the newspaper and radio publicity. In fact, some of the crank replies were quite cruel, though the officers tried to shield the Degnans from them by screening their mail. One man, for example, sent a package with a human ear and the note, "Will cut off your ear next?", though the handwriting didn't match that on the ransom note. Still another person sent a message written in lipstick.[73]

A Chicago *Daily News* staff artist, Frank San Hamel, suggested another way to get clues from the ransom message after he used a photograph of it to put together a chart of handwriting characteristics for a newspaper report. He noticed several darker areas on the note, and when he looked at them under a magnifying glass, he noticed the faint markings of other letters and reported this to Storms. When Storms looked at the note again, he saw that these impressions could be seen when a bright light was focused on the paper at an oblique angle, and realized that this meant the note had been part of a pad and that the impressions were from previous writings. Perhaps this might contain some clues to the killer. Immediately, Storms assigned several detectives to work with Hamel on deciphering the faint markings on the letter. Over the next few weeks they did so. From time to time, they were able to discover a name or part of a telephone number, and there were some tantalizing clues. Several names and numbers led them to students at the University of Chicago, though the students when interviewed knew nothing. Other letters led to a popular student restaurant near the campus. Often they found the letters "eire" grouped together.

Finally, in June, after months of tedious checking, detectives concluded that the pad must have been used by a phone on campus to jot down numbers and messages, and they felt there must be some University of Chicago tie-in with the kidnapping. But they still needed the permission of university officials to do the full-scale inquiry on campus. They made their request to do so on June 20—more than five months after the kidnapping had occurred. College officials were hesitant to disrupt school activities, because almost anyone could have used a pad in a public telephone on the campus. "We'll have to let you know," they said, and for the next six days, detectives waited anxiously while they decided. On June 26, they agreed. The university officials would turn over a complete roster of its students and personnel. Storms felt a sense of renewed hope after so many months of false leads and dead ends.

The very same day, there was another key break in the case. Late that afternoon, a neighbor living in Wayne Manor Apartments in the Rogers Park section of Chicago noticed a young burglar rifling through the living room of the apartment of her neighbor, Mrs. Leonard Pera, and alerted the building janitor and manager, who called the police. Before they arrived, he ran out of the apartment, and the janitor and a tenant ran to try to stop him. When he pulled out a revolver, they stepped back, and he cautiously began backing out of the building, holding his gun in front of him.

At the street, he started running, but in the meantime, the first police officer on the scene, Detective Tiffin P. Constant, arrived and began running after him. The young man ran quickly, speeding through several back yards and over fences. As he dashed up the back steps to a second-floor apartment, Constant a few yards behind him, he fired twice at Constant. But his gun misfired, and after Constant fired at him three times, but missed, he jumped down the steps to flee. In moments, the two were struggling on the ground.[74] An off-duty officer, Abner Cunningham, who lived in the area and had been swimming in Lake Michigan, appeared wearing only beach shoes and bathing trunks. Though he had no weapon, thinking quickly, he saw three flowerpots on the back porch, grabbed them, and crashed them down on the burglar's head, knocking him unconscious.

In moments, the unconscious burglar was on his way to jail. After a brief stop at the Edgewater Hospital where doctors bandaged up his head wound, the police took him to the Bridewell Hospital at the county jail. Because the burglar rested in the hospital, Tiffin took his gun and wallet to the Rogers Park police station and reviewed the incident with Captain Michael Ahern at the police station.

Starting with the identification card in the burglar's wallet, Ahern and Tiffin began unlocking the mysterious secrets that had baffled police for so long. The ID card from the University of Chicago showed that the burglar was a seventeen-year-old student there—William George Heirens, who lived with his parents on Tuohy Avenue in Lincolnwood, a suburb west of Chicago, and he roomed at Gates Hall on the University of Chicago campus. The police also found $1,000 in post office savings certificates in his pockets, along with a mysterious letter signed "George M." that was dated from May 17, a month earlier, and read in part:

> Bill . . .
>
> I haven't heard from you in a long time. I feel for you being in jail. Tough luck. You'll know better next time.
>
> It seems that I'm being caught up with and I'll have to make an exit if I want to enjoy life. Therefore I will entrust with you some of my belongings . . .
>
> It's a good thing the police didn't search your place. I'd probably be in the coop now if they did. I remember once you told me that you wouldn't take the rap. I appreciate you taking those things off my hands when I was being followed.
>
> I could have just as well dumped it but I can't see me losing all that jewelry. I'll give you a phone call before I come for the stuff.
>
> I'm on my way to Milwaukee for a month and then El Paso . . .
>
> I'll see you soon. If this doesn't pan out, the gang might be broken up. We aren't keeping any of our old plans, so burn what you have. We'll burn ours.[75]

The police were puzzled by what the letter was all about and who George M. might be.

Ahern remembered that William Heirens's name sounded familiar to him, and after he checked his records, he discovered that Heirens had been arrested in 1941 and 1942 for over a dozen burglaries. He had spent some months after his first conviction in a private correctional school in Terre Haute, Indiana, before he transferred to a regular private school, St. Bede's Academy in Peru, Illinois. One summer when he was home in Chicago for the summer vacation, he was arrested for five more burglaries, though the Juvenile Court set him free because he seemed remorseful. His father George Heirens, held a high-level position as a special investigator for a large steel company.[76]

Ahern led a police team over to Gates Hall to search Heirens's room. There they found six suitcases full of cameras, clothing, jewelry, furs, watches, surgical instruments, $1,800 in war bonds, and other stolen items. There were also pictures of Hitler, Goebbels, and other Nazis. When searching his family home they found a cache of guns, including two .38 revolvers, a .25 automatic pistol, a .22-caliber rifle, and other guns. Many of these items were subsequently found on lists of stolen property, and some were later found to be taken from the Ross and Brown apartments. Ahern wondered if he might be a member of a gang of burglars because of the note from George.[77]

His parents were shocked by the news, since they had always been law-abiding people, and his father went to see him at Bridewell, where he was recovering from his head wounds. But Heirens said nothing. He acted like he was in a coma, gazing up from his hospital bed with a vacant stare. He wouldn't talk to nurses, doctors, or Ahern. Meanwhile, the press simply reported his arrest as a minor burglar, describing him as a suspected prowler with a juvenile record.

As one headline over a short story put it: "Student Seized in Fight after Revolver Fails."[78]

Suddenly, a discovery came that turned this into the story that shocked America. Laffey, who had already checked about 7,000 sets of fingerprints to find the killer of Suzanne Degnan, was asked to do a routine check of Heirens's prints. He recognized the match. Heirens's left little fingerprint matched the one on the note. His prints linked him to the murder of Miss Brown and the attack on Peterson.

Soon the evidence showed that Heirens was the mysterious burglar and killer that the police had been trying to find for almost a year. Just to verify the prints so they could be used as evidence in court, Laffey sent the prints to the FBI.

Heirens was still in the hospital, not talking, though doctors found no signs of any physical damage in their X-rays. After three days of various neurological and physical exams, doctors believed he was simply pretending to be unconscious. Perhaps there was a way to find out for sure—using a process called narcosynthesis with sodium pentothal. This technique had been developed during the war to help traumatized veterans recall the terrible memories they had repressed because the terror or grief they experienced was too great to remember consciously. When these memories were brought to consciousness by this technique, it helped the men recover.[79]

Prosecutor William Tuohy, who would be handling the case for the district attorney's office, decided to use this process—the first time ever in a criminal case. Though he knew he couldn't use the evidence in court—a confession has to be given voluntarily to be valid—he wanted to learn if Heirens was malingering and discover what he would confess about these crimes, and he felt there was enough other evidence that could be used.

As Tuohy and Storms watched behind a screen, Heirens was wheeled into a small room at the prison hospital and injected with a hypodermic needle. After about ten minutes, he went to sleep, and when he was aroused, he began speaking, sometimes in a low, whispery voice, other times more loudly and animated. After some general questions about his background, schooling, and how he was caught and hit on the head, the doctor began asking Heirens: "Did you kill Suzanne Degnan?" Heirens' strange story began to come out for the first time.

As he described it, no, he didn't do it. But "George did it." George went to a man's home the night before, saw the ladder leaning against the building. He explained how "George is a bad boy," and George was the one who carried her to a place nearby, cut her up, and then carried her to some sewers. After more injections and questions, Heirens identified George as George Murman, a boy five years older than himself who he had met while he was in school in Indiana. He had met George again in Chicago in 1943, and they saw each other frequently after that.[80] Supposedly, Heirens saw George on the morning of January 7, right after the kidnapping, and he accused George of all of the burglaries, too. But now he had gone off to Mexico.

As it soon turned out, there was no George. After an intensive search for him, the police could find no record of George in any hotel; Heirens's parents never heard of him, nor had anyone at Heirens's college seen him during any of his alleged visits. In fact, George was really a creation of Heirens's mind, like the split between Dr. Jekyll and Mr. Hyde. After psychiatrists examined Heirens closely, they concluded that he had created George Murman as his alter ego and that Murman committed the bad acts, while Heirens remained the good boy and good student.[81] They disagreed about whether he was a genuine split personality, or if he used George as a ploy to cover up his desires to do bad things, although when Heirens took a lie detector test and denied committing any of the murders or thefts himself, he passed.

However, the fingerprint, stolen property evidence, and descriptions of the man seen running from the scene of several burglaries and killings were more than enough in court. In return for agreeing to spare Heirens's life, his attorneys offered to have him make a full confession. After reviewing the case with other officials, Tuohy agreed, fearing a jury might decide Heirens was simply insane and not find him guilty of anything.

In his confession, Heirens explained why he did what he did. He even took officials back to the scene of the Degnan and Brown killings to show how he did it and why.

As his story came out, he had grown up feeling sexually frustrated as a child. His puritanical mother had warned him, "All sex is dirty" and "If you touch anyone, you get a disease." Though he had many sexual fantasies, he wasn't able to express his urges in a natural way. Instead, he retreated into expressing his impulses in lonely ways. He secretly obtained female clothing and dressed up in it when alone. He also became fascinated by the Nazi leaders in his early teens and began pasting their pictures into a scrapbook.

He found that his sex urge led him to commit burglaries, starting when he was thirteen. As he told doctors and prosecutors, "I get sexual satisfaction out of breaking into a place. If I got a real thrill, I didn't take anything." But he was never interested in sexually assaulting anyone. The burglary itself provided the thrill.

The burglaries turned to murder when the occupants of the apartment discovered him prowling around in the darkness or tried to resist his attempt to rob them. But he couldn't or wouldn't explain why he had remained alone with the bodies of his nude victims or washed them after the killings. He couldn't explain why he had cut up Suzanne Degnan's body, either. Instead, he said in his confession that a haze came over him after he killed, and he knew nothing until some time later when he came out of his blackout and saw the bodies of his victims.[82]

About a month after his confession, on September 7, 1946, Heirens pleaded guilty to three murders—of Suzanne Degnan, Mrs. Ross, and Miss Brown—and the judge, as Tuohy recommended, sentenced him to three consecutive terms of life imprisonment without the possibility of being pardoned or paroled. Afterward, Heirens spent a brief time in the Illinois State Penitentiary. After several suicide attempts, he was sent to an institution for the criminally insane and as of 1995 was still serving out his sentence—possibly with George Murman in his cell. As he once told doctors, "To me he's very real. He exists. You can accept George as being me, but—well, it's hard to explain. A couple of times I had talks with him. I suppose I was really talking to myself. I wrote lots of notes to him which I kept."[83]

Chapter 6

The 1950s

IN THE 1950S, the United States entered a period of prosperity, characterized by a new wave of consumerism and conformity. It was a time of good feelings, typified by the Eisenhower years; the smiling, placid Ike had been a popular general during the war. It was also a decade characterized by the image of the "organization man"—the new corporate man striving to get to the top (at a time before women joined the corporate struggle for success). Under the surface, there was the growing fear of communism, characterized by the Red Raids, the Ethel and Julius Rosenberg espionage trial and conviction, and the Hollywood blacklist.

Growing like a cancer on the American soul was a spirit of rebellion, especially among the young, that provided a new license to kill without conscience. In some cases, this was an extension of the image of the rebel, striking out against a conformist society, which was typified in many ways. This was seen in the young tough guy played by Marlon Brando in *On the Waterfront* (1954) and the smoldering teenage rebel played by James Dean in the film *Rebel Without a Cause* (1957). It was seen in the growing beatnik movement in the cafés of San Francisco and New York that spread all over the country in 1958 and celebrated a life of freedom on the open road, typified in the writings of Jack Kerouac in *On the Road* or Alan Ginsberg, who screamed out his discontent in the long poem *Howl*. There was also the popular new beat-driven type of music called rock and roll that arose out of the rhythm and blues of the black community and was popularized by the first generation of rockers like Elvis Presley and Bill Haley and the Comets. It was as if the clean-cut image of suburban parents, carefully cut lawns, and high school students trying to be good kids, typified in the image of the family gathered around tame family fare like *Father*

Knows Best and *Leave It to Beaver* had its counterpoint in the rising rock culture of the schools. The boys wore slicked-back hair, the girls wore clingy sweaters, and they necked in cars or watched the tougher boys play chicken, driving their cars toward each other at breakneck speeds to see who would swerve first. There was a growing fear and the beginnings of protests against a computerized, unfeeling America, typified by the fear of the bomb and the drills to duck and cover under schoolroom seats. This sometimes led to nearly deadly protest bombings by dissidents, like the mysterious Mad Bomber who terrorized New York City.

Meanwhile, as murder historian Roger Lane describes it, these new social trends, particularly the rising concern about the cold war, pushed murder out of the headlines for a while. As he observes: "The big news in the postwar era was . . . not crime but communism, and the biggest capital case involved not homicide but espionage, the result of the shock administered by the Soviet Union's explosion of an atomic bomb in September 1949."[1] This scare led to the concern that someone in the United States had slipped information to the Russians, to explain how and why the Russians had so quickly mastered the technology. Klaus Fuchs, a British citizen and communist refugee from Nazi Germany who had worked on a wartime bomb project in Los Alamos, New Mexico, was arrested, and the trail led back to the United States to a Philadelphia chemist named Harry Gold, who worked with David Greenglass, a former technician at Los Alamos, who in turn implicated his brother-in-law Julius Rosenberg and Julius's wife, Ethel.[2] The case fascinated America with shrieking headlines, until the Rosenbergs were finally tried and convicted in 1951, and executed in New York's Sing Sing prison in June 1953.

The news and popular culture of the period reflects a kind of schizophrenic world of growing fear, concern with family and conformity, and rebellion. In 1950, Senator Joe McCarthy began his hunt for communists in government by advising President Harry Truman that the State Department was riddled with communists, which turned into the nationally televised McCarthy witch hunt for spies in the army and Hollywood in 1954. Meanwhile, after Eisenhower's election in 1952, America took an increasingly active role in protecting Europe and the Middle East from the spread of communism, while Nikita Khrushchev became the increasingly scary face of the Soviet Union's intransigent drive for world dominance. And when the Soviets launched *Sputnik* 1 and *Sputnik* 2, the first Earth satellites in 1957, besting the United States in rocketry, America was even more unnerved and embroiled in the arms race.

At the same time, on the home front, as a kind of protection from this disturbing world news, there was a retreat into family domesticity, which was helped along by the spread of TV. By 1951, TV had gone color; three years later, there were TVs in 26 million American homes. Much like families had been united by radio in the 1940s, they now clustered around the TV. This domesticity was expressed in kitschy songs like "If I Knew You Were Coming I'd Have Baked a Cake" (1950), "Come On-a My House" (1951), "I Saw

Mommy Kissing Santa Claus" (1952), and "(How Much Is) That Doggie in the Window?" (1953). Starting in 1954, the new world of Disney on TV celebrated traditional family virtues through its cheery cartoons about Mickey and Minnie Mouse and virtuous frontier heroes like Davy Crockett, celebrated in a hit song of 1955 "The Ballad of Davy Crockett." The popular family comedy shows of the day were *I Love Lucy*, *The Adventures of Ozzie and Harriet*, *The Jack Benny Program*, and *The Amos 'n' Andy Show*. Quiz shows of the mid-1950s were quite popular, too, like *Twenty One* and *The $64,000 Question*; variety shows like *The Ed Sullivan Show* helped bring the family around the tube each night.

Meanwhile, science and technology brought a growing cornucopia of consumer products. The advertising to promote it helped turn America in the 1950s into an eager consumer society. On the medical front, there were new treatments to overcome anxieties, colds, and illness, such as the popularity of the tranquilizer meprobamate and antihistamines in 1950 and the introduction of penicillin in 1951. In the home, there were new improved labor-saving appliances and products, such as washing machines and cake mixes. For teens, an emerging market, there were record players, popular records, and scrapbooks.

Yet the literature and films of the period hinted at an underbelly of restlessness and rebellion growing in American as well as European culture. Some early examples include Budd Schulberg's *The Disenchanted* (1950), J. D. Salinger's book of teen angst, *The Catcher in the Rye* (1951); Tennessee Williams's steamy plays *The Rose Tattoo* (1952) and *Cat on a Hot Tin Roof* (1955); Samuel Beckett's nihilistic dialogue about a never-ending wait for someone who never comes in *Waiting for Godot* (1952); William Golding's *Lord of the Flies* (1954) about a group of British boys on an island who turn to a survival-of-the-fittest ethic; and Vladimir Nabokov's *Lolita* (1955), about the rising passion between an older man and twelve-year-old girl. This rising rebellion was perhaps best expressed mid-decade by Grace Metalious's *Peyton Place* (1956) about the tabloid lives within small-town America, and Kerouac's *On the Road*, about the escape from conformist America to the excitement of the road. There was also an emerging cinema reflecting the release of sexual passion and rebellion. Such films included *A Streetcar Named Desire* (1951) and *On the Waterfront*, both with Marlon Brando; *The Seven Year Itch* with Marilyn Monroe (1955); *Cat on a Hot Tin Roof* (1958) with Elizabeth Taylor; and *Suddenly, Last Summer* with Elizabeth Taylor and Montgomery Clift (1959). A theme in all these films was overthrowing the conventions of traditional society; the star was the rebel, though he often didn't survive, like James Dean in *Rebel Without a Cause*. But then, that was sometimes the price for freedom and rebellion; it made many of the rebellious bad boy actors—like Brando and Dean—and sultry actresses of the period—like Marilyn Monroe and Jane Russell—into big stars.

Though murder might have been less celebrated in the headlines because of concerns with the cold war and a focus on the family, it was becoming more carefully studied. For the first time, an academic—Marvin Wolfgang, a sociologist at the University of Pennsylvania—attempted to analyze patterns of homicide by looking at the statistics compiled by the police to examine types of murders, demographics of killers, arrest rates, conviction rates, and other data. He conducted his five-year analysis on 625 cases reported to the Philadelphia police between 1948 and 1952 and published his study as *Patterns in Criminal Homicide* in 1957.[3] It was a breakthrough study that set the stage for future work in other parts of the country, and it helped supplement the growing mass of national criminal data now being published by the FBI about rates for different kinds of crimes and the homicide rate in different cities. Certain cases in different cities might fascinate the nation, but the data helped provide a more solid grounding in just how common or uncommon these crimes were. For example, in the early 1950s, Wolfgang found that the cities with the highest homicide rates were, in order, Miami (with about 15 homicides per 100,000 people), followed by Dallas; Washington, D.C.; Kansas City, Missouri; Baltimore; Chicago; Cincinnati; and Seattle. In the middle with about 6 homicides per 100,000 was Wolfgang's own city of Philadelphia, followed by Boston, Columbus, Los Angeles, New York, Pittsburgh, Akron, Buffalo, St. Paul, and finally Milwaukee (with only about 2 homicides per 100,000). In turn, the decade's most baffling and publicized crimes came from cities with the highest and lowest rates, showing how these most mysterious crimes could occur anywhere. No place was any more or less safe than another.

Certain patterns also began to emerge about the more likely killers. Before the 1950s, such data hadn't been tracked, and historians had to rely on the hit-or miss collection of newspaper and courtroom records. Now they could turn to numerical data that showed new truths. For example, as was generally true in the past, Wolfgang showed statistically that murder and manslaughter were committed mostly by men—in 82 percent of the cases, especially by young men. Moreover, he was able to make distinctions by age, showing that those between ages twenty and twenty-four had the highest rates (22.7 per 100,000), followed by those between ages twenty-five to twenty-nine and those thirty to thirty-four, whereas teenagers between fifteen to nineteen came in fourth, and those under age fifteen almost never killed.[4] Wolfgang also found that 90–95 percent of all offenders were at the "low end of the occupational scale" as skilled or unskilled workers. Typically killers killed members of their own racial group (94 percent), whereas men were more likely to kill women than women to kill men, since there were significantly more female victims (24 percent) than female offenders (18 percent); though both sexes killed mostly men. When women killed, it was usually their husbands or lovers.[5]

As the decade went on and in subsequent decades, such data became increasingly used in trying to explain homicides, added on to the psychological explanations that began to play a role in the 1930s and 1940s, especially when a growing number of killers began to take the role of rebels against society and social conventions. More frequently as this new type of crime came to fascinate America by the mid to late 1950s, sociologists began to ask these questions. Was there something about the social character of America and other industrial societies that was contributing to the rise of crime? Before, the dynamics were sought in traditional motives like love, jealousy, revenge, and greed, and then in psychological factors that caused particular individuals to become abnormal, such as in the cases of Albert Fish (see Chapter 5), William Heirens, and Raymond Fernandez and Martha Beck. Sociologists began to look to social dynamics, too, and they advanced theories like alienation, anomie, and social deprivation to explain why the new generation of killers did what they did.

These data also helped starkly document what was becoming the new weapon of choice in homicide—the gun, part of a growing trend to violence in murder generally. In previous decades, the widely publicized difficult-to-solve homicides were more typically committed by stealthy and quiet methods—poison or knives were common, apart from the gangland killings and bank robberies of the 1920s and 1930s. Guns were more often used in the 1950s, making killings faster and bloodier, especially in the domestic killings that characterized this decade, as more homicides occurred in the home, in part because people stayed at home more now, and partly because it was a decade that celebrated the close, loving family. A popular image was the family grouped around the radio and, as the decade wore on, the TV. This family closeness might lead to murder—especially violent ones because of the close emotional relationship of killer and victim. Or as murder historian Lane, citing Wolfgang's report, observed:

> [There was] a "domestication" of homicide by the 1950s. . . . The home had become by far the most frequent site, with over half of all cases, only partly because homes by then were more attractive places to be in at night, with central heating often, radios usually, and television sometimes. . . . The victims . . . in over half the cases, were close friends or family of the offenders . . . and most of the rest were acquaintances. . . .
>
> In general, murderous attacks tended . . . to grow wilder as the relationship between victim and killers grew closer, as the fury of betrayal, or years of anger, were reflected in the number of shots, blows, or cuts inflicted, often on an already lifeless body. What "domestication" means . . . is that as homicide was more fully restricted to the home, and to a circle of family and friends, fewer strangers were in danger.[6]

Wolfgang's data showed another pattern beyond the family circle—a growing number of violent offenders, many with prior police records, who were often involved in drinking before they killed someone. In a period of high employment and prosperity, the most common time for these killings were on the weekend between Friday and Sunday—about two-thirds of all killings occurred then, especially on Saturday night.[7] Meanwhile, the civil rights struggle in the South, which resulted in a growing number of racially motivated killings of blacks was just beginning, fueled by the U.S. Supreme Court's *Brown v. Board of Education* decision in 1954 ordering the end to segregation in schools.

Buried within these statistics was another disturbing trend reflected in the types of homicides that increasingly fascinated and baffled America—the growing number of murders by people with a compulsion to kill. It's a trend crime writer Colin Wilson observes in *The Killers among Us*, where he profiles some of the major British, American, and European killers of each decade from the nineteenth century to the present. As he notes, many of the 1950s killers represent an older type of sex killer who might be characterized as a "conventional little man with a violent sexual appetite that drives him to rape in much the same furtive spirit as a poacher stealing game." A new type of killer who became increasingly familiar in the following decades was the social rebel. This is the "rebel against society who seems to feel that he has a *right* to kill."[8] Such a killer draws on the glamorized image of the rebel of films and literature portrayed by Brando, Dean, and Kerouac—but then takes that rebellion a step further, into killing to strike out at both his particular victims and at society as a whole. Although there was a growing number of such killers in Britain and Europe, they were especially likely to appear in the United States, with its long tradition of celebrating the individual, lone cowboy, frontiersman, and other figures of rebellion.

For example, Wilson describes Peter Manuel, a serial killer of at least nine people—mostly women—who was born in Manhattan in 1927, returning to England at age five with his British parents, as someone who loved to kill and justified his killing as his way of getting back at society. As Manuel once told police, "If I can't be a part of society—with the pre-eminence I deserve—then I'm going to do my best to screw things up, until the bastards feel sorry they *didn't* pay me more attention."[9] It was an attitude that more serial killers began to take to explain and justify their crimes.

A glance at some of the more high-profile murders of the decade reflects this attitude. Whether the crimes are motivated by a desire for sex, greed, love, revenge, or other reasons, they were marked by a growing level of violence and even overkill. In some cases, the murderer takes many other victims along with his intended target, or just kills for the excitement of killing itself.

For example, in 1955, Jack Graham of Colorado killed his mother for her insurance money. He took out three insurance policies for her on a United Airlines Flight and then blew up the whole plane, killing all thirty-nine passengers. In 1957–58, Charles Starkweather, who was infatuated with the James Dean image, and his fourteen-year-old girlfriend, Caril Ann Fugate, went on a killing spree throughout the Midwest. It started after Caril's mother began yelling at Charles, since she didn't like him and was tired of him hanging around her daughter. After she slapped him, he shot her and then her husband. After spending a couple of days watching TV and eating hamburgers in the house with the bodies, the two went on a spree, killing more people before a search with over 1,000 lawmen tracked them down—later immortalized in the film *Badlands* in 1974. In 1959, Richard Hickock and Perry Smith didn't just try to rob farmer Herbert Clutter—the original motive for going to his farm in Holcolm, Kansas—they tied up and killed him, his wife, and two daughters by slashing their throats—a story that later became the subject of a celebrated book and movie by Truman Capote, *In Cold Blood*.

This was also the decade when a TV repairman, Harvey Murray Glatman, terrorized the L.A. community in 1957–58 by posing as a photographer and taking girls who thought he was hiring them as models into the desert, where he tied them up, raped them, and killed them. He was caught when one of his would-be victims fought back and a police officer caught them fighting.

Then there was Edward Gein, a seemingly quiet retiring farmer in Plainfield, Wisconsin, who lived with his brother and ailing mother. After his brother died in 1944 and his mother in 1945, he sealed off his mother's bedroom and parlor, where he left her mummified body and lived downstairs in a small bedroom and kitchen. After voraciously reading books on anatomy and fascinated by the bodies of women, he began digging up corpses from remote graves generally at the time of the full moon to more closely study their bodies. He began turning the skins of these bodies into vests, lampshades, household decorations, and wall hangings. Between 1954 and 1957, he killed at least two elderly women to add to his collection before he was caught.[10]

Such killings showed a hardened attitude toward human life, as well as a release from the restraints of society—the dark underside of an Eisenhower *I Love Lucy* company man America.

Detectives had to develop new tools and strategies to fight this trend. One method was the better coordination of networks of law enforcement officials from federal to state to county police and even the National Guard, such as when a multistate manhunt was organized to go after Starkweather and Fugate. The FBI was continuing to collect even more fingerprints and make searches available to the local police. There was some further development in DNA exploration, in that Francis Crick and James Watson were finally able to decode the DNA molecule in the early 1950s, winning the Nobel Prize for Medicine for their efforts. They discovered that DNA consists of a double helix structure that resembles two interlocking spirals of genetic material consisting of four types of chemicals—adenine, guanine, cytosine, and thymine—linked together in different combinations. These combinations determine the characteristics of any human being, much like the letters of the alphabet form a word or a sentence. At the time, there was no practical application of this discovery—but it later provided the basis for DNA identification.[11] Meanwhile, there were some scientific discoveries in other fields that later became applicable to the crime lab as well, such as the discovery and identification of new elements and isotopes in medicine and industry, including plutonium and berkelium. There were new discoveries about ultra high-frequency waves produced at the Massachusetts Institute of Technology (1955), and the development of the field ion microscope by E.W. Müller in 1951. Also, the creation of a transatlantic cable telephone service in 1956 opened the way to better connect police departments from the United States to Britain and Europe.

It took time for many of these scientific breakthroughs to be translated into day-to-day investigative work. For the most part, the 1950s seemed to be a time of expanding, consolidating, and systematizing investigative methods that had already developed. As it became apparent there was a new kind of killer on the loose, investigators became aware of the need to develop other methods, leading to new techniques like psychological profiling, which emerged in the 1960s and 1970s. For the time being, during the 1950s investigators did the best they could to cope with the more violent and alienated killers, which so fascinated America and sometimes baffled investigators.

Following are some cases illustrating these trends and developments in investigative techniques.

THE CASE OF MELVIN DAVID REES

Baltimore, Maryland, and Fredricksburg, Virginia, 1957–59

When they arrived at the farmhouse near Route 450 outside of Annapolis, Maryland, on June 26, 1957, the police found a terrified army sergeant, who was shaking and breathing heavily after running a mile down the road. "He just stopped our car and shot her," he babbled, barely able to speak.

The shooting came as a shock because at this time, apparently random, motiveless shootings were rare, especially in the peaceful countryside. The late 1950s were characterized by a kind of calm around the country. Though there was growing fear of communism, the McCarthy witch hunts of the mid-1950s were over, and family life in the suburbs had an air of friendly conformity typified by two loving parents, two well-behaved teenagers, and their kid sister. Though a growing number of kids drove around in their Chevys, Fords, and Oldsmobiles, and cruising had become a popular way of checking out the girls and guys, the soc's with their blazers and slacks and girls with long skirts, sweaters, and ponytails still dominated the scene. The number of teenagers and young adults attracted to the rock or greaser lifestyle was still small, and the rise of the beatnik philosophy popularized by Kerouac was just beginning. A sudden, out-of-the-blue killing on a country road was very much out of the ordinary.

As the police listened sympathetically, the sergeant told them this strange story. He had been driving with his girl, Margaret Harold, on a country road near Annapolis and had just stopped at a roadside where wildflowers were growing to admire the view. As they drove on, a green Chrysler suddenly sped by and jackknifed in front of them. To avoid an accident, they swerved over to the side of the road and stopped. The sergeant saw a tall, thin-faced man with long hair jump out of the Chrysler and run over to his car.

The man looked liked he was leering at Margaret, and when the sergeant asked what the man wanted, he pulled out a gleaming revolver, pulled open the back door, and climbed in. As he aimed the gun at the sergeant's head, he reached forward and began caressing Margaret's head and neck, running his fingers through her hair. When she shuddered, groaned in disgust, and tried to pull away, the man jerked his gun and shot Margaret in the head.

As she fell sideways, the sergeant, terrified, pushed open his car door and began running down the highway as fast as he could. "I thought for sure he would fire after me," he told police, "but he didn't. He just drove away."

Following the sergeant's directions, the police took him back down the road to the car. There it was, along the side of the road where the sergeant had left it. On the passenger side, Margaret's body was slumped forward, her dark hair hanging limply, a large bullet hole covered with blood on the side of her head.

At once, the police asked for a team of fingerprint specialists to check the car. They were able to raise a few prints, but later analysis showed they were only the prints of the sergeant and Margaret.

The police thoroughly searched the surrounding area that night, looking for any sign of the suspect or his car. But nothing turned up. Police chief William Wade and Lieutenant Hagner noticed a small cinderblock building with a broken basement window on one side. It was dark and seemed to be unoccupied, so they went closer to check. Through the window they could see some pictures of apparently nude women on the walls, and they squeezed in through the opening to check.

They were amazed by what they saw. The basement walls were covered from floor to ceiling by hundreds of pornographic pictures featuring women in lewd poses. In some cases, the women seemed to be in poses showing them cowering, being whipped or otherwise tormented, suggesting that whoever put them there had sadistic interests. But there was no evidence of anyone who lived there.

The officers noticed one picture that looked different from the rest. It was a very pretty girl who was fully dressed, and the photo was printed on a heavy glossy paper. Thinking it might provide a clue, Wade took the photo and sent it to the FBI to analyze the paper and the picture. After carefully documenting the scene with photographs, the officers left, feeling there was nothing more they could do. They would have to wait to hear from the FBI.

A few days later, a small clue came back. The FBI reported that the paper on which the picture was printed was the kind often used in college yearbooks, and it sent out a team of FBI agents to check the colleges in the area around Annapolis. Normally, this might be a task for the local police department. But in this case the killing was near the state line with Virginia, only about twenty miles from Washington, D.C., leading the FBI to step in. They pored through the yearbooks, going back several years, and finally found what they were looking for at the University of Maryland in Baltimore—about thirty miles from Margaret's murder. It was the same photo that was plastered up in the cinderblock building. It was a picture of Wanda Tipson, a 1955 graduate. But when the FBI questioned her to learn if she knew a tall, thin-faced man like the sergeant described, she had no idea who he was. She had gone on a few dates with several tall men with long hair. Her leads proved fruitless. The Margaret Harold murder case became one more unsolved case in police and FBI files.

In January 1959, there was another odd roadside killing that brought to mind this buried case from eighteen months before. It occurred in Fredericksburg, Virginia, about forty miles south of Washington and about sixty miles from Annapolis. A twenty-nine-year-old tall burly feed-truck driver, Carroll Jackson, his twenty-eight-year-old wife, Mildred, and their two children (five-year-old Susan and eighteen-month-old Janet) had been visiting Mildred's parents in Louisa County south of Fredericksburg, and set off for home in Applegrove. As usual, they took Route 609, a country road, as they drove home in the early evening. As they waved goodbye, Mildred was holding little Janet, and Susan sat in the back seat.

The next day, after Mildred's parents didn't hear from their daughter as usual, they began to worry and asked a relative, Mrs. H. M. Ballard, who lived near the Jacksons' home, to check on them. When she did, she spotted the Jacksons' truck abandoned on the side of Route 609, and she called the local sheriff. In a few minutes, Sheriff Willis E. Proffitt was on the scene investigating. He found the keys still in the truck, and Mildred's purse and the children's dolls were there as well. He noticed skid marks directly in front of the car and concluded the Jacksons must have been forced off the road by another car, and that the other driver had probably forced them out of the truck. He was probably armed, Proffitt concluded, because Carroll was a strong, tough guy. Again, there were no prints, no clue leading to the criminal, though the local police, county officers, and the FBI searched the truck and the surrounding area. There was also no ransom note and no trace of the missing Jackson family.

Almost two months later, on March 4, a nearby neighbor of the Jacksons, James Beach, was walking along a shallow depression near an abandoned sawmill to gather sawdust for his roses when he found Carroll Jackson's body lying face-down in some brush, his hands tied with a necktie. When the police arrived, they found that there was a bullet hole through his head, and under his corpse was the dead body of Janet, who had apparently been either suffocated or died of exposure.[12]

At this point, the police and the FBI hadn't connected the two killings in Maryland and Virginia. About two weeks later, on March 21, there came more grim news. Two thirteen-year-old boys, John Russell and Johnny Brolin, playing near the cinderblock house near the site of Margaret Harold's murder, discovered what looked like a rat's nest or gopher hole in the ground. They had been climbing the roof of a nearby house to look for a kite, and when they went down to look more closely, they discovered that the rat's nest was actually an exposed bit of human hair. Frightened, they ran to get the police, and again Chief Wade and Lieutenant Hagner, who had investigated the Jackson killing, came to the scene. This time, as they dug away the shallow pile of earth, they discovered the body of a woman, who turned out to be Mildred Jackson, with a silk stocking tied around her neck. Lying on top of her body was another corpse, that of a small child with a fractured skull, who turned out to be Susan. The Maryland medical examiner reported that Mrs. Jackson had been beaten severely before or after she had been strangled, and she had been repeatedly and brutally raped before she was killed. In fact, it was one of the most brutal rapes he had ever seen.

But where had it occurred and how? Wade and Hagner recalled the collection of pornographic pictures they had found in the cinderblock house from nearly two years before, and when they went back to check, wondering if there was any connection, they found a red button in the basement room that matched the buttons on Mildred's dress. They knew that not only had the rape probably occurred in this shack, but whoever did so was probably the same man who had killed Margaret Harold. The use of the cinderblock house and the modus operandi—a night killing on a lonely country road, a car pushed off the road, a shot in the head, an obviously brutal killer who attacked women—all pointed to the same man, a tall, thin man with some connection to the University of Maryland.

At this point the FBI stepped in to work with the police, because the crime had led from the first murder in Virginia to the recent two in Maryland, making it an interstate crime. With the help of the press, the FBI began an intensive manhunt, using the description given by the sergeant to ask anyone for knowledge of a tall, thin-faced man who drove a blue or green Ford. That turned out to be the break they needed that helped unravel the strange puzzle of the sadistic killer who came to be called the "Sex Beast" by the press and public.

The FBI soon began to get letters from people describing such a man with that make of car who acted strangely. The first leads went nowhere. But among the letters, they received one from the killer himself, who had been following the publicity of the manhunt with a perverse fascination. He attached a newspaper photo of Mildred and her little girl, with a drawing of a hand across the mother's mouth, followed by a letter describing just how he had captured and killed the Jackson family, killing first Carroll and the baby, and then terrorizing Mildred for several hours before raping and killing her and then killing their daughter.[13] The killer seemed to take obvious delight in not only the acts themselves but writing about them later, like he was boasting with pride about what he had done and at the same time mocking the police and FBI with their failure to catch him. The note read in part (with the obscene references in the note tastefully omitted by the newspaper that published it): "caught on a lonely road . . . After pulling them over . . . I leveled the pistol . . . I ordered them out and him into the car trunk . . . both bound . . . I drove to a select area . . . and killed the husband and baby. Now the mother and daughter were all mine." After describing how he brutally raped her and how she failed to satisfy his sexual desires, he concluded with these chilling words: "And so . . . I killed her . . . then I gagged her, and led her to her place of execution . . . and buried her."

At this point, the police, press, and public concluded that whoever killed the Jacksons "must have been a sex pervert," although one psychiatrist, Dr.

Benjamin Karpman, tried to offer an alternate opinion. This was a time when psychiatrists were starting to play a greater role in understanding the new type of sexual predators and serial killers that had become more a part of the American crime scene. In Karpman's view, as he wrote to the *Washington Star* in a letter appearing March 28, the killer was "not a pervert" but a victim of a "much deeper disease." These are not, he continued "the crimes of a sex pervert. . . . They are not in the pattern of a sex criminal," explaining that he had never "encountered a case of a sexual pervert who killed a whole family for no overt reason. . . . Mental illness undoubtedly enters the case . . . and . . . some sexual factors might be involved." Karpman went on to try to explain the factors and causes of what was obviously an "illness . . . more severe" than just being a sex pervert. This view reflected the growing interest of psychiatrists in seeking to explain crimes as mental illness, and it contributed to a polarizing of views of those who sought to understand and sympathize with the criminal versus those who wanted to crack down on them.

Meanwhile, as the hunt for the killer and the debate about his mental state went on, the police and the FBI were still stymied. Finally, a letter from Norfolk, Virginia, arrived from a man who initially sent his letter anonymously and later wrote back with his name—Glen Moser, a salesman, and friend of a man he suspected might be the killer, Melvin David Rees. As Moser explained, he had been with Rees, a musician with long dark hair, on the night that Margaret Harold was killed, and he noticed that Rees was "hopped up" on amphetamines at the time and acting wild. When he asked Rees if he had killed the family, Rees didn't deny it; he evaded the question, leaving the friend suspicious. Currently, Moser didn't know where Rees was, but the FBI began checking Rees's background, and soon various clues began to fall into place pointing right to him.

Investigators found that Rees had attended the University of Maryland in 1953, which could be why he had been able to get Wanda Tipson's picture from the student yearbook. They also discovered an earlier charge in Maryland dating back to March 12, 1955, when Rees had been picked up for pulling a thirty-six-year-old woman into his car and then assaulting her after he offered her a ride and she refused. When she didn't want to press charges against him, the local police had dropped the case.

Rees's salesman friend got a letter from Rees from West Memphis, Arkansas, where he worked as a piano salesman in a music store. After he told the FBI, they finally found Rees and arrested him, bringing him back to Maryland. "But I'm innocent. Innocent," he yelled in protest. When the FBI agents put him in a police line-up and asked the army sergeant if he could identify the man who strong-armed his car two years before, he successfully picked out Rees.

With Rees in jail under arrest, the FBI agents investigated further. It was almost like Rees was a Dr. Jekyll and Mr. Hyde character, with well-respected parents who had raised him to be a well-behaved, upstanding young man. His father, for example, worked for the Potomac Telephone Company in Hyattsville,

Maryland, and had lived there for almost forty years, while his wife worked for the U.S. Department of the Interior. Both had been active in civic affairs, and their two daughters, older than Rees, were married and highly esteemed in the community, too.

Even Rees had a good local reputation. He was an aspiring jazz musician, and in the 1950s, band musicians were very much a part of the respectable community. They played at church socials, weddings, and local clubs; his parents had absolutely no suspicions that their son could be the sex-mad killer of five brutally murdered victims as described in the press. The impression was one of disbelief. As they told investigators, Rees was "of a kind and sympathetic nature. . . . He would not hurt any living thing." They explained that he had been married and divorced and was the father of one son. Despite his divorce, he and his wife remained on good terms, and "he loved our grandchildren and his own son and they loved him greatly."[14]

Thus, when the investigators proffered a warrant to search their home, Rees's parents felt they had no reason to worry or fear what investigators might find. They felt sure the arrest had all been a terrible mistake, a problem of mistaken identity.

In the attic, the police found a nickel-plated .38 pistol in a saxophone case—which later turned out to be the gun that killed both Margaret Harold and Carroll Jackson. Along with it, they found numerous letters and notes written by Rees in which he described in detail how he had committed various crimes against women, including a copy of the note he had sent to the newspaper describing how he had killed the Jacksons.

The evidence against him was overwhelming, and at his 1961 trial in Baltimore he was convicted for the Harold slaying and sentenced to life imprisonment. When he was tried by the Circuit Court in Virginia for the murders of the Jackson family, he was readily convicted again and this time sentenced to death on September 28, 1961.[15]

Even though his crimes were obvious, the underlying psychology of Rees presented a curious picture, as his family, friends, neighbors, and associates spoke about him after his arrest and at his trials. One young man who played in a band with described him thus: "The killer was . . . a pretty nice boy . . . He was rather cold and reserved . . . but a gentleman."[16] One neighbor described him as "the quiet type . . . always ready to lend a helping hand,"[17] and another said, "He used to stop occasionally and chat with me . . . I was always impressed by his poise, his good manners and his quiet dignified way of speaking. . . . I never though of him as distant or noticeably reserved."[18] Even his girlfriend of two years when he was arrested—Pat, an exotic dancer in her twenties, who Rees met in a night club—was unaware of his sadistic side, describing him as someone who "loved music and played it well" and who had "never tried anything on me."[19] Observers who saw him shortly after he killed noticed nothing strange. For example, on the night of January 12, 1959, after he killed the Jacksons, he went to the music studio where he taught as usual and taught seven students and two band groups. "I noted nothing unusual about him," said the storekeeper.[20]

Yet a few acquaintances noted that he sometimes had strange ideas or was interested in unusual books. One man remarked that Rees had an unusual interest in "the supernatural and the Hereafter," and the manager of the piano store where Rees worked said he seemed lackadaisical about his job and hadn't sold a single piano in the six weeks he was there. One day he found that Rees had left a stack of books in a back room of the store—books that showed an interest in Freudian psychology and personal anxieties, such as *Our Inner Conflicts*, *The History of Frustration*, *A Constructive Study of Neurosis*, and *The Future of an Illusion*. He also found comics and sexy magazines.[21]

It was like Rees was split into two different people—the outwardly reserved, shy, well-behaved jazz musician, music teacher, and piano salesman, with the raging Sex Beast inside. As he sat calmly in the courtroom at his final trial in Virginia, he looked exactly like the ordinary good boy everyone knew, while the jurors sentenced him for this inner beast. Or as one writer described this split:

> The impulse of life came, night by night, under a compulsive obsession to find *sadistic* outlets. All sense of guilt disappeared. There was no place left for remorse. . . . Cruel fantasy had violated no moral imperatives that Rees knew. He could keep the surface polished. . . . Then there came a time when imaginary acts could no longer be contained within the bounds of fantasy. Alone, he became restless and his imagination took him along "car parked" lanes that he had traveled before.[22]

Then he sadistically attacked and killed.

It had been a difficult case to solve. What was even more puzzling and disturbing was the way the case mirrored a kind of split that was growing within American culture—between the outwardly calm and conformist surface of a prosperous postwar nation devoted to family, consumerism, and the good life, and the underbelly of society that was fighting for release in the growing image of the outlaw and rebel. Rees was like the glamorized image of Marlon Brando or James Dean turned to real sex and violence. He was a harbinger of the spread of sex and violence that lay ahead.

THE CASE OF PENNY BJORKLAND

Daly City, California, 1959

When police found August Norry's body high up in the Daly City hills on Monday, February 2, 1959, near a pile of grass clippings the day after he was killed, it didn't make sense. It looked like he or someone else might have just dumped the large pile of drying grass, and then someone had pumped eighteen bullets into him. The bloody wounds spattered his body like he had just been used for target practice, but there was no sign of a car or truck that he might have used to get to the isolated spot, although it seemed clear that he had been shot at the scene the day before from the state of the body. Police soon knew who he was from the prints taken off the body. A short time later, they found Norry's blood-stained truck parked in a lover's lane in the hills. They theorized that whoever killed him must have driven away in his truck—unless it was stolen by someone else—after the killing. But as to who killed him or why, they didn't have a clue, though they put out a call in the press for leads, asking the *San Francisco Chronicle* for help.

The *Chronicle* reporters were only too glad to help, since by now they had become known for a trendy pop style of journalism, featuring a mix of sensationalism and gossip along with the news. The local crime beat had become a growing staple, along with Herb Caen, who started the new style of three-dot celebrity journalism in a column he called *Baghdad-by-the-Bay*. There was a growing footloose pop culture, and people enjoyed reading about the trendy rebels, as the lifestyle of the beatniks and outlaws were becoming part of more mainstream culture. Many teenagers, for example, adopted this pose of being wild and hip in high school; it was becoming classy to take the role of the déclassé, and many songs, books, and films of the day expressed this attraction of the outlaw. Examples include the popular song "Mack the Knife," about a cool killer with a knife; the films *Anatomy of a Murder* (1959) and *Our Man in Havana* (1959), and the book *Casino Royale* by Ian Fleming (1953), which introduced the blasé agent James Bond to the world. The folk movement was big on the college circuit, with clean-scrubbed singers like The Kingston Trio singing upbeat ballads like "Tom Dooley." A more cynical Tom Lehrer expressed a kind of rebel mockery of this straight suburban life in one of his songs in which the singer dances around with his dead lover. Meanwhile, bad-boy novelist Norman Mailer was at the height of his glory, presenting an image of the tough outlaw writer as his own hero, as in his big book of 1959, *Advertisements for Myself*. Mailer very much had the look of a petty crook or Brooklyn hood himself—and America gloried in this new cooler-than-cool outlaw as celebrity image, while foreign films like Federico Fellini's *La Dolce Vita* (1960) helped open the door to this new amorality that was spreading through American culture.

Soon the police began to get some leads in the Norry case, and at first, they thought were dealing with a spurned lover. As it turned out, Norry, age twenty-seven, worked as a landscape gardener and was married with a wife, twenty, who was expecting their first child. Family and friends reported they were mystified by his shooting because he was "a man without an enemy."[23] But he also had a local reputation as a philanderer and womanizer. Before his marriage, he had boasted about his many conquests, and some speculated that perhaps a jealous woman or boyfriend might have had it in for him. Then the police got a call from a boy who lived in the Daly City hills and reported that he had seen a "freckle-faced blonde" on the day of the murder, "driving like mad" in a truck that looked like the description of Norry's.[24] Daly City and the San Francisco area were full of freckle-faced blondes, so that clue didn't lead anywhere.

As if to help out the frustrated police, the *Chronicle* got a mysterious, anonymous handwritten letter in which the writer stated that "a girlfriend" of his committed the crime and even gave the registration numbers on Norry's truck, which hadn't been reported in the newspapers, to indicate that the writer was knowledgeable about the crime. The numbers had been copied from the registration papers taken from his car. Is there a reward for turning in the murderer, the writer wanted to know? If so, the writer would name the girlfriend. But after the *Chronicle* published this strange letter and no reward offer was forthcoming from anyone, the publicity about it and its offer died down, and the police still had no solid leads.

Three inspectors at the San Mateo County Sheriff's office along with two police officers in Daly City decided to follow the trail of the bullets.[25] They noticed that Norry's bullet-peppered body had been shot with a special kind of .38 bullet called wadcutters used in target practice. Besides the slugs taken from Norry's body, they found a box of the unusually shaped wadcutter bullets near the body.

Using a careful process of deduction, they began to trace down where the bullets came from. First, they recognized that these were hand-loaded bullets—a common practice among target-shooting enthusiasts who like to load and reload their own bullets by buying gunpowder separately and putting it into molds to suit their own tastes. Second, they theorized that whoever loaded these bullets might have resold them to someone else if he didn't use them himself. Target shooters often do this to help cover the costs of buying gunpowder and bullets.

The next step was to trace down whoever created the bullets. The detectives learned that the bullets had three cannelures, which are the indentations around the base of the bullet's cartridge that hold the lubricating grease. They found that there was only one manufacturer, in Connecticut, who made a model with three cannelures, and they got the names of four local distributors of this manufacturer. Still, it seemed almost hopeless, since the distributors reported selling dozens of molds throughout the southern San Francisco Bay area.

Inspector Eugene Stewart in San Mateo took several unfired cartridges from the box found near the body and found that they each had more than the usual amount of gunpowder—which meant they were loaded to fire especially fast and hot—an approach called hot loading. It wasn't much to go on, but Stewart and several other officers visited every store selling guns in San Francisco and northern San Mateo County, where Daly City is located, to learn the names of customers who were known to buy molds, hot load three-cannelure bullets, and perhaps sell some of their extras.[26]

Eventually, the search led them to five men, one of them Lawrence Schultze, a young man who lived in Colma, a city mostly known for graveyards and cemeteries, located next to Daly City. When they arrived, Schultze was initially reluctant to say anything, because he was already charged by the police as part of an auto theft ring. After police assured him their questions had nothing to do with that, he agreed to cooperate, though he told them that two boxes of his hot loads had been stolen from his car a few months before. "What about the lead you use in casting?" one officer asked, and Schultze gave the officers a sample of the lead. The police sent the sample off to a spectrograph laboratory in San Francisco.

The results proved to be the break the police needed. The spectrographic analysis showed the lead was the same as that in one of the slugs in Norry's body. On Tuesday, April 14, Inspector Stewart and others went back to see Schultze, dubious about his stolen-from-the-car story. He was now their number one suspect. "Let me talk to my attorney," Schultze told them, and shortly after, he told them another story. "Around the beginning of the year," he admitted, "I sold a box of fifty cartridges for $3."

To whom might that be, the detectives wanted to know. "To Penny Bjorkland," Schultze explained, describing how he had known her for some time, and one day she brought him a .38 revolver and said she needed some ammunition for it so she could practice target shooting. A few evenings after he had loaded the bullets for her, he took her to the hills around Daly City and they fired off a few shots to be sure the bullets were okay. "And they were," Schultze told the detectives.

At once, the detectives headed straight over to Bjorklands house at 241 Olive Street in Daly City, where she lived with her parents and three brothers, ages fifteen, thirteen, and nine. They waited for her to come home from her job as a mail clerk for a San Francisco business office, as her bewildered parents expressed surprise that their daughter could be in any kind of trouble. "We'll just wait," said the police officers.

After Penny arrived, she would only acknowledge buying the bullets but would say nothing about the murder. As her parents looked on in shock and amazement, the officers took her to the San Mateo County Jail in Redwood City, the county seat, about twenty miles from Daly City.

The next morning, Penny began confessing to the county jail matron, Esther Brown, who turned on the intercom as officers in the booking department listened and took notes. Penny's calm, unfeeling confession came like a shock to the public when the San Francisco newspapers reported it. As she explained, she killed Norry simply because she "wanted to kill someone." Or as Penny told Matron Brown, "For about a year or a year and a half I've had the urge to kill someone. I'll admit that the motive sounds crazy. But I wanted to know if a person could commit a crime like this and not worry about the police looking for her or have it on her conscience. I've felt better ever since I killed him."[27]

Over the next few hours, she poured out her story, and police officers quickly corroborated what she said. She explained that she had dumped the bullets in a street drain in front of her house and had thrown the revolver into a street drain in San Francisco. Within a few hours, a crew of sewer workers had retrieved both the gun and the bullets. She also described how she got the gun from the bedroom of a friend, William Freeman, she had visited two weeks before the murder. "I simply stole it," she said.

She also led Sheriff Earl Whitmore, Chief Assistant District Attorney Howard Hartley, and Mrs. Brown to the scene of the killing, where she described in more detail exactly how she killed Norry, noting that "I've wanted to kill somebody ever since I started target shooting. I used to go up in the hills and point my pistol at a target and pretend it was a human target." Almost by chance, she happened to meet Norry and pick him as her victim. Initially, she had met him about a month earlier, when he was in the hills dumping lawn clippings from his truck. They chatted briefly, and after they stopped at a drive-in for some food, he drove her home. Norry told her he was twenty-three and unmarried, though he was actually twenty-seven or twenty-eight with a young wife, but he "never did anything improper or out of the way," she said. However, thinking he was single perhaps made it easier for her to choose him as her victim.

In any case, Penny was carrying her .38-caliber revolver in the waistband of her pedal pushers and had a box of ammunition in her purse. She invited Norry to join her for target shooting, and after she fired a single test shot, she suddenly decided to kill Norry, who was seated behind the wheel.

As she demonstrated for Whitmore, Hartley, and Brown, she got out of the passenger seat of the car, turned, and fired five bullets into Norry. As he slumped forward, she reloaded, walked around the rear of the car, and fired at him from the driver's window. Then, back at her own side, she fired again. Finally, she dragged him out on the ground and drove off.[28]

The investigators looked at her, amazed at her odd indifference and callousness. How could she have simply done this so coldly? "Had he mistreated you, or kissed you, or made any improper suggestions?" one of the investigators asked. Penny simply shook her head to say no. She had killed out of a curiosity to see how it felt, and now she didn't want to talk about it anymore. When Mrs. Brown asked if she shot him again after she pulled his body out of the car, she said, "I don't want to talk about it. It makes me sick."

The case, now referred to as an "urge slaying," created a local sensation. The next day, when reporters spoke to her at a press conference, they asked if she considered herself mentally ill. But Penny came back with a firm "no!", insisting that she had been completely free of her urge to kill somebody since she had killed Norry. She seemed oddly unconcerned about the consequences, telling reporters she wasn't even particularly bothered by the thought of getting caught. "I figured if I got caught, I got caught." She seemed strangely disconnected from her parents, though she told reporters that her home life didn't have anything to do with the killings. She admitted that she had deliberately picked fights with her mother and realized that her parents would suffer due to what she had done. She quickly brushed off any concern with the comment, "But that's not my affair."[29]

After her detailed confession and comments to the press, the only question was whether Penny was sane and what penalty she would get. On April 23, the San Mateo County grand jury formally indicted her for murder. After her arraignment was postponed to permit a full psychiatric examination, she waived a jury trial and pled guilty on May 26 before Superior Court Judge Frank Blum in return for the prosecution agreeing not to seek the death penalty. Now it was up to the judge to decide her sentence, based on hearing medical and psychiatric testimony from a panel of seven specialists, including three court-appointed psychiatrists who examined her. A key consideration was whether the murder was premeditated and whether she was sane or legally insane.

Oddly, when Penny casually pled guilty, as if she was "bidding our spades in a friendly game of bridge," as one newspaper reporter described it,[30] the psychiatrists reported that she seemed to actually like being in jail because she hated her family and this kept her away from them. After her plea, "she trotted happily back to her cell, her lips smiling."

At her July 28 psychiatric hearing, six of the seven psychiatrists agreed she was sane, but emotionally unstable. As one doctor, Dr. Walter Rappaport, superintendent of Agnews State Hospital reported, he found her "alert, in good contact with reality, responsible, outgoing, and fully oriented."[31] Most of the others agreed.

Finally, on August 6, after finding that the facts of the crime showed a premeditated murder, Judge Blum sentenced Penny to prison for life. He felt she had planned the crime many months in advance, picked out the type of victim she wanted, found the victim fitting her description, and proceeded to kill him. Also, she stole the gun she used far in advance of the crime and got the bullets in advance, too. "The facts of the crime show willful premeditated killing," Judge Blum said.[32]

As she heard the sentence, she expressed the first bit of emotion since the court proceedings began, perhaps because she had told reporters the week before that she hoped for a second-degree verdict, which would mean about five years in the Corona prison for women. The sentence meant she would have to spend at least about seven years in prison before she could be considered for parole. "I am unhappy. This is not what I expected," she told the judge. As she was led away by the matron, she had only one question, "Was my mother in court?" The matron shook her head no. Apparently, according to one psychiatrist, her underlying purpose in killing Norry was to "wreak vengeance on her mother."[33] Her reaction, as her lawyer told reporters, reflected her first realization of what she had really done. As he stated, "Until this moment, she didn't appear to care one way or another. I think she now realizes what she has done."

After that, she spent the next few years in Corona, though she briefly convinced the prison psychiatrists she needed special psychiatric care and was transferred to Patton State Hospital. Once there, she announced that all her symptoms were gone and she had simply fooled the doctors at Corona. She said hopefully, because she was in a mental hospital and proved she was sane, "You'll have to release me as cured." It didn't quite work that way. The hospital shipped her right back to Corona, where she was likely to spend at least nine years in prison—the average term then served for life sentences in California.

THE CASE OF BURTON ABBOTT

Berkeley and Alameda, California, 1955–56

When fourteen-year-old Stephanie Bryan disappeared one warm afternoon on April 28, 1955, in the city of Berkeley, across the bay from San Francisco, everyone was mystified. She was a ninth-grade student at Willard Junior High School in a community that was known nationally for the prestigious University of California and was considered to be very safe. It was a close-knit community of scholars and civic-minded townspeople in the days before Berkeley became known for civil rights and free speech protests. It was a time when academics was much in vogue, featured in the popular quiz shows of the day like *The $64,000 Question* and *Twenty One*. Outside of academia the conformist image of the corporate man as written about in the best seller *The Organization Man* by American sociologist William H. Whyte was very much in vogue.

When Stephanie vanished, it brought about widespread shock, especially because she was such a well-behaved, quiet, studious girl who carefully adhered to her parents' schedules for coming home directly after school. As the police and press pieced together the story, Stephanie had left Willard Junior High at 3:30 p.m. that afternoon with her classmate, Mary Anne Stewart. From there, they had stopped briefly at the Berkeley Public Library, where she borrowed two books; headed to a store where she bought a paperback on parakeets; and after stopping at a doughnut shop, headed home. A brisk walk led the girls to the entrance of the Claremont Hotel, a beautiful luxury resort in the foothills near Tilden Park, with manicured gardens and lawns, tennis courts, and patios. There, Stephanie said goodbye to Mary Anne and took her usual shortcut across the hotel grounds to get to her home—and that's the last anyone saw of her.

By 4:15 p.m., Mrs. Bryan was worried that her prompt daughter hadn't returned. She tried walking through Stephanie's usual path and calling several of her daughter's friends to find out what happened, but nothing turned up. No one had heard from her. After her husband, Dr. Charles Bryan Jr., a radiologist who worked at a nearby Oakland hospital, arrived around 5:30 p.m., they called more friends. Her disappearance was even more surprising to them because Stephanie was an unusually studious and shy girl, not at all like some of the teenagers who were starting to be attracted to rock music and the sounds of a recently recorded singer named Elvis Presley. Moreover, the Bryans were very strict disciplinarians who kept a very close watch on their daughter. They believed her to be very unlikely to even talk to a stranger, much less go off with one.

With growing concern, at 6:15 p.m., Dr. Bryan called the police, who had gained a reputation nationally for a new style of scientific policing, led by chief August Vollmer. In fact, the Berkeley police had been in the forefront of using scientific investigators back in the 1920s, when Berkeley chemist and criminologist Edward Heinrich cracked the D'Autremont brothers case using hair, fiber, and handwriting evidence. After receiving Bryan's call and interviewing Dr. and Mrs. Bryan, the police carefully retraced Stephanie's movements from the moment she left school to when she left her friend at the Claremont Hotel. They carefully searched the nearby neighborhood of small shops and stately homes and spread out through the hotel's grounds and into the foothills that led to Tilden Park. Still they found nothing.

At this point, the police sent out the alert to every officer on the beat and notified the press for their help. The next day, the *San Francisco Chronicle*, which by then had become a lively newspaper given to featuring crime and lifestyle stories over the more serious national and international news of the day, headlined the story of the missing teenager, including her picture, and all sorts of leads and tips poured in. The police rushed to check them all out, though many proved unfounded. There were dozens of reports of seeing Stephanie—or at least girls who looked like her—in various places, each one raising and then dashing hopes. A half-dozen men and women reported seeing a girl who looked like Stephanie in a car near the Claremont Hotel, where she was struggling with a young man. A few callers reported seeing a car with a young man and girl of Stephanie's description on Highway 24 leading from Berkeley into Contra Costa County. But the descriptions were vague, and no one had written down a license number, so the police had little to go on. They weren't even sure the callers really had seen Stephanie—or if they had, they had no idea what kind of car to look for, since the descriptions were so different. Then, too, the police felt that part of the problem was that eight days after Stephanie disappeared, Dr. Bryan had offered a $2,500 reward for information that led to solving the mystery of her disappearance, resulting in an unusually large number of calls.

For a brief moment, there was a ray of hope. A man called saying he had Dr. Bryan's daughter. But when police traced the call, the man turned out to be a recently released mental patient. It was another dead end to what the *San Francisco Chronicle* now called "one of the most intensive searches in the West's history" since Stephanie's disappearance.[34]

On May 9, eleven days after Stephanie's disappearance, there was the first solid clue. David Tyree, an electrician, called to say he had discovered a French textbook belonging to Stephanie in a field in Franklin Canyon, in Contra Costa County. He had already thrown away the book's soiled paper cover when he gave it to his son, a student in high school, but then he had read about the search for Stephanie Bryan, so he called to turn it in. Though there were no fingerprints, the discovery at least confirmed that Stephanie had been driven somewhere and tended to support the callers who had claimed they had seen a girl struggling with a man in a car headed toward Contra Costa County.

At once, the police organized a search of the entire canyon area, thinking perhaps they might find more of her possessions, maybe even her body. Again, nothing turned up, and the press reported the growing frustration. The police felt they could only wait for some other lead or clue.

For the next two months, there was nothing more. Suddenly, the police got a phone call that opened up the case—in a way that raised even more puzzling questions. A woman named Georgia Abbott, who sometimes took part in amateur theatricals, called to say that she had been looking in the basement of her home in Alameda in a scrap box for some materials for a costume when she found a red leather handbag she had never seen before. When she opened it, she found a wallet inside that contained a student's identification card, photographs of young teenage girls, and an unfinished letter to a girl in Dartmouth, Massachusetts. When she saw Stephanie's name on the ID, she knew she was the missing girl that the whole Bay area was looking for, and so she had called the police.

It was, to the police, an amazing phone call. Why would the wife of the man who would become the number one suspect in the case call, since the pocketbook must have most likely been put in the basement by her husband? As it happened, that night she and her husband, Burton, and her mother who lived with them, had two guests, Otto Dezman, a longtime family friend, and the husband of Georgia's employer, Leona, who operated a small beauty parlor. After she found the pocketbook, without thinking to hide it to protect her husband or asking him about it after their guests left, she simply brought it upstairs and asked, "Isn't this the girl who disappeared?"[35]

There was some discussion about what to do. Abbott himself seemed very calm, as if this was just an ordinary mislaid possession. He just commented matter-of-factly, "I can't figure out how it got there. I'm positive I didn't put it there." After some further discussion, Dezman suggested that they should call the police, and Abbott made no effort to discourage them, perhaps not thinking about the importance of this circumstantial evidence turning up in his basement.

Very soon the police arrived, and Burton calmly met them at the door. In response to their questions, he calmly told them, just as his wife and the Dezmans had, that he had no idea how Stephanie's handbag happened to turn up in his basement. "I didn't know her and I never saw her," he assured them, and when the police pressed on with their questions, he suggested that maybe the bag was dropped there in May when their garage was used as a polling place in the election. Perhaps someone casting a ballot had put the bag in the basement. The police looked at him skeptically, wondering whether it was reasonable to think a voter had come with the dead girl's belongings in his pockets and after casting his ballot had hid the evidence of a murder in the basement. For the time being, they made no arrest, simply informing the Abbotts that they would like to return the following morning to search the basement and garden outside. "Certainly, you can search," Abbott readily agreed, and after they left, the family sat down to dinner. Afterward, Abbott calmly played chess with his friend.

It was as if nothing unusual had happened, certainly nothing to be concerned about. Later, Abbott's calm was one of the most baffling things about the case.

The next day, the police arrived with their picks and shovels and began digging and searching. They found nothing in the garden, but as they dug into the dirt walls around the cellar, they uncovered other possessions belonging to Stephanie—several school books, some notebooks, the two library books she had borrowed, and her brassiere.

How did her possessions get here? the police wanted to know, as they grilled Abbott. Again, he remained calm, insisting he had no idea how Stephanie's property turned up at his home and suggesting that perhaps something had happened on that May election day. When the police grilled him further, wanting to know what he did on April 28, the day Stephanie disappeared, he had a detailed explanation. He was going up to his family's cabin in the mountains in Trinity County, 300 miles away, to be there a day ahead of the opening of fishing season, because fishing was one of his few hobbies. He had left early in the morning, about 11 a.m., he explained, so it would be physically impossible for him to have been in Berkeley at the time Stephanie disappeared.

The police were not immediately convinced. Though they didn't immediately arrest him, they told him they would obviously have to check his alibi. Who did you see on the way and exactly how did you drive there?, they wanted to know. Immediately, Abbott had a detailed list for the officers, as if he had expected this request. His list included a gas station where he had stopped for gas, a restaurant where he had gotten some coffee, even a twenty-minute stop to look for the State Land Office in Sacramento on the way to the cabin. He had arrived there around 9 p.m., and the next day, Friday, he said he went fishing, and was joined on Saturday by his brother Harold and Harold's wife. He stayed with them at the cabin until he returned home in Alameda on Sunday night. "We'll check it out," said the officers, as they left.

Over the next few days, officers not only carefully visited the places Abbott mentioned, they learned what they could about him. The *San Francisco Chronicle* reported their progress—an early harbinger of the day-by-day murder investigation coverage in high-profile cases today.

The profile that emerged of Burton Abbott was puzzling—he certainly didn't seem like someone who could have possibly had the desire to kill anyone, much less the physical strength to do so. As detectives and newspaper reporters soon discovered, Abbott, a twenty-seven-year-old accounting student at the University of California, was highly regarded by his friends and relatives as an apparently ordinary man. He was considered a "good son, husband, and father" to his young child. Before enrolling at Berkeley under the G.I. Bill, he had been a war veteran who was disabled, as a result of suffering from double pneumonia, which triggered a renewed attack of latent tuberculoses when he was stationed at a camp in Kentucky. As a result, he spent two years in a hospital; during that time, all of one lung and five ribs had been removed. He had a large scar, almost a foot long, on his back. He was very thin, weighing only 130 pounds, and according to his wife, he even had trouble breathing, as well as lifting heavy objects. As his brother Mark later commented, "He is still in constant pain and is so weak that he can't lift his four-year-old son."[36] His only physical recreation seemed to be going on an occasional fishing trip in the mountains; otherwise, he spent most of his leisure time reading or visiting with friends at a coffee shop near his home. His wife and family described him as having a very gentle disposition, as someone who was very "gentle and kind and good."[37] He went for biweekly medical check-ups because of his disabled condition.

Thus, Burton Abbott seemed a most unlikely murder suspect. He even offered to take a lie detector test, though the results turned out to be inconclusive. Yet there was the circumstantial evidence of her murder buried around his house.

Besides checking out Abbott's alibi, the police went to search in the vicinity of his cabin in the Trinity Mountains, and to this end they enlisted the help of Trinity County Deputy Sheriff Harold Jackson, who had two half-bloodhound bear-hunting dogs. As Jackson later described to the *San Francisco Chronicle*, he went to Abbott's ramshackle cabin, which was on a little country road two and a half miles north of the tiny hamlet of Wildwood, the nearest human habitation. After he gave the dogs Stephanie's brassiere, found in Abbott's basement wall, to sniff, he let them loose. After they ranged for a while, they headed up a steep hillside to a thicket of manzanita bushes, about 600 feet up the hill beyond the cabin, and began baying for him to come look. When he did, he found a pile of loose earth, and under it he found a badly decomposed and animal-mangled body. It was the long-missing Stephanie Bryan. Jackson wondered, how could Abbott, who was weak and sickly, have carried a 105-pound girl up the hill? Even if they both walked, how could he have managed it? As Jackson remembered, it had been snowing and raining heavily on April 28, and this was a rugged, steep slope—"steeper than hell," as he described it. A brutal murder by this frail accounting student seemed to make no sense. Yet there was the body near Abbott's cabin, after other evidence of Stephanie's property had appeared at his home.

At once, Jackson roped off the area and notified the Trinity County Sheriff Harold Wilson. Wilson, along with Coroner E. G. Chapman and every available deputy in the county, headed for the scene. At the same time, Wilson notified the police in Berkeley of the find, and a contingent of Berkeley police, headed by Lt. R. T. Sherry, headed for the scene with Stephanie's fingerprints and dental charts to positively ID the body. An hour later, other Alameda County officials were on their way as well, including the district attorney and a pathologist. Stephanie's dentist joined the group, too.[38]

Soon the officials confirmed the grim news. Though the body was badly decomposed, the torn clothing was what Stephanie had been wearing the day she disappeared, and her underwear was tied around her neck, perhaps to either strangle or gag her. Though there was no sign of a weapon, the condition of her skull indicated that she had been battered by some heavy instrument. The detectives couldn't tell from the decomposition of the body whether she had been sexually assaulted, though they theorized she might have been.

In any case, it was enough circumstantial evidence to arrest Abbott. After deciding with the Trinity officials that the Berkeley police and Alameda district attorney's office would pursue the case, the Berkeley police headed to Abbott's home, arrested him, and took him to the station for questioning. Among those questioning him were a university criminologist and psychiatrist and a lie detector expert.[39]

Abbott seemed oddly dazed as police came to arrest him. They had already notified his attorney to prepared for their arrival, and when they appeared, Burton was seated in the living room with Georgia, his mother, Elsie Abbott, and attorney Stanley D. Whitney. "It just can't be. It just can't be," he told his family and attorney before the police arrived. "All I want to say is I didn't do this." Shortly after, the police arrived to take Abbott away.

The next day, the press had a field day, describing Abbott and the investigation at length. In fact, the *San Francisco Chronicle* observed that if Abbott turned out to be the long-sought Bryan killer, his own Georgia would be eligible to apply for the $2,500 reward posted by Bryan's parents, though the Abbott attorney quickly denied she was even thinking about that. "She's too stunned to even think about such a thing," he told a curious press.[40]

Meanwhile, in jail, Abbott continued to protest his innocence, telling the press he had an ironclad timetable alibi for every minute of the day Stephanie disappeared that would vindicate him. His family rallied behind him, too. Besides hiring two well-known attorneys, Stanley Whitney and Harold Hove, to handle his defense, his mother offered $2,500 for information vindicating her son.[41]

Detectives were not convinced, suspicious that his alibi for the day in question was so precise, while Abbott was vague about many other days, including the day before. They continued to talk to alibi witnesses, and they also brought in a criminalist, Dr. Paul Kirk, who was well known as a member of the Department of Criminology at the University of California.

At Abbott's trial, which began November 7 before Alameda County Superior Court Judge Charles W. Snook, the case hinged on his alibi, assessments of his strength, dueling alibi witnesses, and the testimony of criminalist Kirk. There were so many seeming contradictions in this completely circumstantial case that led a fascinated public to wonder what really happened. During the trial, the longest in Alameda County, which went on until January 25, 1956, one of the big questions was how could a "sickly young man, so frail that he could not lift his son of four" carry Stephanie, dead or alive, to the place where her body was found? It seemed so unlikely that she would have willingly walked up the steep slope to the hills behind his cabin. Then, too, if Abbott discarded one of Stephanie's books on the way to the mountains, why take the other possessions back to his home and leave them there to be discovered later?[42] Why not bury them with the body?

The defense portrayed Abbott as a weak, sickly, and gentle family man who couldn't possibly have done it. The prosecution chipped away with other facts that had been uncovered by detectives. For one thing, a medical doctor from a veteran's hospital he tried to reenter sometime after Stephanie's disappearance said the hospital turned him down for further treatment on the grounds his condition was "almost that of a nontuberculous male."[43] Although there were witnesses who said they had seen him in Berkeley on the afternoon of April 28 (including Mrs. Dezman, the owner of the beauty shop where Georgia worked, who was certain Abbott had visited his wife at her shop at 2:30 that day), other witnesses said they had seen him miles away at the same time. Especially critical was the testimony of one casual acquaintance at the Wildwood restaurant and bar, where Abbott said he stopped in briefly on the night of April 28 and also came in the following morning. According to the man, Tom Daly, a University of Chicago graduate who was staying in lumberjack country, when Abbott came in on the morning of April 29, Wildwood owner Delbert Cox exclaimed, "Why, Bud Abbott, what the hell are you doing here at this time of year?"[44] Meanwhile, Cox himself didn't recall whether he had seen Abbott at the Wildwood on the night of April 28 or not.

The testimony of various people who might have seen a man struggling with a young girl in a car was too vague or contradictory. When Abbott himself took the stand, he was cool and polished, calmly detailing every moment of his alibi; firmly protesting his innocence; and saying he could not explain how Stephanie's possessions turned up in his basement, except perhaps that they were left there by someone that day when their house was used for voting. Mostly, as the days of testimony wore on, Abbott sat listening, expressionless, although from time to time he would smile slightly.

The testimony seemed so contradictory it was hard to predict how the jury would respond. Perhaps most critical was the dramatic testimony given by criminalist Kirk, who described in detail the intensive analysis of the trace evidence found at the scene of the crime and taken from Abbott's home and car. Several decades before, such tests might not have been possible, but Kirk mesmerized the courtroom with his careful account of what he discovered from hours of study using a high-powered microscope.

For one thing, he had taken a few thin woolen fibers and a few hairs that detectives had found in Abbott's car, and he compared them under the microscope with some fibers taken from the sweater Stephanie had been wearing that April day and with several of her own hairs. "They were identical," he said on the stand.[45] He analyzed a small amount of clay from the boots Abbott had worn that day, and he discovered that this clay matched the earth at the bottom of Stephanie's grave. Moreover, when he examined the floor mat taken from Abbott's car, he found tiny specks of human blood. He also found that a small piece of cleaning tissue discovered near the body was the same type as that used by Abbott.[46]

Kirk's testimony didn't seem to shake Abbott as he listened coolly, nor when he later took the stand, but it was damning nonetheless. The prosecution had still more incriminating evidence in rebuttal to Abbott's carefully constructed alibi. District Attorney Coakley confidentially came forward waving Abbott's gasoline credit cards and then presented evidence to show that Abbott had bought gasoline many blocks from the route he claimed he took to the mountains.[47] In his closing arguments, Coakley told the jury that Abbott had done all of these things because he was a "sexual psychopath, and that his attitude of deliberate politeness was a symptom of the disordered personality."[48] Conversely, Abbott's attorneys tried to present the case as an unsolved mystery in which Abbott's alibi showed he couldn't have been in Berkeley that fateful day to kidnap and kill Stephanie, since he arrived in Wildwood 8:30 p.m. that night.

Finally, on January 19, 1956, the jury retired after a forty-eight-day trial with 106 witnesses and spent six days deliberating the verdict. After seven days, the jurors returned January 25 with their verdict, finding Abbott guilty of both kidnapping and murder. The jurors had taken a long time to decide because there were so many contradictions. But as one juror told a *San Francisco Chronicle* reporter the day after the verdict, it had been the mass of evidence, including the testimony by Kirk, that the prosecution had presented as the "latest thing in crime detection." Kirk's testimony had been weighed in with all the rest, and as this juror reported, "It was the weight of all the witnesses, tied into the chain of events and the fact there was no other reasonable explanation offered by Abbott. There were a lot of holes."[49] In setting the verdict, the jurors agreed on death.

In response, Abbott told the *Chronicle* when interviewed at his county jail cell, "I guess the jurors feel they're correct, but they're wrong. That's all there is to it. They're wrong, wrong, wrong."

Afterward, there were numerous appeals. Finally, on March 15, 1957, Burton Abbott was executed in San Quentin Prison's gas chamber, still protesting his innocence. Perhaps for the first time, he showed some emotion. As he gripped the arms of the death chair tightly, his jaws were clenched and there were tears in his eyes. Taking the secret of exactly what happened to Stephanie Bryan two years before, he died a few minutes later. He took a deep breath just before the gas pellets dropped and held it as long as he could before he died.[50]

Notes

CHAPTER 1

1. Roger Lane, *Murder in America: A History* (Columbus: Ohio State University Press, 1997), p. 107.

2. Ibid., pp. 112–16.

3. Brian Marriner, *On Death's Bloody Trail: Murder and the Art of Forensic Science* (New York: St. Martin's Press, 1993), pp. 8–9.

4. Ibid., pp. 171–78.

5. Ibid., p. 9.

6. Ibid., pp. 201–2.

7. Lane, *Murder in America*, pp. 201–2.

8. Ibid., p. 210.

9. Janet L. Langlois, *Belle Gunness: The Lady Bluebeard* (Bloomington: Indiana University Press, 1985), pp. 1–3.

10. Ibid., pp. 106–7.

11. Named John Heldgren in the *New York Times*.

12. "Bodies of Five Slain Unearthed in Yard," *New York Times*, May 6, 1908, p. 1:3.

13. "Four More Skeletons in Indiana Mystery," *New York Times*, May 7, 1908, pp. 1:1; 2:6.

14. Ibid.

15. "Indiana Murders Laid to Fanatic," *New York Times*, May 8, 1908, p. 1:7.

16. "The Laporte Mystery," *New York Times*, May 8, 1908, p. 6:3.

17. Langlois, *Belle Gunness*, p. 121.

18. Ibid., p. 87.

19. Ibid., p. 129.
20. Ibid.
21. Ibid., p. 131.
22. Ibid., p. 134.

CHAPTER 2

1. Roger Lane, *Murder in America: A History* (Columbus: Ohio State University Press, 1997), p. 188.
2. Brian Marriner, *On Death's Bloody Trail: Murder and the Art of Forensic Science* (New York, St. Martin's Press, 1993), pp. 197–98.
3. Ibid., pp. 215, 222.
4. Ibid., p. 222.
5. Ibid., pp. 178–79.
6. Ibid., pp. 138–39.
7. Jay Robert Nash, *Bloodletters and Badmen* (New York: M. Evans, 1995), pp. 580–82.
8. "Admits He Killed Fourteen Persons," *New York Times*, October 6, 1913, p. 1:3.
9. Ibid.
10. "Cut Chicago Man's Murder List to Two," *New York Times*, October 7, 1913, p. 1:6.
11. Ibid.
12. Ibid.
13. Martin Fido, *The Chronicle of Crime* (New York: Carroll and Graf, 1993).
14. Nash, *Bloodletters and Badmen.*
15. "Think Girl Was Duped and Slain by German," *New York Times*, April 23, 1918, p. 8:6.
16. "Admits Killing Girl, Then Ends His Life," *New York Times*, April 24, 1918, p. 8:1.
17. Nash, *Bloodletters and Badmen*, p. 550.
18. "Find Body of Woman Buried by Schmidt," *New York Times*, May 3, 1918, p. 10:3.

CHAPTER 3

1. Roger Lane, *Murder in America: A History* (Columbus: Ohio State University Press, 1997), p. 215.
2. H. C. Brearley, *Homicide in the United States* (1932; Glen Ridge, NJ: Patterson Smith, 1969), p. 229.
3. Lane, *Murder in America*, p. 219.
4. Ibid., p. 231.
5. Ibid.
6. Ibid., p. 221.
7. Ibid.
8. John Brophy, *The Meaning of Murder* (New York: Thomas Y. Crowell, 1966), pp. 220–21.

9. Ibid., p. 44.
10. Lane, *Murder in America*, p. 235.
11. Ibid., p. 237.
12. Ibid., pp. 238–39.
13. Ibid., p. 230.
14. Ibid., pp. 224–28.
15. Eugene B. Block, *The Wizard of Berkeley* (New York: Coward-McCann, 1958), pp. 41–44.
16. Jay Robert Nash, *Bloodletters and Badmen* (New York: M. Evans, 1995), p. 424.
17. Block, *The Wizard of Berkeley*, p. 42.
18. Ibid., pp. 42–43.
19. Ibid., p. 44.
20. Ibid., p. 45.
21. Jay Robert Nash, *The Dark Fountain* (New York: A & W, 1982), p. 123.
22. Ibid., p. 124.
23. Ibid., p. 138.
24. Ibid., p. 145.
25. Ibid., p. 155.
26. Colin Wilson and Damon Wilson, *The Killers among Us: Book 2: Sex, Madness and Mass Murder* (New York: Warner Books, 1997), p. 173.
27. Nash, *The Dark Fountain*, p. 172.
28. Harold Schechter and David Everitt, *The A to Z Encyclopedia of Serial Killers* (New York: Pocket Books, 1996), p. 196.
29. Nash, *Bloodletters and Badmen*, pp. 460–61; much of this echoed in Wilson and Wilson, *The Killers among Us*, p. 2:175.
30. Nash, *Bloodletters and Badmen*, p. 464.
31. There are a number of versions of events in the various sources on Nelson's crimes. I've tried to synthesize them together into what seems to make the most sense. For example, it's not clear if Richard Newman actually passed Clara Newman on the stairs and saw the killer, or if he arrived and saw her later. It's also not clear if Richard actually saw the Bible at this time, or whether Nelson was actually carrying the Bible on this first killing, though he did later. Some of this information comes from a novelized version of the case, which does have accurate dates and some accurate names but changes others. Other differences are whether the woman Nelson married was an older spinster or a young schoolteacher; whether he lived with an aunt in Philadelphia or in San Francisco when he was orphaned; whether he was accused of rape and served time in an institution in Philadelphia or in San Quentin; and whether his accident with a street car was due to his riding a bike or playing ball in the streets. The basic story is the same in all accounts; discrepancies turn up in various details. Also, the novel suggests a single San Francisco cop followed the case around the country; although it seems likely from the other accounts that the police in various jurisdictions were sharing information—and the press in various cities were also passing along the story. But the story never hit the *New York Times* or any indexed papers, so newspaper accounts aren't available.
32. Charles Boswell and Lewis Thompson, *The Girl in Lover's Lane* (Greenwich, CT: Gold Medal Books, 1962), pp. 5–6.
33. Ibid., p. 20.
34. Ibid., p. 21.

35. Jay Robert Nash, *The Almanac of World Crime* (New York: Anchor Press, 1981), p. 1430.

36. Boswell and Thompson, *The Girl in Lover's Lane*, p. 21.

37. Ibid., p. 23.

38. Nash, *Almanac*, p. 1431; Boswell and Thompson, *The Girl in Lover's Lane*, pp. 26–27.

39. Boswell and Thompson, *The Girl in Lover's Lane*, p. 8.

40. Ibid., pp. 30–31.

41. Ibid., p. 31.

42. Nash, *Almanac*, p. 1431; Boswell and Thompson, *The Girl in Lover's Lane*, p. 35.

43. Nash, *Almanac*, p. 1431; Boswell and Thompson, *The Girl in Lover's Lane*, p. 67.

44. $15,000 in Nash, *Almanac*, p. 1431; $15,000 and $40,000 in Boswell and Thompson, *The Girl in Lover's Lane*, p. 39.

45. Nash, *Almanac*, p. 1431.

46. Marvin J. Wolf and Katherine Mader, "Enigma: The Unsolved Murder of William Desmond Taylor," in their *Fallen Angels: Chronicles of L.A. Crime and Mystery* (New York: Ballantine Books, 1986), p. 82.

47. Ibid., p. 82.

48. Sidney D. Kirkpatrick, *A Cast of Killers* (New York: Penguin Books, 1986), p. 168.

49. Wolf and Mader, "Enigma," pp. 77–80.

50. Ibid., pp. 78–79.

51. Kirkpatrick, *A Cast of Killers*, pp. 88–90.

52. Wolf and Mader, "Enigma," p. 79.

53. Ibid., p. 83.

54. Kirkpatrick, *A Cast of Killers*, pp. 228–32.

55. Wolf and Mader, "Enigma," p. 84.

56. Kirkpatrick, *A Cast of Killers*, p. 156.

57. Ibid., pp. 39–48.

58. Ibid., p. 131.

59. Ibid., pp. 265–78.

60. Ibid., pp. 258–69.

61. Ibid., p. 269.

62. Ibid., pp. 202–7.

63. Ibid., pp. 256–57.

64. Ibid., pp. 279–80.

65. Ibid., pp. 282–83.

66. Ibid., p. 285.

67. Larry Sturholm and John Howard, *All for Nothing: The True Story of the Last Great American Train Robbery* (Portland, OR: BLS Publishing, 1976), pp. 33–35.

68. Ibid., p. 44.

69. Ibid., pp. 44–47.

70. Ibid., pp. 47–50.

71. Ibid., pp. 50–52.

72. Block, *The Wizard of Berkeley*, pp. 14–15.

73. Ibid., p. 15.

74. Sturholm and Howard, *All for Nothing*, pp. 54–55.
75. Ibid., pp. 59–64.
76. Block, "Great Train Robberies of the West," in *The Wizard of Berkeley*, p. 17.
77. Ibid., pp. 17–19.
78. Ibid., p. 22.
79. Sturholm and Howard, *All for Nothing*, pp. 64–67.
80. Ibid., pp. 72–73.
81. Ibid., p. 71.
82. Ibid., p. 80.
83. Ibid., pp. 82–89.
84. Ibid., p. 91.
85. Ibid., pp. 97–98.
86. Ibid., p. 106.

CHAPTER 4

1. Roger Lane, *Murder in America: A History* (Columbus: Ohio State University Press, 1997), p. 244.
2. Ibid., pp. 244–45.
3. Ibid.
4. Ibid.
5. Ibid., p. 245.
6. Ibid., p. 246.
7. Martin Fido, *The Chronicle of Crime* (New York: Carroll and Graf, 1993), pp. 178–79.
8. Lane, *Murder in America*, p. 247.
9. Ibid.
10. Colin Wilson and Damon Wilson, *Written in Blood: Book 2: Detectives and Detection* (New York: Warner Books, 1989), p. 188.
11. Brian Marriner, *On Death's Bloody Trail: Murder and the Art of Forensic Science* (New York, St. Martin's Press, 1993), p. 82.
12. Ibid., p. 82.
13. Ibid., p. 84.
14. Ibid., pp. 178–79.
15. Jay Robert Nash, *Bloodletters and Badmen* (New York: M. Evans, 1995), pp. 470–71.
16. Ibid., pp. 612–14.
17. Ibid., pp. 345–46.
18. Harold Schechter, *Deranged* (New York: Pocket Books, 1990), pp. 11–17.
19. Ibid., pp. 19–23.
20. Ibid., p. 27.
21. Mel Heimer, *The Cannibal* (New York: Pinnacle Books, 1971), p. 49.
22. Schechter, *Deranged*, p. 76.
23. Heimer, *The Cannibal*, p. 15.
24. Ibid., p. 17.
25. Schechter, *Deranged*, p. 51.
26. Ibid., p. 52.

27. Ibid., p. 59.
28. Ibid., p. 66.
29. Ibid., pp. 64–65.
30. Ibid., pp. 68–69.
31. Ibid., pp. 72–77.
32. Ibid., p. 78.
33. Ibid., pp. 77–79.
34. Ibid., pp. 79–80.
35. Ibid., pp. 80–86.
36. Ibid., pp. 87–88.
37. Ibid., pp. 90–96.
38. Ibid., pp. 98–100.
39. Ibid., pp. 103–8.
40. Ibid., pp. 110–12.
41. Ibid., pp. 114–15.
42. Heimer, *The Cannibal*, pp. 69–70.
43. Ibid., p. 70.
44. Schechter, *Deranged*, pp. 120–21; Heimer, *The Cannibal*, pp. 70–72.
45. Room 7 in Schechter, *Deranged*, p. 122; room 11 in Heimer, *The Cannibal*, pp. 72–73.
46. Heimer, *The Cannibal*, p. 73.
47. Schechter, *Deranged*, pp. 129–43.
48. Ibid., pp. 204–5.
49. Ibid., pp. 291–92.
50. Helen Reilly, "1935: Robert James: The Reluctant Rattlesnakes," in Richard Glyn Jones, ed., *The Mammoth Book of Murder* (New York: Carroll and Graf, 1990), pp. 429–30.
51. Ibid., p. 430.
52. Eugene D. Williams, "1936: The Rattlesnake Murder," in Craig Rice, ed., *Los Angeles Murders* (New York: Duell, Sloan and Pearce, 1947), pp. 179–98.
53. Ibid., p. 187.
54. Ibid., pp. 182–83.
55. Ibid., p. 183.
56. Ibid., p. 184.
57. Ibid.
58. Ibid., p. 191.
59. Ibid., p. 193.
60. Ibid.
61. Marvin J. Wolf, and Katherine Mader, "The Rattlesnake Murders: Robert James, 1936," in their *Fallen Angels* (New York: Ballantine Books, 1986), pp. 155–62. Reprint of Eugene Williams account, p. 162.
62. Nash, *Bloodletters and Badmen*, p. 558.
63. Ibid.
64. Ibid.
65. Ibid.
66. Ernest Kahlar Alix, *Ransom Kidnapping in America: 1874–1974* (Carbondale: Southern Illinois University Press, 1978), p. 120.

67. Hank Messick and Burt Goldblatt, *Kidnapping: The Illustrated History* (New York: Dial Press, 1974), p. 112.

68. Nash, *Bloodletters and Badmen*, p. 559.

CHAPTER 5

1. Roger Lane, *Murder in America: A History* (Columbus: Ohio State University Press, 1997), p. 250.

2. Ibid.

3. Ibid., p. 249.

4. Ibid., p. 251.

5. Ibid., p. 249.

6. Ibid., p. 255.

7. Ibid., pp. 257–58.

8. Ibid., p. 251.

9. Ibid.

10. Colin Wilson, and Damon Wilson, *The Killers among Us: Book 2: Sex, Madness and Mass Murder* (New York: Warner Books, 1997), p. 227.

11. Ibid., pp. 226–27.

12. Brian Marriner, *On Death's Bloody Trail: Murder and the Art of Forensic Science* (New York, St. Martin's Press, 1993), pp. 65 and 181.

13. Ibid., p. 271.

14. Ibid.

15. Ibid., pp. 271–72.

16. Ibid., p. 91.

17. Colin Wilson and Damon Wilson, *Written in Blood: Book 2: Detectives & Detection* (New York: Warner Books, 1989), pp. 278–79.

18. Marriner, *On Death's Bloody Trail*, p. 230.

19. Wilson and Wilson, *Written in Blood*, p. 278.

20. Martin Fido, *The Chronicle of Crime* (New York: Carroll and Graf, 1993); Jay Robert Nash, *Crime Chronology: A Worldwide Record: 1900–1983* (New York: Facts on File, 1984); Jay Robert Nash, *Bloodletters and Badmen* (New York: M. Evans, 1995).

21. John Gilmore, *Severed: The True Story of the Black Dahlia Murder* (San Francisco: Zanja Press, 1994), p. 146.

22. Marvin J. Wolf and Katherine Mader, "Famous in Death: Elizabeth Short (1947)," in their *Fallen Angels: Chronicles of L.A. Crime and Mystery* (New York: Ballantine, 1986), p. 202.

23. Gilmore, *Severed*, p. 113.

24. Ibid., pp. 166–67.

25. Ibid., p. 140.

26. Ibid., pp. 137–38.

27. Ibid., p. 154.

28. Ibid., pp. 157, 161.

29. Janice Knowlton with Michael Newton, *Daddy Was the Black Dahlia Killer* (New York: Pocket Books, 1995), p. 33.

30. Ibid., pp. 199–200.

31. Ibid., p. 308.
32. Gilmore, *Severed*, p. 218.
33. Ibid., pp. 196–216.
34. Ibid., pp. 226–27.
35. Ibid., p. 225.
36. Ibid., p. 236.
37. James Ellroy, *The Black Dahlia* (New York: Mysterious Press, 1987).
38. Knowlton, *Daddy Was the Black Dahlia Killer*, p. 36.
39. Ibid., pp. 140–61.
40. Ibid., p. 321.
41. Jonathan Goodman, "Lonely Hearts," in his *Posts-Mortem: The Correspondence of Murder* (New York: St. Martin's Press, 1971), pp. 44–45.
42. Wenzell Brown, *Introduction to Murder* (New York: Greenberg, 1952), p. 48.
43. Ibid., pp. 74–79.
44. Ibid., pp. 79.
45. Ibid., pp. 84–88.
46. Ibid., pp. 88–95.
47. Ibid., pp. 11–21.
48. Ibid., pp. 29–36.
49. Ibid., pp. 36–37.
50. Ibid., pp. 38–44.
51. Ibid., pp. 52–58.
52. Ibid., pp. 55–65.
53. Goodman, *Posts-Mortem*, p. 42.
54. Brown, *Introduction to Murder*, p. 133.
55. Goodman, *Posts-Mortem*, p. 46 (had a search warrant); Brown, *Introduction to Murder*, p. 144.
56. Brown, *Introduction to Murder*, p. 148.
57. Ibid., p. 149.
58. Ibid., pp. 149–62.
59. Ibid., p. 168.
60. Ibid., p. 174.
61. Goodman, *Posts-Mortem*, p. 49.
62. Edward D. Radin, *Crimes of Passion* (New York: G. P. Putnam's Sons, 1953), pp. 216–18.
63. Ibid., p. 218.
64. Lucy Freeman, *Before I Kill More . . .* (New York: Crown, 1955), p. 22; Radin, *Crimes of Passion*, pp. 220–21.
65. Freeman, *Before I Kill More . . .*, p. 23.
66. Freeman, *Before I Kill More . . .*, pp. 22–23; Radin, *Crimes of Passion*, pp. 221–22.
67. Radin, *Crimes of Passion*, p. 222.
68. This extensive matching is only described in Radin, *Crimes of Passion*, pp. 225–26; he has more detail on the investigative process than other accounts.
69. Radin, *Crimes of Passion*, p. 226; Jay Robert Nash, *Encyclopedia of World Crime, Volume 1* (New York: Crime Books, 1990), p. 1510.
70. Freeman, *Before I Kill More . . .*, p. 12.
71. Radin, *Crimes of Passion*, p. 230.

72. Ibid., pp. 231–32.

73. Ibid., p. 234.

74. An alternate account in Freeman has Cunningham leaving the beach and chasing Heirens first, when Tiffin Constant (rather than Constant Tiffin) arrives, and then Cunningham hits him on the head. There are also differences in accounts of who saw Heirens in the Pera house.

75. Freeman, *Before I Kill More . . .* , pp. 30–31.

76. Radin, *Crimes of Passion*, pp. 237–38.

77. Freeman, *Before I Kill More . . .* , p. 32.

78. Ibid., p. 33.

79. Ibid., p. 36.

80. Ibid., pp. 38; Radin, *Crimes of Passion*, p. 242.

81. Radin, *Crimes of Passion*, p. 244.

82. Ibid., p. 245.

83. Nash, *Bloodletters and Badmen*, p. 309; Radin, *Crimes of Passion*, p. 246.

CHAPTER 6

1. Roger Lane, *Murder in America: A History* (Columbus: Ohio State University Press, 1997), p. 252.

2. Ibid.

3. Ibid., pp. 254–55.

4. Ibid., p. 256.

5. Ibid.

6. Ibid., p. 259.

7. Ibid., pp. 259–60.

8. Colin Wilson and Damon Wilson, *The Killers among Us: Book 2: Sex, Madness and Mass Murder* (New York: Warner Books, 1997), pp. 229–30.

9. Ibid., p. 251.

10. Jay Robert Nash, *Crime Chronology: A Worldwide Record: 1900–1983* (New York: Facts on File, 1984), pp. 255–56; Wilson and Wilson, *Killers among Us*, pp. 293–94.

11. Brian Marriner, *On Death's Bloody Trail: Murder and the Art of Forensic Science* (New York, St. Martin's Press, 1993), pp. 91–92.

12. Jay Robert Nash, *Bloodletters and Badmen* (New York: M. Evans, 1995), p. 466 (suffocation); James Melvin Reinhardt, *The Psychology of Strange Killers* (Springfield, IL: Charles C Thomas, 1962), pp. 165–77 (exposure).

13. Reinhardt, *The Psychology of Strange Killers*, p. 173.

14. Ibid., p. 169.

15. "Musician Gets Death," *New York Times*, September 29, 1961, p. 71:5.

16. Reinhardt, *The Psychology of Strange Killers*, p. 167.

17. Ibid.

18. Ibid.

19. Ibid., p. 170.

20. Ibid., p. 171.

21. Ibid., pp. 168–69.

22. Ibid., p. 177.

23. Charles Raudebaugh, "Girl Confesses Daly City Slaying—'Longed to Kill,'" *San Francisco Chronicle*, April, 16, 1959, pp. 1–1, 4–3.

24. Miriam Allen DeFord, *Murders Sane and Mad: Case Histories of the Motivation and Rationale of Murder* (New York: Abelard-Schuman, 1965), p. 141; Raudebaugh, "Girl Confesses," p. 1–1.

25. DeFord, *Murders Sane and Mad*, p. 142.

26. Ibid.

27. Raudebaugh, "Girl Confesses," p. 1–1.

28. Ibid., p. 4–3.

29. "Urge Killer Talks at Jail: 'I'm Sane, a Normal Girl,'" *San Francisco Chronicle*, April 17, 1959, p. 5–1.

30. Carolyn Anspacher, "Penny Casually Pleads Guilty of Murder," *San Francisco Chronicle*, July 21, 1959, p. 5.

31. DeFord, *Murders Sane and Mad*, p. 145.

32. "Penny Gets Life for Urge Slaying," *San Francisco Chronicle*, August 7, 1959, p. 3–1.

33. Ibid.

34. "Stephanie's Body Found Buried: Grave at Abbott's Cabin; Murder Booking: Student Arrested, Denies He Did It," *San Francisco Chronicle*, July 21, 1955.

35. DeFord, *Murders Sane and Mad*, p. 33.

36. DeFord, *Murders Sane and Mad*, p. 28.

37. Ibid.

38. "Stephanie's Body Found," July 21, 1955.

39. Ibid.

40. "Abbott's Wife Is Eligible for the Reward," *San Francisco Chronicle*, July 21, 1991, p. 1.

41. Eugene B. Block, *The Fabric of Guilt* (Garden City, NY: Doubleday, 1968), pp. 182–83.

42. Ibid., p. 183.

43. Robert Colby, "Stephanie Bryan Is Missing," in *California Crime Book* (New York: Pyramid Books, 1971), p. 98.

44. DeFord, *Murders Sane and Mad*, p. 37.

45. Ibid., p. 185.

46. Ibid.

47. Ibid., p. 186.

48. George Draper, "Jury Convicts Him on Both Counts," *San Francisco Chronicle*, January 26, 1956, p. 4.

49. James Benet, "Juror's Full Story of the Verdict," *San Francisco Chronicle*, January 26, 1956, p. A1.

50. George Draper, "Gas Chamber: Stephanie Bryan Slayer Executed," *San Francisco Chronicle*, March 16, 1957, p. 2.

Selected Bibliography

"Abbott Tells Feelings, Insists He's Innocent," *San Francisco Chronicle*, January 26, 1956.

Alix, Ernest Kahlar. *Ransom Kidnapping in America: 1874–1974.* Carbondale: Southern Illinois University Press, 1978.

Block, Eugene B. *The Wizard of Berkeley*. New York: Coward-McCann, 1958.

Block, Eugene B. *The Fabric of Guilt*. Garden City, NY: Doubleday, 1968.

Boswell, Charles, and Lewis Thompson. *The Girl in Lover's Lane.* Greenwich, CT: Gold Medal Books, 1962.

Brearley, H.C. *Homicide in the United States*. 1932; Glen Ridge, NJ: Patterson Smith, 1969.

Brophy, John. *The Meaning of Murder*. New York: Thomas Y. Crowell, 1966.

Brown, Wenzell. *Introduction to Murder*. New York: Greenberg, 1952.

Colby, Robert. "Stephanie Bryan Is Missing," in *California Crime Book*. New York: Pyramid Books, 1971, pp. 92–102.

DeFord, Miriam Allen. *Murders Sane and Mad: Case Histories of the Motivation and Rationale of Murder*. New York: Abelard-Schuman, 1965.

Ellroy, James. *The Black Dahlia*. New York, Warner Books, 1987.

Fido, Martin. *The Chronicle of Crime*. New York: Carroll and Graf, 1993.

Freeman, Lucy. *Before I Kill More . . .* New York: Crown, 1955.

Gilmore, John. *Severed: The True Story of the Black Dahlia Murder*. San Francisco: Zanja Press, 1994.

Goodman, Jonathan. "Lonely Hearts," in *Posts-Mortem: The Correspondence of Murder*. New York: St. Martin's Press, 1971, pp. 40–50.

Green, Jonathan. *The Greatest Criminals of All Time*. New York: Stein and Day, 1980.

Heimer, Mel. *The Cannibal*. New York: Pinnacle Books, 1971.

Jones, Richard Glyn, ed. *The Mammoth Book of Murder*. New York: Carroll and Graf, 1990.

Kirkpatrick, Sidney D. *A Cast of Killers*. New York: Penguin Books, 1986.

Knowlton, Janice, with Michael Newton. *Daddy Was the Black Dahlia Killer*. New York: Pocket Books, 1995.

Lane, Roger. *Murder in America: A History*. Columbus: Ohio State University Press, 1997.

Langlois, Janet L. *Belle Gunness: The Lady Bluebeard*. Bloomington: Indiana University Press, 1985.

Marriner, Brian. *On Death's Bloody Trail: Murder and the Art of Forensic Science*. New York: St. Martin's Press, 1993.

Messick, Hank, and Burt Goldblatt. *Kidnapping: The Illustrated History*. New York: Dial Press, 1974.

Nash, Jay Robert. *The Almanac of World Crime*. New York: Anchor Press, 1981.

Nash, Jay Robert. *The Dark Fountain*. New York: A & W, 1982.

Nash, Jay Robert. *Crime Chronology: A Worldwide Record: 1900–1983*. New York: Facts on File, 1984.

Nash, Jay Robert. *Encyclopedia of World Crime, Volume 1*. New York: Crime Books, 1990.

Nash, Jay Robert. *Bloodletters and Badmen*. New York: M. Evans, 1995.

Radin, Edward D. *Crimes of Passion*. New York: G. P. Putnam's Sons, 1953.

Reilly, Helen. "1935: Robert James: The Reluctant Rattlesnakes," in Richard Glyn Jones, ed., *The Mammoth Book of Murder*. New York: Carroll and Graf Publishers, 1990, pp. 429–32.

Reinhardt, James Melvin. *The Psychology of Strange Killers*. Springfield, IL: Charles C Thomas, 1962.

Schechter, Harold. *Deranged*. New York: Pocket Books, 1990.

Schechter, Harold, and David Everitt. *The A to Z Encyclopedia of Serial Killers*. New York: Pocket Books, 1997.

Sturholm, Larry, and John Howard. *All for Nothing: The True Story of the Last Great American Train Robbery*. Portland, OR: BLS Publishing, 1976.

Williams, Eugene D. "1936: The Rattlesnake Murder," in Craig Rice, ed. *Los Angeles Murders*. New York: Duell, Sloan and Pearce, 1947, pp. 179–98.

Wilson, Colin. *Murder in the 1930s*. New York: Carroll and Graf, 1992.

Wilson, Colin, and Damon Wilson. *Written in Blood: Book 2: Detectives and Detection*. New York: Warner Books, 1989.

Wilson, Colin, and Damon Wilson. *The Killers among Us: Book 1: Motives behind Their Madness*. New York: Warner Books, 1996.

Wilson, Colin, and Damon Wilson. *The Killers among Us: Book 2: Sex, Madness and Mass Murder*. New York: Warner Books, 1997.

Wolf, Marvin J., and Katherine Mader. *Fallen Angels: Chronicles of L.A. Crime and Mystery*. New York: Ballantine Books, 1986.

Index

ABOUT THE AUTHOR

GINI GRAHAM SCOTT is a professional writer with over 40 books to her credit including *Homicide by the Rich and Famous: A Century of Prominent Killers* (Praeger, 2005), *Disagreements, Disputes, and All Out War*, and *A Survival Guide for Working with Humans*, among others.